D0965479

REPEAL THE
SECOND AMENDMENT

REPEAL
THE SECOND
AMENDMENT

THE CASE FOR
A SAFER AMERICA

ALLAN J. LICHTMAN

ST. MARTIN'S PRESS
New York

First published in the United States by St. Martin's Press, an imprint of
St. Martin's Publishing Group

www.stmartins.com

Designed by Steven Seighman

The Library of Congress Cataloging-in-Publication Data
is available upon request.

ISBN 978-1-250-24440-6 (hardcover)
ISBN 978-1-250-24441-3 (ebook)

First Edition: January 2020

10 9 8 7 6 5 4 3 2 1

This book is dedicated to the loved ones and victims of needless gun violence in America. It is a call to action for the majority of Americans who believe in real solutions to the plague of gun violence, not just empty thoughts and prayers.

CONTENTS

The Book That Must Be Written

A constitutional amendment to get rid of the Second Amendment would be simple and would do more to weaken the NRA's ability to stymie legislative debate and block constructive gun control legislation than any other available option.

—RETIRED US SUPREME COURT JUSTICE
JOHN PAUL STEVENS, 2018[1]

On April 28, 1996, twenty-eight-year-old Martin Bryant stopped at an inn near his home of New Town in Tasmania, Australia, and shot to death its two owners. He then drove to the former penal colony and tourist attraction of Port Arthur, where he lunched at a café. After eating, Bryant pulled from his sports bag a semiautomatic rifle with a thirty-round magazine that he had legally purchased through a newspaper ad. With no provocation, he began firing at patrons in the café and its gift shop. Before the police stopped his shooting spree, Bryant had murdered thirty-five and wounded eighteen others. His motive remains unknown.

"There were people everywhere—bodies," said witness Lynne Beavis. "I thought at the time, being a nurse, 'I've seen dead people, I've seen blood, I've seen things like this.' But what I saw in there, nobody but perhaps a soldier would know what it was like."[2]

The leadership of a shocked nation responded to the Port Arthur massacre not with thoughts and prayers, but with decisive action. The country's conservative-led government rebuffed their gun lobby, and its American ally, the National Rifle Association (NRA), to adopt comprehensive national gun controls. In a 2015 broadside labeled "Australia: There Will Be Blood," the NRA charged that these regulations, which Australia significantly tightened as of 2002, have "robbed Australians of their right to self-defense and empowered criminals."[3]

If the NRA was right, America with its lax controls over firearms for alleged self-defense should be one of the world's safest countries, certainly far safer than Australia, where criminals presumably evade gun controls to prey on defenseless, law-abiding citizens. Yet, in the latest reporting year, gun homicides claimed 14,542 American lives, compared to 27 in Australia, and all homicides took 19,510 American lives compared to 222 in Australia. Since the NRA issued its warning, firearm homicides have declined in Australia, while soaring by 3,534 in the U.S. An American is now over 30 times more likely per capita than an Australian to be murdered by a gun and seven times more likely to be murdered by any means. If we had rates comparable today to Australia's, some fourteen thousand American lives would have been saved from firearms homicides in 2017 alone.[4]

By the gun lobby's twisted logic, Japan, which has one of the world's strictest gun control laws, should be drenched in innocent blood. Yet, out of a population of 127 million, shooters in Japan murdered only three persons and injured only five in firearms assaults throughout 2017. Australia and Japan are not outliers. As compared to residents of our closest peer democracies in the G7 group of nations plus Australia, an American in 2017 was over twenty times more likely to die from a gun homicide.[5]

The gun lobby would have you forget that gun deaths are not limited to murders; in 2017 23,854 Americans died from gun suicides, 64 percent more than were killed in firearms homicides. As compared to the peer nations, the 2017 per capita rate of firearms suicides in the United States was *seven times higher,* while the rate of suicides by other means was *40 percent lower.* These other democracies all have strict firearms regulations. None has a constitutional right to keep or bear arms, a distinction the United States shares worldwide only with Guatemala, whose gun murder rate is the third highest of some 195 nations worldwide.[6]

Why has America lagged behind the democratic world in protecting its citizens from needless death and injury? The culprit is not spending by the NRA on campaigns and lobbying, which other pressure groups exceed.

The real problem is that which gun control advocates fear to name: the Second Amendment. Led by the NRA, the gun lobby exploits a historically defective, perverse reinvention of this amendment to inspire their grassroots supporters, sell guns, and provide constitutional cover for their opposition to making us safer by regulating firearms.[7]

The competing movement for gun control has floundered in response to the gun lobby's triumphant marketing of the Second Amendment. Gun control advocates have righteous zeal and noble motives but lack a winning strategy. Instead of forthrightly refuting the lobby's bogus claims, the gun control movement has instead fallen into the trap of lamely insisting, "We support the Second Amendment, *but* we also support responsible gun control." With such a self-defeating strategy, the movement can never win. It plays on the gun lobby's home turf and fails to rally the American majority that favors stricter firearms regulations. It provokes only scorn from a gun lobby that dismisses "yes, but" assurances as rank hypocrisy. And it ignores the clear history and the true meaning of the Second Amendment itself.

The movement for gun control must strike hard with a new strategy. Repeal of the Second Amendment is not only right, but realistic. It would break open the political logjam and open a path for the comprehensive, national gun control and safety measures that have eluded the American people for so long. None of these measures would confiscate firearms or stop Americans from using guns for hunting, sports shooting, antique collecting, or legitimate self-defense.

"A well regulated Militia, being necessary to the security of a free State, the right of the people to keep and bear Arms, shall not be infringed." These two brief phrases, knitted together by a comma, form the Second Amendment to the US Constitution, which Congress enacted in 1789 and the states ratified in 1791. "From all the direct and indirect evidence, the Second Amendment appears to apply to a collective, not an individual, right to bear arms," wrote Jack Basil, the National Rifle Association's in-house expert on constitutional law, in a 1955 memo to the association's CEO. Twenty years later the NRA publicly conceded in its 1975 *Fact Book* that the amendment had "limited practical utility" in combating gun control.[8]

As even the NRA recognized, the amendment protected only the maintenance of a well-regulated militia, not private gun ownership for self-defense or checking an allegedly oppressive government. For some two hundred years it remained largely irrelevant to enacting and implementing gun control laws. Then, late in the twentieth century, after members voted in a new militant leadership, the NRA erased from memory its own prior findings to reinvent the Second Amendment and distort its meaning to claim a virtually unlimited right to keep and bear private arms.

The NRA's reinvention of the Second Amendment as

a hammer against gun control was the most audacious and successful public relations coup in the history of the United States. It rested not on new discoveries, but on the marketing of a false, alternative history of guns and gun control in America, propagated largely by attorneys with ties to the NRA.

Ironically, the lobby resurrected the Second Amendment at a time when the militia of the framers no longer existed. In the early twentieth century, Congress replaced the citizen militia with the National Guard, armed not with personally kept firearms, but with military weapons issued by the government. The early NRA lobbied for the creation of the National Guard and has since backed the growth of a massive military establishment, even as it claims that the Second Amendment arms private citizens to check an oppressive government. Yet, the gun lobby sold its fraudulent version of the Second Amendment to the American people with little resistance, culminating in a 5–4 decision of the US Supreme Court that overturned precedent in the 2008 case of *D.C. v. Heller* and embraced an individual-rights construction of the Second Amendment.

For America's framers a central purpose of a well-regulated militia was to defend the government from internal insurrections from aggrieved citizens taking the law into their own hands. James Madison, the Second Amendment's framer, said in 1788, "if resistance should be made to the execution of the laws it ought to be overcome," and "the best way . . . was to put the militia on a good and sure footing." In 1790, as states were ratifying the Second Amendment, General Henry Knox, President George Washington's secretary of war, warned, "Convulsive events . . . require that the government should possess a strong corrective arm." He drafted plans for a well-regulated militia to ensure that "rebellions would be suppressed or prevented with ease." With the National Guard and police forces assuming that corrective function, privately armed militia groups, encouraged by the gun lobby's inflammatory rhetoric, have turned the Second Amendment on its head by claiming an inherent right to rebel against their government. These dangerous, self-appointed private militias owe allegiance only to themselves and obedience to no laws but their own.[9]

Since the 1990s, the survivors of gun violence and the families and friends of victims have failed to achieve any gun control or safety measures in Washington, despite public support and the loss of nearly a million lives from gun violence. A Quinnipiac University poll from May 2019 found that 61 percent of registered voters backed stricter gun controls. Instead, the gun control cause has slipped backward. Congress has enacted not a single significant gun control law since the assault weapons ban in 1994. It let the ban lapse in 2004 and shielded gun makers from liability lawsuits in 2005. Few states have comprehensive gun controls, and with firearms flying across state lines, the needed national solution to gun violence remains elusive.[10]

At the time of this writing in August 2019, gun

massacres in El Paso, Texas, and Dayton, Ohio, have rekindled hopes for congressional action on gun control. It is unclear, however, whether President Donald Trump and Republican Senate Majority Leader Mitch McConnell will back *any* new legislation, much less the comprehensive regulations needed to cope with America's epidemic of gun murders, suicides, and accidents (see chapter 14). After consulting with the NRA, Trump seems to have reverted to its strategy of deflecting and delaying under the shield of the Second Amendment.

The NRA hijacked the Second Amendment just a few decades ago—and Americans who care about gun safety must now take it back. My aim, with this book, is to do just that. By shedding light on how America's gun lobby—led by the NRA—has distorted the long-settled meaning of the amendment to block gun control and safety laws and pad gun industry profits, as well as by reexamining the repeal of the Prohibition Amendment, I prove that Americans can and must rid themselves of a counterproductive amendment that puts our lives at risk. We need not remain enslaved to the gun lobby's corrupt version of our history and Constitution.

Like the addicts in the movie *Trainspotting,* whose answer to every drug tragedy was more drugs, the gun lobby's answer to every gun tragedy is more guns. The dirty secret behind the gun lobby is that, to satisfy the gun industry, which pays much of its bills, it exploits the Second Amendment to call for near-universal access to firearms without the slightest concern about who gets the guns. The gun lobby backs the unrestricted open and concealed carrying of firearms and opposes every measure to keep guns from the hands of hardened criminals, drug dealers, gang members, terrorists, potential suicides, and domestic abusers. In 2019, for example, the NRA lobbied furiously against reauthorization of the Violence Against Women Act because of an amendment that would bar domestic abusers from buying guns.[11]

The gun lobby claims that good guys with guns are needed to stop bad guns with guns. Was drug dealer Tavarious China Smith a "good guy" when he shot and killed another dealer during a drug trade gone bad? Was Joe Horn a "good guy" when he chased down and blew away with his shotgun two men he suspected of robbing a neighbor's home, after police told him they were en route and he should stay home? "Property's not worth killing somebody over," the dispatcher said.[12]

These men, and many others in episodes of needless gunplay, escaped retribution under NRA-sponsored stand-your-ground laws that authorize lethal violence rather than retreat when faced with a perceived threat. "Stand Your Ground laws encourage the use of deadly force," said Duke University criminologist Philip J. Cook. "These laws open the door to a more dangerous world where everyone feels pressure to carry a gun—and if they feel threatened, to shoot first and tell their stories later."[13]

Members of the gun lobby would go so far as to arm kindergarten children with firearms. In his satire *Who Is America?* comedian Sacha Baron Cohen, posing as an

Israeli security expert, gets gun rights advocates to endorse his fictitious "Kinderguardians" scheme to arm kindergarten kids for defense against school shooters. Former Republican congressman Joe Walsh, who was "A" rated by the NRA, gushed that Kinderguardians "introduces specially selected [children], from twelve to four years old, to pistols, rifles, semiautomatics, and a rudimentary knowledge of mortars. In less than a month, a first-grader can become a first grenader." Philip Van Cleave, president of the Virginia Citizens Defense League, on-air paraded kid-friendly firearms camouflaged as stuffed toys, such as the "Puppy Pistol" and the "Uzicorn."[14]

While the show was farcical, these gun rights proponents were dead serious, and Cohen struck close to reality. Although the "Uzicorn" is fiction, the NRA has promoted the HotShot rifle (since discontinued), "a tiny gun intended for the very youngest shooters." With this miniature but still deadly rifle—available in pink for girls—"we're targeting the six- to twelve-year-old range," said Craig Cushman, marketing director for the manufacturer, Thompson/Center Arms. Keystone Sporting Arms markets similar Crickett rifles, with ads that feature armed children in camouflage gear and a cute Davey Crickett Beanie Baby brandishing a rifle.[15]

The gun lobby expansively markets the Second Amendment as arming citizens both for self-protection and thwarting government tyranny. Yet, just as America trails other nations in public safety, it also lags in the quality of its democracy. In the *Economist*'s respected index of democracies worldwide, the United States ranks as a "flawed democracy," finishing twenty-fifth among nations. The twenty "full democracies" all have much stricter gun control laws, no constitutional right to keep and bear arms, and much lower rates of firearms death per capita than the United States.[16]

So long as the Second Amendment remains in the Constitution, it sustains gun lobby propaganda and puts in legal jeopardy gun controls, current and future. Following *Heller*'s individual-rights interpretation, courts could strike down as unconstitutional any firearms regulation, especially now that gun-friendly judges hold a majority on the US Supreme Court and are salted across the federal judiciary through President Donald Trump's appointments.

On January 3, 2019, Linda Greenhouse warned in *The New York Times* that even if it is "wildly out of sync" with public support for tougher gun controls, the conservative US Supreme Court may be ready to follow the call of Justice Clarence Thomas to stop treating the Second Amendment as a "second-class right" and start invalidating firearms regulations. Less than three weeks later, the Supreme Court agreed to take up its first gun rights case in nearly a decade.[17]

My interest in gun control and safety is both academic and personal. I was born in 1947 and grew up in a tough neighborhood of Brooklyn, New York. The boys in my neighborhood fought one another, but no one that I knew of was ever killed or seriously injured, for the simple reason that we didn't have guns. Yet, many who share my commitment to reasonable gun control urged me not to write this book. They said that the gun lobby has been screaming for years that gun control is a ploy for confiscating firearms. A book proposing the Second Amendment's repeal would play into their hands and undermine the movement for gun control.

But I remain convinced that this book must be written, especially after the persuasive and eloquent plea for repeal made by the late US Supreme Court justice John Paul Stevens in *The New York Times*. A free people should never let political expediency impede truth or stifle inquiry. Besides, the current gun control movement has stalled and cannot recover with its failed defensive maneuvers. The great majority of Americans who favor tougher gun controls should come to realize that their aim can only be achieved by a forthright movement to repeal the Second Amendment and not by a push for incremental change.[18]

In a 2014 address, the NRA's CEO, Wayne LaPierre, evoked a bleak *Blade Runner* nation redeemable only by armed citizens: "There are terrorists and home invaders and drug cartels and carjackers and knockout gamers and rapers, haters, campus killers, airport killers, shopping mall killers, road rage killers . . . I ask you, Do you trust the government to protect you? We are on our own."[19]

Such fear-driven precautions in a gun-ridden society have not made people safer, not at any time, not anywhere in the world. But fear works for the gun lobby. "People don't donate as much when they're not afraid," said Daniel Sheppard, a grassroots coordinator for the

NRA in 2018. The peoples of other advanced democracies have rejected this dystopian vision of a gun-toting nation. Every American should do so as well.[20]

Contrary to the intent of its framers, the Second Amendment today has become an impediment to reasonable gun control legislation, a marketing ploy for the gun industry, a cultural icon, and a political weapon for the gun lobby and their captive politicians. The NRA has become a self-serving racket that under the umbrella of the Second Amendment enriches its leaders with exorbitant salaries and outrageous perks. In 2017, the NRA ran a deficit of $15 million but paid its CEO, Wayne LaPierre, $1.4 million and its head lobbyist, Chris Cox, $1.2 million, not counting the $39,000 that LaPierre reportedly billed for a day of clothes shopping in Beverly Hills, the $18,300 for a car and driver in Europe, and $200,000 in one month for air transportation expenses, including a two-week trip to the Bahamas. Yet these self-serving, self-appointed apostles of guns dare to dictate how to interpret our Constitution and ensure our safety.[21]

As President John F. Kennedy said of America's mission to reach the moon, repealing the Second Amendment and reclaiming our heritage of gun control will be hard, not easy. But I assure you that like the moon voyage it can be done. Repeal will take a concerted effort from Americans who are well briefed on the true history of the Second Amendment and the calamity of gun violence today. The first twelve chapters probe these issues in depth and will provide you with all the facts you need to refute the gun lobby's lies. The final two chapters outline a plan of action for repeal and the reforms that would replace the amendment. Repeal will take people with a strong will and a sound strategy to bring about the change that is needed for a safer America. As Kennedy promised about our venture into space, "That goal will serve to organize and measure the best of our energies and skills, because that challenge is one that we are willing to accept, one we are unwilling to postpone."[22]

1

The Toll of Gun Violence

There is no more contemptible sound than a gunshot.

— JONATHAN HEATT, POET, 2015[1]

Dylan Hockley, a six-year-old boy, and Anne Marie Murphy, his special needs aide, are among the many— too many—victims of gun violence in the United States. The NRA would have us forget them, but we must not. The victims' stories put human names and faces on the otherwise cold statistics that document the more than three hundred women, men, and children killed or injured by gunfire every day in America. Dylan and his guardian died in each other's arms when twenty-year-old Adam Lanza riddled their bodies with bullets fired from a Bushmaster semiautomatic assault rifle at Sandy Hook Elementary School in 2012. Lanza, who slaughtered twenty students and six staff members, had earlier killed his mother and stolen the Bushmaster, which she had purchased legally after the lapse of the national assault weapons ban.

Dylan's mother, Nicole Hockley, asked, "Who is responsible for delivering the changes we need to prevent further violence, injury, and death? Is it the gun manufacturer? The purchaser? Is it the boy holding the gun? Is it the frozen statesman who allows the cycle to continue? . . . One man murdered my son but so many others took no action to intervene in the shooter's destructive life or to prevent his easy access to firearms. My beautiful boy's murder could have been prevented."[2]

Most children murdered at Sandy Hook were first-graders, aged between six and seven. This prompted West Virginia's Joe Manchin—the recipient of a rare NRA "A" rating for a Democratic senator—to say, "Seeing the massacre of so many innocent children, it's changed. It's changed America . . . Everything has to be on the table." Manchin was wrong. More than seven years after Lanza murdered Dylan and his classmates, the gun control debate remains frozen, and thousands more parents have mourned offspring killed by guns at school, on the street, or in their homes. "Every year the leaves bury memory of those juvenile graves—the cracking umbers and rusts muting to umbrage what otherwise should be rage," wrote the poet Kyle Dargan.[3]

Undercover reporter Rodger Muller, who embedded himself within the NRA, explained in March 2019 how the group defused the nation's response to gun massacres: "First, 'Say nothing.' If media queries persist, go on the 'offense, offense, offense.' Smear gun-control groups. 'Shame them' with statements such as—'How dare you stand on the graves of those children to put forward your political agenda?'" To manipulate media coverage of gun violence, said NRA spokesperson Lars Dalseide, "We want to print up stories about people who were robbed, had their home invaded, were beaten or whatever it might be and that could have been helped had they had a gun"[4]

Catherine Mortensen, an NRA media liaison officer, added, "A lot of the times, we'll write them for like a local sheriff in Wisconsin or whatever. And he'll draft it or she will help us draft it. . . . You know, that it's coming from that community. But we will have a role behind the scenes." A couple of months later, emails obtained through a public records request revealed that during debates over firearms regulation in New Mexico, the NRA had drafted anti-gun-control op-eds for county sheriffs that the law enforcers published under their own names in local newspapers. Adding irony to deceit, Mortensen tried to explain away the manuever, saying that the disclosure "is a distraction being pitched to reporters by the Michael Bloomberg–financed gun control lobby."[5]

Although mass shootings stir outrage across the land, they account for only a fraction of the 14,542 Americans murdered by gunfire in 2017. Gun homicides soared by 32 percent since 2014, while nongun murders inched up only by 2 percent. Homicide by firearms was more than eight times higher than by stabbing, twenty-eight times higher than by suffocation, seventy times higher than by bludgeoning, and ninety-six times higher than by poisoning. So much for the myth that "guns don't kill people, people kill people."[6]

Murder "leaves a taint, like the mark of Cain, on everyone murder touches," wrote investigative journalist Eric Schlosser. In East Oakland, California, after a shooter killed fifteen-year-old Hadari Askari, his friends, mostly teenagers themselves, sought revenge on a fourteen-year-old boy they suspected of the shooting. The avengers fired twenty shots at the boy with their semiautomatic weapons. They only wounded him in the leg but killed an innocent bystander, Jubrille Jordan, a fifteen-year-old girl on her way to the mall. Several young men convicted of her murder face lengthy prison terms. Their terrified target, whom police did not implicate in Askari's murder, went into hiding.

"An innocent girl killed. Every time New Year's rolls around, her sister and friends will relive the horror," wrote Tammerlin Drummond in Oakland's *Mercury News*. "Young African American men will spend much of the rest of their lives in prison. Another child who is not yet a man is hiding out in fear for his life. The families of both victims and perpetrators have suffered a tremendous loss."[7]

African Americans suffer most from gun murders and assaults. Aalayah Eastmond, an African American who survived the school shooting that claimed the lives of seventeen students and staff members at Marjory Stoneman Douglas High School in Parkland, Florida, said that her uncle Patrick Edwards had been "shot in the streets of Brooklyn, New York. He was shot in the back; the bullet then pierced his heart. He was only eighteen. With his whole life ahead of him, and evidently that's the same story of thousands of black and brown families across the country." Homicide, mostly by firearms, is the leading cause of death for black men aged fifteen to thirty-four. The 2017 rate of firearm homicides for black men and black children, male or female, was about ten times higher than the rate for their white counterparts.[8]

Although the dead mesmerize and terrify us, wounded Americans are the hidden victims of gun violence. Many tens of thousands Americans suffered physical injuries from firearm assaults, accidents, and self-harm annually. Jalil Frazier is a hero who hurled his body at armed robbers at a Philadelphia barbershop in 2018 to protect three children who were in the shop. One of the intruders fired multiple shots that ricocheted through Frazier's insides, leaving him paralyzed in a wheelchair and confined to a hospital bed at the age of twenty-eight. He suffers from bouts of depression and his family struggles financially to meet his needs.[9]

In 1991, a bullet fired accidentally by a young boy playing with his father's unsecured gun struck eleven-year-old Benedict Jones in the neck, slicing an artery and slamming bone fragments into his spinal cord. For nearly three decades, Jones has suffered paralysis from the chest down and psychological trauma from his injury and disability.[10]

In 2009, Lisette Johnson's husband shot her multiple

times, before turning the gun on himself. The bullets struck her lung and diaphragm, back, and liver. Although saved by emergency surgery, Johnson continues to suffer from pain, exhaustion, and nightmares. She has coped by working with other women to deal with the aftereffects of domestic violence.[11]

In 2013, a gunman shot journalist Deborah Cotton while she filmed New Orleans' second line parade on Mother's Day, May 12. One of nineteen victims wounded in this infamous mass shooting, she suffered injuries that required close to thirty surgeries. Cotton became a victims' rights advocate but never fully recovered, and in 2017 she died at the age of fifty-two.[12]

Each year, firearms injuries cost the nation billions of dollars in medical bills and diminished productivity. From 2006 to 2014, according to researchers from the Johns Hopkins School of Medicine, medical care for shooting victims cost an average of $2.8 billion per year, and as much as $45 billion after factoring in lost wages.[13]

The least visible victims of firearms violence are the survivors and witnesses who escape bodily harm, but not damage to their psyche and spirit. The National Crime Victimization Survey reported 456,270 nonfatal violent firearms victimizations in 2017, up from 284,910 in 2015. The survey counts episodes reported (56 percent) and not reported to police (44 percent) and in which offenders either fired a gun or showed a gun without firing, for example, in a gunpoint robbery.[14]

Witnesses to shootings and survivors often suffer from

PTSD, depression, sleep disruption, diminished academic performance, risky sexual behavior, and impaired physical health. The National Center for PTSD estimates that 28 percent of people who have witnessed a mass shooting develop PTSD (Post-Traumatic Stress Disorder), and about a third develop acute stress disorder. In the year 2014 alone, 4.2 percent of children in the United States witnessed a shooting, placing them at risk for lifelong problems. From 1999 to 2017, 215,000 students experienced gun violence directly; that's not counting family members and school staff. "Post-traumatic stress disorder can strike even those who have not witnessed a trauma directly," wrote journalist Dave Cullen, a researcher of school shootings. "First responders, therapists, victim advocates, and journalists are among the most vulnerable professions, but I had never heard of secondary traumatic stress, or vicarious traumatization (VT), until it took me down twice."[15]

Aalayah Eastmond has told of her life-shattering experience as a school-shooting survivor. Eastmond's high school was nestled in a quiet suburban neighborhood in Parkland, Florida, where teachers assured her that gun violence "would absolutely never happen here." Then on Valentine's Day, February 14, 2018, she heard loud pops that sounded like gunshots. She said, "I needed to get behind something. The only thing in front of me was Nicholas Dworet. Helena Ramsay began passing books so we could shield ourselves from the bullets, yet everyone thought it was a drill." Then Eastmond looked up and "saw Helena Ramsay slump over with her back against the wall. Then Nicholas Dworet rapidly fell over in front of me." Eastmond said, "I knew I was going to die. I asked please make it fast. I didn't want to feel anything. I asked for the bullet to go through my head so I wouldn't endure any pain."

In this moment of terror, she called her mother. "I told her my last goodbye, and I told her how much I loved her. I apologized for all the things I might've done in my lifetime to upset her." Eastmond survived without physical injury only because Nicholas Dworet's dead body covered her own. When the police rescued her, they had to pick body matter from her hair. "The shooting didn't only impact me on February fourteenth. It impacts me every day of my life," she said.[16]

Eastmond's classmates Sydney Aiello and Calvin Desir survived the Parkland shooting unscathed externally but torn up inside. On March 17, 2019, a year and a month after the massacre, Sydney took her own life with a gunshot to the head. She was nineteen years old. A week later Calvin shot himself dead. He was sixteen years old.

The devastation for survivors of mass murder has no limit in time. Seven years after the Sandy Hook massacre, Jeremy Richman, the father of a murdered six-year-old child, took his own life. Richman had cofounded the Avielle Foundation, a nonprofit named after Richman's daughter, which he dedicated to preventing violence through research and grassroots activism. "The love of my life," said his wife, now widow, Jennifer Hensel, "succumbed to the grief that he could not escape." Richman left behind two young children born after the massacre.[17]

Compounding the trauma of mass shooting survivors are allegations by extreme right-wing allies of the gun lobby that parents and gun control advocates had staged the slaughters, with "crisis actors" rather than real murdered victims. In a lawsuit filed against InfoWars conspiracy theorist Alex Jones, Sandy Hook parents charged that by calling the massacre of their children a "hoax," Jones prompted "online, telephone, and in-person harassment, abuse, and death threats." Lenny Pozner, the parent of a murdered child, said that death threats forced him to move his residence eight times.[18]

Charges of a staged event reemerged in 2018 against survivors of the Parkland high school massacre. These falsehoods, which PolitiFact ranked as the "Lie of the Year" for 2018, did not come directly from the NRA, but were only a baby step up from the association's inflammatory rhetoric. If backers of gun control aim to destroy the nation, as the NRA insists, they would plausibly stage gun massacres to advance their agenda. A week after the mass shooting, the number one trending video on YouTube purported to show that student survivor David Hogg, an outspoken proponent of gun control, "was an actor." Several survivors reported receiving death threats, and authorities arrested two men for threatening family members and friends. A letter sent to Hogg's mother read, "Keep F—— with the NRA and you will be DOA."

Twitter accounts linked to the Russians piled on against the Parkland survivors.[19]

For America's children, school is no longer a safe haven in this age of mass shootings. After another massacre on May 18, 2018, that killed eight students and two teachers at Santa Fe High School in Texas, a reporter asked student survivor Paige Curry if she thought that such a tragedy would ever befall her small-town school. Curry responded, "It's been happening everywhere. I've always felt like eventually it was going to happen here, too." In 2017–18, schools and colleges in the nation's thirty-one largest cities had sixty-two hundred lockdowns affecting some 4.1 million students; shooting threats prompted 61 percent of the lockdowns.[20]

After each killing of schoolchildren and innocent persons in public places, frozen politicians continued to offer their "thoughts and prayers," but no remedy. "'No Way to Prevent This,' Says Only Nation Where This Regularly Happens," *The Onion* satirized.[21]

The gun lobby would have you forget that gun violence is not limited to murder and assaults. Many more Americans die from suicide by gunfire than from firearms homicides. In 2017, 23,854 Americans committed suicide with firearms. Firearms accounted for 39,773 American deaths from all causes that year, up 18 percent from 2014, and more than the number who perished from vehicle accidents on America's roads. Suicide rates demonstrate the ubiquity of gun violence across racial lines in America. Unlike with gun homicides, non-Hispanic white Americans are by far the most prevalent victims of gun suicides. In 2017, non-Hispanic whites accounted for 85 percent of all firearm suicides, with a rate of 9.1 per 100,000 compared to 3.4 for non-Hispanic blacks and 2.5 for Hispanics.[22]

"When someone dies by suicide, their family, loved ones, and communities are often forever changed," wrote suicide researchers Julie Cerel and Rebecca L. Sanford. Not just family members and close friends, but "schools, workplaces, places of worship, and communities are also shaken by suicides." Some "will experience a minor impact on their lives from the suicide," but others will find "the death impacting their life in a devastating way." In comparisons to the nonbereaved, "samples have shown suicide loss survivors to have higher risk of death by suicide; more suicidal ideation and attempts; and greater levels of depression, anxiety, and PTSD."[23]

After John Smith, a sixteen-year-old high school football player, took his own life in 2016, his girlfriend checked into a psychiatric hospital with thoughts of suicide. Two other football players from John's school later committed suicide, and his preteen stepsister sought treatment for PTSD. His stepfather began drinking heavily, and his father endured a life-changing loss. The school's football coach entered grief counseling.[24]

The proliferation of guns in America also leads to accidental shootings that killed 486 people in 2017, including 62 children under the age of fifteen. But the sad story of firearms accidents is only fully told in the estimated

20,488 injuries that they caused in 2017, forty-two times more than the number of deaths.[25]

On March 15, 2019, extreme gun violence struck New Zealand when white supremacist Brenton Tarrant slaughtered fifty-one worshippers at mosques in the city of Christchurch, using semiautomatic firearms. The killer said he used guns not just for their killing power, but also "for the affect [sic] it would have on social discourse" in America, nearly nine thousand miles away. "The US is torn into many factions by its Second Amendment, along state, social, cultural, and, most importantly, racial lines." Echoing US gun lobby arguments, he said, "With enough pressure the left wing within the United States will seek to abolish the Second Amendment, and the right wing within the US will see this as an attack on their very freedom and liberty."[26]

Like leaders in Australia after the Port Arthur massacre, New Zealand's prime minister, Jacinda Ardern, wasn't intimidated into offering thoughts and prayers and then moving on. Within a month, her government, with only one dissenting vote in its Parliament, had joined neighboring Australia and most of the democratic world by banning assault weapons and high-capacity magazines. "The NRA for a long time has held out New Zealand as a place where there are lots of guns and where there are no mass shootings," said Stanford law professor John Donohue. "I guess they're going to change their tune." Don't count on it.[27]

Four months before the Christchurch massacre, Ian

David Long fatally gunned down twelve victims at a country music bar in Thousand Oaks, California. Like Tarrant, Long killed with an agenda—in his case, to mock the hypocrisy of America's pro-gun advocates who respond to mass shootings with empty thoughts and prayers. Before his killing spree and suicide, Long posted on Instagram, "It's too bad I won't get to see all the illogical and pathetic reasons people will put in my mouth as to why I did it. Fact is I had no reason to do it, and I just thought . . . [expletive], life is boring so why not?

"I hope people call me insane [two smiley face emojis] would that just be a big ball of irony? Yeah . . . I'm insane, but the only thing you people do after these shootings is 'hopes and prayers' . . . or 'keep you in my thoughts.' Every time . . . and wonder why these keep happening . . . [two smiley face emojis]."[28]

Less than three months after Long's massacre, Zephen Xaver killed five victims with his semiautomatic 9mm handgun at a SunTrust bank in Sebring, Florida. The response of the NRA "A"-rated state leaders? More thoughts and prayers:

> GOVERNOR RON DESANTIS: "Please continue to keep the victims and their families in your prayers."
> LIEUTENANT GOVERNOR JEANETTE NÚÑEZ: "Our thoughts and prayers are with the victims and families."[29]

Ian David Long must be laughing in hell.

2

Guns in Early America

*You know very well when the white people came first here,
they were poor; but now they have got lands and are by
them become rich, and we are now poor.*

—GACHRADODOW, IROQUOIS LEADER, 1744[1]

Pro-gun advocates do not just tolerate guns as a necessary evil in a dangerous world. They celebrate firearms as part of their mythology of America's founding. In his book *A Way Through the Wilderness: The Natchez Trace and the Civilization of the Southern Frontier,* historian William C. Davis rhapsodizes about the independent armed pioneer of early America who stands as an icon of the gun lobby's remaking of American history: "Every cabin had at least one rifle and perhaps an old pistol or two, virtually of them, up to 1830, working on the old flintlock system. They put meat on the table, defended the home against intruders, and provided some entertainment to the men. A man was not a man without knowledge of firearms and some skill in their use." This narrative of the "good guy with the gun" crumbles against the historical record of early America.[2]

In early America, guns were military weapons, not means of self-defense. Davis cites not a single example of individual self-defense with firearms, even on the lawless frontier. The unwieldy, inaccurate, and unreliable muskets, rifles, and flintlock pistols of the seventeenth and eighteenth centuries had minimal value for individual self-defense, especially if not meticulously maintained or properly deployed.

Pamela Haag writes in her study of gun manufacturing that in the late eighteenth century "many patriots had broken weapons or weapons that were nearly useless. Even the best were hard to use. They were heavy, ungainly, and encumbered by accoutrements ranging from ramrods and powder horns to bullet molds. Many were badly balanced and had to be rested on forked sticks when used." Davis concedes, "The flintlocks could be cantankerous, of course." To function, the hammer had to properly strike the flint and open the covering of a small pan of powder. The sparks from the flint had to ignite the powder, which in turn fired the main charge in the barrel of the gun. "If all these things went well, the gun fired. Often, it did not."[3]

In a rare gun-crime trial of the eighteenth century, prosecutors charged Dr. James Reynolds in 1799 with assault with intent to kill after he drew a pistol, allegedly to defend himself from an angry mob during a political dispute on the grounds of St. Mary's Church in

Philadelphia. To downplay the danger posed by Reynolds's pistol, his defense attorney disparaged the notion of using a pistol for self-defense given the state of firearms. He argued "that a pistol was an uncertain defense; it was liable to so many accidents . . . that there is no security in a pistol, that the danger was such as to require a more secure weapons of defense such as a dirk [long dagger]." After thirty minutes of deliberation, the jury acquitted Reynolds.[4]

In his book *Armed America: The Remarkable Story of How and Why Guns Became as American as Apple Pie,* which he wrote to demonstrate the ubiquity of guns and their use in early America, gun rights advocate Clayton E. Cramer includes a section on firearms accidents, but no narratives of individual self-defense with guns. Nor does the word *self-defense* appear in the book's lengthy index.[5]

An individual right to keep and bear private arms is not rooted in early-American traditions, but is an anachronism imposed on history by modern gun rights activists. British practice established a precedent for gun control adopted by many colonies and early state governments. State constitutions did not typically establish rights to private arms, and governments authorized the seizure of private arms to maintain a well-organized and supplied militia. For eighteenth-century Americans, the keeping and bearing of arms mattered not for self-defense or checking government tyranny, but rather for defense against external enemies, and most immediately for controlling slaves and fighting the Indian wars. Not just the quest for political freedom, but also restrictive British policies on western expansion and paranoia about imperial threats to slavery, Washington biographer Colin G. Calloway wrote, "turned Washington and other Americans to revolution and independence. . . . The revolution was not only a war for independence and a new political order; it was also a war for the North American continent."[6]

Colonial militias—military forces raised from the civilian population—battled Indians throughout the seventeenth and eighteenth centuries over the most precious commodity in North America: land, which the Indians possessed, and white settlers craved. Military historian John Grenier explained that by eliminating Indians "the settlers could make North America their own," but not through limited wars that "did little to drive the Indians from their lands." Instead, white Americans waged unlimited war by sending "groups of men . . . to attack Indian villages and homes, kill Indian women and children, and raze Indian fields." The savagery of Indian warriors was more than matched by settler forces.[7]

In the colony of South Carolina, from 1715 to 1717, British settlers fought the Yamasee Indians and allied tribes in the most destructive war per capita in American history. With the survival of British and Indian civilizations at stake, the settlers' militia forces ultimately prevailed, but at the cost of 7 percent of South Carolina's population. The Yamasees lost more than a quarter of their people to death or slavery, and the remnant fled to the Southern swamps, abandoning their lands to white settlers and ultimately disappearing as a people.[8]

In 1739, South Carolina's settlers battled slaves in the Stono Rebellion, which threatened to turn slaves into masters and masters into slaves. "Our Negroes," South Carolina's lieutenant governor, Thomas Broughton, had warned in 1737, "are very numerous and more dreadful to our safety than any Spanish invader." After settler militias crushed the rebellion at the cost of more than twenty white and more than forty black lives, the South Carolina government upgraded its militia and strengthened the slave patrol, which confiscated weapons and other contraband from slaves, checked on slaves traveling from their home properties, dispersed gatherings of slaves, and chased down runaways. An investigative committee of the state assembly said that in Stono the slave "fought for liberty and life," and the whites "for their country and everything that was dear to them."[9]

In New York, which had a large slave population and was a hub of the slave trade, some two dozen slaves attacked whites with guns, knives, and axes in 1712, killing nine and wounding six, before an armed militia crushed the uprising and authorities executed twenty-one rebels. New York did not abolish slavery until 1799. The New England states and Pennsylvania did so in the 1780s, and New Jersey delayed until 1804. Yet, Northern merchants still profited from the coastal slave trade and the transatlantic trade, which ended at least legally in 1808.

Only white men had a right and responsibility to serve in militias and slave patrols. According to the historian Benjamin Quarles, although "each colony maintained and controlled its own independent militia force [one] policy became uniform throughout the colonies. Slave or free, Negroes were excluded from the militia, save as noncombatants or in unusual emergencies. This policy of semi-exclusion became so prevalent as to constitute a basic tenet of American military tradition." Some critics of gun control draw on the formal colonial exclusion of nonwhites from gun possession and military service to prove the "racist roots" of gun control. However, gun policy was only one of many colonial practices that enabled white settlers to control slaves and fight Indians.[10]

Constitutions of the original thirteen states, from the onset of America's revolution through Congress's adoption of the Second Amendment, provide singular insight into Americans' thinking about firearms just prior to adoption of the Second Amendment. With but one exception, the latest state constitutions either omitted any mention of firearms rights or linked the bearing of arms to militia service and defense of the community, uncoupled from any individual right to private arms. Only the 1776 constitution of Pennsylvania seemed to provide for firearms rights beyond the common defense, saying, "The people have a right to bear arms for the defence of themselves and the state."

Although Pennsylvania adopted its constitution before Georgia, Massachusetts, New Hampshire, New York, and South Carolina, none followed even approximately the Pennsylvania model. Massachusetts confined the right to keep and bear arms for "the common defense." New Hampshire referred only to "a well regulated militia" as "the proper, natural, and sure defense of a state." New York declared that the militia "as well in peace as in war, shall be armed and disciplined, and in readiness for service." Georgia and South Carolina did not mention arms in any context.[11]

Even in the Pennsylvania constitution, as the historian Nathan R. Kozuskanich explains, the phrase "defense of themselves" is not "synonymous with personal self-defense." In context, this phrase likely references communities armed for defense of themselves, notably from Indian incursions, and did not preclude gun control regulations. In the 1799 gun assault case in Philadelphia, Dr. Reynolds's defense attorney did not invoke a right to bear arms for self-defense either under the Second Amendment or the Pennsylvania constitution. Instead, he relied on "the law of nature and the law of reason," which he said allowed deadly force "if necessary to [one's] own safety." According to Kozuskanich, "The case clearly demonstrates that using a gun in self-defense was legally different from bearing arms in 'defense of themselves and the state.'"[12]

In Britain, weapons control had a long history, beginning centuries before its colonization of North America. Compilations of firearms and weapons legislation identify more than forty English statutes and decrees regulating the possession and bearing of arms, prior to America's independence. In 1285, a statute for the City of London prohibited persons from traveling the streets of the city after curfew with "Arms for doing Mischief . . . unless he be a great Man or other lawful Person of good repute, or their certain Messenger." In 1299, King Edward I prohibited anyone from "going armed within the realm without the King's special license."[13]

The 1328 Statute of Northampton declared that persons could "bring no force in affray of the peace, nor to go nor ride armed by night nor by day." An enactment of 1541 prohibited the possession of "little short handguns, and little hagbuts," which were a "great peril and continual fear and danger of the King's loving subjects." The Militia Act of 1662 authorized militia lieutenants to disarm persons deemed to be a threat to the state. A parliamentary statute of 1671 stipulated, "No person who had not lands of the yearly value of 100 pounds other than the son and heir of an esquire or other person of higher degree, should be allowed to own a gun."

Pro-gun rights advocates cite, as precedent for their reading of the Second Amendment, Article VII of the 1689 English Declaration of Rights, which says, "That the subjects which are Protestants may have arms for their defence suitable to their conditions and as allowed by law." Yet, a new government adopted the article as a counterattack against a Catholic king who had disarmed Protestants. And they hemmed it in with the catch-all qualification of "as allowed by law."

A historian of seventeenth-century England, Lois G. Schwoerer, wrote that "no one urged in this or any other debate" on the Declaration of Rights "that the individual had a right to bear arms," and that there "was no ancient political or legal precedent for the right to arms." In restricting arms possession as "suitable to their conditions," the declaration refers to the prior English legislation making the possession of firearms "dependent on the holders' social and economic status," which restricted the right to have a gun to the wealthy elite. "The fact is," Schwoerer concluded, "there was no unrestricted English right of the individual to possess guns for the colonists to inherit." A decade after adoption of the Declaration of Rights, officials of London, alarmed about persons going armed without proper licenses, decreed, "We have for the Remedying the said evil, thought fit to Re-call all Licenses whatsoever."[14]

Consistent with this English precedent, all thirteen governments of pre–Second Amendment America regulated the keeping and bearing of private arms. Colonial and early state governments restricted the carrying, brandishing, and firing of weapons and banned the gathering of armed men or the bearing of arms in sensitive areas. They imposed hunting limitations, enhanced penalties for gun crimes, required the safe storage of gunpowder or firearms, and in a few cases taxed or registered firearms.[15]

Also following English precedent, some of the colonial and early state governments required able-bodied men of military age to possess arms, but for militia service, not

private use. The militia only existed as authorized, organized, and commanded by government. In what would
be anathema to the gun lobby today, governments conducted censuses of arms possessed by militiamen or men
eligible for militia service. When deemed necessary, officials armed militiamen, sometimes through the seizure
of private arms.

During the Revolution, the Continental Congress
directed colonial governments to seize arms from those
who declined to support the rebellion—Tories and neu-
trals alike—and to transfer the weapons to patriot forces.
Pennsylvania responded, in the same year that it adopted
its constitution, by empowering the commanders "of every
Battalion of Militia in this State . . . to collect, receive and
take all the Arms in his District or Township nearest to
such officer which are in the hands of Non-Associators
[nonrevolutionaries] in the most expeditious and effectual
manner in his power." The Pennsylvania legislature saw no
conflict between confiscation and the state constitution's
guarantee of people's right to bear arms for "defense of
themselves, with no exceptions for wars or emergencies."[16]

After independence, the staid, law-and-order Federalists, who adopted the Constitution and the Bill of
Rights, had no intention of protecting a right to private
arms so that aggrieved citizens could rebel against their
new government. For these men, private, arms-toting
militias were a threat, not a boon to their fledgling democracy. Unlike the orderly and verifiable expression
of the people's will through the vote, popular uprisings

risked imposing minority views on the majority and sub-verting lawfully elected governments. The people exer-cised sovereignty, wrote prominent Federalist Benjamin Rush, "only on the days of their election." Once voting and counting is completed, sovereignty is "the property of their rulers." Thomas Paine, the preeminent theorist of the American Revolution, said that unlike King George's monarchy, America's new "republican" government "leaves no room for insurrection because it provides and estab-lishes a rightful means in its stead," whereby elected repre-sentatives "may be displaced by the same power that placed them there, and others elected."[17]

Early American laws routinely restricted the gathering of privately armed persons as a danger to law and order. Massachusetts in 1750 prohibited the gathering of "any persons to the number of twelve or more, being armed with clubs or other weapons" and "unlawfully, riotously, or tumultuously assembled." New Jersey in 1758 banned "several Persons [from] wearing" edged weapons, pistols, "or any other unusual and unlawful Weapons [in pub-lic because it induced] great Fear and Quarrels." Maine in 1786 required that "if any persons, to the number of twelve, or more, being armed with clubs or other weap-ons . . . any Justice of the Peace, Sheriff, or Deputy . . . or Constable . . . shall openly make [a] proclamation asking them to disperse."

George Washington and other framers applauded the mustering of militia forces to suppress Shays's Rebel-lion in Massachusetts in 1786 and 1787, in which farmers protested high taxes. Washington and other framers supported the Massachusetts law prohibiting congregations of armed men and supported the Disqualification Act, which for three years barred rebels from serving on juries, holding public office, voting, or working as schoolmasters, innkeepers, and liquor salesmen. During the rebellion, Washington wrote to the Confederation's secretary of war, General Henry Knox, "There are combustibles in every State, which a spark may set fire to."[18]

During the colonial era, conflict with Indians and control of slaves preoccupied white British settlers. Britain's policies that threatened slavery and limited incursions into Indian territory alarmed settler leaders. Although Britain would not formally abolish slavery until 1833, it alarmed slaveholders in 1772 when the Court of King's Bench ruled that a slave brought from Boston to England could not be sold to slaveholders in Jamaica and must be set free because England and Wales had not authorized slavery by statute law and the institution had no standing in the unwritten or common law.[19]

With the outbreak of revolution, Lord Dunmore, the royal governor of Virginia, used the prospect of freeing slaves against the American patriots. He promised freedom for slaves who would join "His Majesty's Troops." Virginia's revolutionaries responded by imposing the death penalty on all fugitive slaves who fled to the British army. In 1779, Sir Henry Clinton, the British commander in North America, offered protection to slaves who deserted the rebels. General Washington then urged his commanders to recruit slaves and free black people. Ultimately at least several thousand African Americans served in some capacity in the rebel forces. Realizing slaveholders' worst fears, many thousands of slaves fled from bondage, with some joining the British military. Service in Washington's army did not typically earn slaves their freedom; most were returned to bondage along with many runaways apprehended during and after the war.[20]

In the Declaration of Independence, Thomas Jefferson denounced King George III for having "endeavoured to bring on the inhabitants of our frontiers, the merciless Indian Savages whose known rule of warfare, is an undistinguished destruction of all ages, sexes and conditions." Beyond the many injustices inflicted by the British on their colonial subjects, revolutionaries objected to a British proclamation in 1763 that restricted settlement to the lands east of the Appalachian Mountains and left vast territories to the Indian nations. Although later modified, important limitations of the proclamation remained in place, especially on westward expansion in Virginia, an epicenter of the revolution.

Although many settlers crossed the porous barrier between open and prohibited territory, their landholdings lacked legal title, and speculators such as revolutionary leaders George Washington, Patrick Henry, and George Mason found it difficult to sell or lease western holdings. Washington complained in 1771 that in western lands "no man is certain of his property, or can tell how, or in what manner to dispose of it." After the break with England, speculators scooped up tens of thousands of frontier acreage previously occupied by Indians. None, however, matched Washington, who had acquired some forty-five thousand acres of western land by the end of his life.[21]

Calloway wrote that slavery and western expansion were integral to the worldview of Washington, who "from cradle to grave inhabited a world built on the labor of African people and on the land of disposed Indian people." Washington "knew that the frontier was Indian Country and that the future he envisioned would be realized at the expense of the people that lived there." American "independence marked a fundamental shift" in the balance of power between white settlers and Indians, explained historian Edward Countryman. Imperial Britain had provided Indians the means "for protecting themselves," which "would be denied by the young republic. . . . The western land that Indians held on their own terms under the old order became the huge trove of free capital that was the basis for the young republic's commercial agricultural expansion, north and south alike." In 1780, Jefferson said of Indians, "The same world will scarcely do for them and us." The new republic of freedom, he prophesied, would "add to the Empire of liberty an extensive and fertile Country."[22]

3

Adoption of the Second Amendment

When you actually go back and look at the debate that went into drafting of the amendment, you can squint and look really hard, but there's simply no evidence of it being about individual gun ownership for self-protection or for hunting. Emphatically, the focus was on the militias.

—MICHAEL WALDMAN, AUTHOR, *THE SECOND AMENDMENT: A BIOGRAPHY*, 2014[1]

In 1787, the then fifty-five-year-old George Washington, who had already outlived his father by seven years, decided to sacrifice his "love of retirement" and "a mind at ease." He donned his best breeches and frock coat, powdered his hair, and pushed his body, debilitated by seven years of war, to serve his country once more, this time as the indispensable president of a Constitutional Convention in the Philadelphia summer.

Convention delegates never debated the individual right to keep and bear private arms. They focused on the militia, which they viewed as an organized, controlled, and regulated force, not as the entirety of the people privately armed. The delegates considered the militia as "the joint object of congressional and state legislation," explained historian Jack N. Rakove. "Nothing that was said during the principal discussions of August 18 and 23, 1787, supports the contention that the militia would henceforth exist as a spontaneous manifestation of the community at large."[2]

Rather than recognizing the right of armed citizens to resist alleged tyranny by government, the delegates authorized the militias to suppress internal rebellions. Their new Constitution provided "for calling forth the Militia to execute the Laws of the Union, suppress Insurrections and repel Invasions." It empowered the federal government "to provide for organizing, arming, and disciplining, the Militia, and for governing such Part of them as may be employed in the Service of the United States, reserving to the States respectively, the Appointment of the Officers, and the Authority of training the Militia according to the discipline prescribed by Congress."

The militia did not fully substitute for a regular military, despite the misgivings of some delegates about the dangers of a standing army. Article I of the Constitution empowered Congress "to raise and support Armies," and "to provide and maintain a Navy." However, the Constitution limited army appropriations to no "longer Term than two Years" and required periodic reauthorization of its budget. The new republic, then, had a two-tiered military system: the regular armed forces plus the organized militia.

At the Constitutional Convention, delegate George

Mason of Virginia said that he "wished the plan had been prefaced with a Bill of Rights. . . . It would give great quiet to the people." Without a dissenting vote, the convention rejected his proposal for what James Madison called "parchment barriers" that could not fully spell out all rights reserved to the American people. To protect people's liberties, Madison relied on checks and balances within government, and on the virtue of Americans. "No theoretical checks—no form of government can render us secure," he wrote. "To suppose that any form of government will secure liberty or happiness without any virtue in the people, is a chimerical idea."[3]

Through a circuitous route, however, the Federalists, led improbably by Madison, agreed to a Bill of Rights. When Madison ran for the first Congress in 1788, his Anti-Federalist opponents, who had opposed ratification of the Constitution but now held a majority in the Virginia legislature, cabined him within a geographically elongated district packed with opposition voters. Madison beat his opponent—another future president, James Monroe—despite what we today call a gerrymander, by co-opting Anti-Federalist demands for a Bill of Rights, which he hoped would reconcile skeptics to their new government.[4]

States recommended Bill of Rights amendments relating to arms and defense. Most followed the precedents of state constitutions and linked the keeping and bearing of arms to sustaining a well-regulated militia. Even Pennsylvania's ratifying convention, which Federalists dominated, decisively voted down a proposal for a right to keep and bear arms for self-defense and "killing game." The majority declined even to include the proposal in the journal of the convention, although the minority circulated it among Anti-Federalists, who mostly disregarded it. Yet, the proposal for firearm rights granted broad discretion for gun control by adding, "No law shall be passed for disarming the people or any of them, unless for crimes committed, or real danger of public injury from individuals."[5]

The ratifying convention in New Hampshire proposed a negatively framed provision that "Congress shall never disarm any citizen unless such as are or have been in Actual Rebellion." Although seemingly more explicit than the Second Amendment on the right to private arms, the proposal exempted the states and did not prohibit Congress from enacting firearms regulations short of confiscation.

James Madison and the first Congress rejected proposals of the Pennsylvania dissenters and the New Hampshire convention, or any approximation. Instead, they adopted a markedly different amendment aimed at sustaining a well-regulated militia, not a right to private arms. At Congress's first session in 1789, Madison proposed nearly twenty amendments to the Constitution as part of a Bill of Rights, after sifting through some two hundred proposals from the states. Twelve survived congressional review in some form. His first draft of the future Second Amendment read:

> The right of the people to keep and bear arms
> shall not be infringed; a well armed and well
> regulated militia being the best security of a free

country: but no person religiously scrupulous of bearing arms shall be compelled to render military service in person.

If Madison had intended his draft to secure an individual right to keep and bear arms, uncoupled to militia service, he would not have needed the clause exempting certain persons from military service.

A House committee substituted the phrase "free state" in place of "free country," a small change with large consequences. As Northern states abolished slavery, the nation moved closer to a division between free and slave states. To control slaves through militias and patrols, the slave states needed an amendment that referenced the security of the states, not the country. The committee also shifted the order of the amendment's phrases, putting the explanatory phrase before the operative clause. It replaced the original semicolon with a comma, tying the two more closely together. These amendments further demonstrated that the first clause of the amendment was hardly irrelevant, but of real concern to its framers.

After members dropped the phrase on religious exemption, the Second Amendment assumed its final form, as enacted by Congress in 1789 and ratified by the states in 1791 as part of the Bill of Rights:

A well regulated Militia, being necessary to the security of a free State, the right of the people to keep and bear Arms, shall not be infringed.

The Senate also rejected a motion to insert "for the common defense" after "bear Arms." Although gun rights advocates claim that the Senate had thus recognized an individual right to keep and bear arms, no evidence backs up this interpretation. Senate debates were not recorded for this first Congress. A more plausible explanation, given House debates, is that the phrase was redundant. Moreover, the proposed amendment could well have contradicted the use of the militia for the purpose of quelling internal rebellion, a high priority of the Federalist majority in the first Senate. Tellingly, the Senate struck from the final version an amendment that defined the militia as "composed of the body of the people."[6]

The NRA's contention that the Second Amendment had primacy in the Bill of Rights as "America's First Freedom, the one right that protects all the others," is another gun lobby myth. No member of Congress or a state ratifying convention made any such claim, which framer Madison rejected, saying that the "essential rights" are trial by jury and freedom of conscience, speech, and the press.[7]

The sparsely recorded House debates centered on religious exemptions for military service. Congress dropped the exemption clause not because it muddled an individual-rights construction, but because members feared that pleas of religious scruples, legitimate or not, could weaken the nation's well-regulated militias. Pennsylvania representative Thomas Scott said that if the exemption clause "becomes part of the constitution, such persons can neither be called upon for their services, nor can an equivalent be demanded; it is also attended with still further difficulties, for a militia can never be depended upon." He worried that those "with no religion" would "have recourse to these pretexts to get excused." No participant in this debate or any other contemporary commentator questioned the authority of government to protect public health and safety by regulating the keeping and bearing of dangerous weapons such as pistols, muskets, swords, and daggers.[8]

As a panel of linguists and professors of English explained in an amicus brief submitted for the *Heller* case, people at the time would not have read the Second Amendment as protecting an individual right to bear arms, independent of militia service. Rather, the first phrase limited the application of the subsequent, operative clause "under longstanding linguistic principles that were well understood and recognized" by contemporaries. "The 'well regulated Militia' clause necessarily adds meaning to the 'keep and bear Arms' clause." The crucial modifier *well regulated* "suggests a militia that not only is 'subject to' regulation under the militia laws, but also is in possession of the qualities that flow from participation in regular military exercises—orderliness, discipline, proficiency with arms, knowledge about maneuvers and so on." These attributes did not apply to the citizenry at large, even those subject to militia service.[9]

Washington recognized the difference between the militia as armed citizens and a trained, disciplined, and organized military body. Early in the Revolutionary War,

Washington disparaged the military value of an unregulated militia: "I am wearied to death all day with a variety of perplexing circumstances, disturbed at the conduct of the militia, whose behavior and want of discipline has done great injury to the other troops, who never had officers, except in a few instances, worth the bread they eat." A year later he wrote, "The irregular and disjointed State of the Militia of this province, makes it necessary for me to inform you, that unless a Law is passed by your Legislature to reduce them to some order, and oblige them to turn out in a different Manner from what they have hitherto done, we shall bring very few into the Feild [*sic*], and even those few, will render little or no Service." As president in 1794, Washington urgently called for the "devising and establishing of a well regulated militia" through "organizing, arming, and disciplining the militia; and thus providing, in the language of the Constitution, for calling them forth to execute the laws of the Union, suppress insurrections, and repel invasions."[10]

The authorities on early American usage demonstrate that "the term 'bear arms' is an idiomatic expression that means 'to serve as a soldier, do military service, fight.'" They found that "examples of the idiomatic usage of 'bear arms' during the time of the founding abound. In each instance where 'bear arms' (or 'bearing arms' or 'bear arms against') is used without additional language modifying the phrase, it is unquestionably used in its ordinary idiomatic sense." Unless there is additional modifying language, "the idiom is apparent."[11]

In the Library of Congress's database on debates in the Continental and US Congress from 1774 to 1821, the term *bear arms* surfaces thirty times. In every case, the linguists explain, "The usage was unquestionably the military usage." In historian Saul Cornell's compilation of language in "books, pamphlets, broadsides and newspapers from the period between the Declaration of Independence and the adoption of the Second Amendment," there were more than 100 instances of the term, in which all but five "conformed to the military understanding of the term." A review of these outliers found that in four of five, "the use was expressly qualified by further language indicating a different meaning (e.g., 'bear arms in times of peace' or 'bear arms . . . for the purpose of killing game')."[12]

Nathan Kozuskanich searched *bear arms* in "120 American newspapers from 1690 to 1800," plus numerous newspapers, pamphlets, and broadsides in the Library of Congress online database. He found that virtually all the sources "use the phrase 'bear arms' within an explicitly collective or military context to indicate military action." He concludes that Americans in the eighteenth century "overwhelmingly used 'bear arms' in a military sense both in times of war and in times of peace." Similarly, a scan of early-American newspapers and compilations of 135,000 colonial texts by Brigham Young University fails to turn up narratives of self-defense with firearms, and scarcely any references to the right to bear arms outside of a military context.[13]

If the originators of the Second Amendment had

meant for it to confer an individual right to private arms, then its explanatory clause would have been redundant and unnecessary. An individual right to private arms is much broader than a right to keep and bear arms for service in a well-regulated militia. It would include firearms rights for every man eligible for militia service as well as men too young, too old, or too disabled to serve, women, and at least free, if not enslaved, African Americans.

Gun rights advocates argue that gun control was racist and that the Second Amendment liberated African Americans to keep and bear private arms. Yet, the opposite is true. Contrary to the gun lobby's claim, the well-regulated militia did not include the entire people of the land. Recall that in its final version Congress rejected this definition of the militia. At the time of the Second Amendment's adoption and ratification, women, Native Americans, and African Americans (except under extraordinary circumstances) were barred from armed militia service. A year after ratification of the Second Amendment, the federal Militia Act of 1792 limited service to white males, with no one in Congress or the press objecting on Second Amendment grounds. The federal government did not open the militias to African Americans until the Civil War, more than seventy years after ratification of the Second Amendment.[14]

Thus, the amendment's first phrase, that tied the keeping and bearing of arms to a well-organized militia, had the effect of excluding African Americans. Gun rights advocates conveniently ignore this. Southern senators, congressmen, or state legislators, including slaveholders such as Madison, would hardly have backed the Second Amendment if they believed for a moment that it guaranteed a constitutional right for black people to keep and bear private arms. No Southerner, or one of many Northerners with antipathies to African Americans, during debates over the Second Amendment in Congress or in the state ratifying bodies, is recorded as having expressed any such objection. My purpose here is not to critique the framers as racist, but rather to show that they never intended to provide a private right to arms in the Second Amendment.[15]

Of the thousands involved in framing, adopting, or ratifying the Second Amendment, not a single person said that it protected an individual right to keep and bear arms. A panel of pro-gun-rights law professors claimed to have discovered two exceptions, neither of which withstands scrutiny. They cite James Madison's note on the 1689 English Declaration of Rights, which reads, "fallacy on both sides—espcy as to English Decln of Rts—Attainders—arms to Protestts." Beyond relying on an impossibly cryptic reference that could be affirming or disputing the Declaration of Rights, the lawyers ignore the its second clause, which limits the arming of Protestants as "suitable to their conditions and as allowed by law."[16]

They additionally cite a book written nearly forty years later by William Rawle, who they claim had sat in the Pennsylvania Assembly that ratified the Bill of Rights. However, the primary source on his political career documents that "in October 1787, he was chosen a member of the Assembly . . . but he would serve no longer than the year for which he had been elected," predating the enactment and ratification of the Second Amendment.[17]

Faced with this embarrassing silence from participants, gun rights advocates canvassed all opinion makers from the time of the Second Amendment's adoption. Yet, confirmation of the advocates' views remained so lacking that true believers have compensated with distorted and fabricated quotations, integrating these frauds into the popular culture of gun rights. Here are a few of the more prominent examples.

George Washington

A free people ought not only be armed and disciplined, but they should have sufficient arms and ammunition to maintain a status of independence from any who might attempt to abuse them, which would include their own government.[18]

Fact-checkers at Snopes.com note that this quotation has been making the online rounds for several years. The first ten words of the quotation, before the *but*, are from Washington's address to Congress on January 8, 1790. The rest is fabricated. Washington made no such claim about the synergy between arms and independence in this address or in any other context. As explained by Ron Chernow, author of the Pulitzer Prize–winning *Washington: A*

Life, "Washington is talking about national defense policy, not individuals arming themselves, and the need for national self-sufficiency in creating military supplies."[19]

George Washington

Firearms are second only to the Constitution in importance; they are the people's liberty's teeth.[20]

This bogus Washington quotation has circulated online and in print. Scholars at the National Library for the Study of George Washington at Mount Vernon say that it "does not show up in any of Washington's writings, nor does any closely related quote."[21]

Thomas Jefferson

No free man shall ever be debarred the use of arms. The strongest reason for people to retain the right to keep and bear arms is, as a last resort, to protect themselves against tyranny in government.[22]

Gun rights advocates have disseminated this purported Jefferson quotation online for many years. The first sentence is from Jefferson's first-draft proposal for the

1776 Constitution of Virginia. The third and final draft, however, conveys a different meaning: "No Freeman shall be debarred the use of arms [in his own lands or tenements]." None of his drafts made it into the Virginia Constitution. The Thomas Jefferson Foundation debunks the second sentence as a fraud, which "does not appear in the Virginia Constitution drafts or text as adopted, nor in any other known Jefferson writings."[23]

Thomas Jefferson

One loves to possess arms, though they hope
never to have occasion for them.

This quotation has appeared on the NRA website and many other pro-gun sites. Retailers sell T-shirts and plaques emblazoned with this supposed Jeffersonian wisdom. However, Jefferson is referring to arming himself with facts not weaponry. On June 19, 1796, Jefferson asked President Washington for a document that would help Jefferson resolve a political controversy. "While on the subject of papers permit me to ask one from you," Jefferson wrote. "Tho' I do not know that it will ever be of the least importance to me yet one loves to possess arms tho' they hope never to have occasion for them. They possess my paper in my own handwriting. It is just I should possess theirs."[24]

John Adams

Arms in the hands of citizens may be used at
individual discretion in private self-defence.

This quote appears online; in NRA spokesperson
Dana Loesch's 2014 book, *Hands Off My Gun;* and in a
slightly different version in pro-gun advocate Stephen P.
Halbrook's 1989 book, *A Right to Bear Arms.* Loesch and
Halbrook truncated this quotation to make it appear to
support an unlimited right to keep and bear private arms.
Yet, Adams actually said that privately armed, untrained
citizens pose a serious threat to liberty and the Constitution, and that arms should be restricted to persons who
support established governments.[25] The full and correct
Adams quote reads as follows:

> To suppose arms in the hands of citizens, to be
> used at individual discretion, except in private
> self-defence, or by partial orders of towns,
> countries or districts of a state, is to demolish
> every constitution, and lay the laws prostrate,
> so that liberty can be enjoyed by no man; it is a
> dissolution of the government. The fundamental
> law of the militia is, that it be created, directed
> and commanded by the laws, and ever for the
> support of the laws. This truth is acknowledged
> by our author when he says, "The arms of the
> Commonwealth should be lodged in the hands

of that part of the people which are firm to its establishment."[26]

George Mason

To disarm the people is the best and most effectual way to enslave them.[27]

This snippet from George Mason's speech during Virginia's convention to ratify the Constitution appears in Loesch's book, online, and as a gun-lobby bumper sticker, decal, and magnet. In context, Mason had argued not for an individual right to private arms, but for arming, training, and disciplining a well-regulated militia. The complete version of this incomplete fragment reads, "To disarm the people; that it was the best and most effectual way to enslave them; but that they should not do it openly, but weaken them, and let them sink gradually, *by totally disusing and neglecting the militia*" (emphasis added).

Clearly the full, not the truncated, version of Mason's remark shows that he was referring to the neglect of the militia, not the deprivation of private arms. Mason goes on to reject the notion that an unorganized, unregulated, but armed citizenry can preserve freedom: "When, against a regular and disciplined army, yeomanry are the only defence, —yeomanry, unskillful and unarmed,— what chance is there for preserving freedom? . . . Why should we not provide against the danger of having our militia, our real and natural strength, destroyed? . . . If they neglect to arm them, and prescribe proper discipline, they will be of no use."[28]

Loesch also cites an anti-gun-control passage from Italian philosopher Cesare Beccaria, which Jefferson copied in his commonplace book (in original Italian), implying that it represented Jefferson's own views. Jefferson put numerous quotations from many sources in his copy books. His only comment on Beccaria's passage was "False idee di utilità." ("False ideas of utility"), which just encapsulated Beccaria's argument. Although Jefferson adopted other elements of Beccaria's thought, not once in his voluminous public writing or speaking did he endorse Beccaria's critique of gun control or represent Beccaria's views as his own. Yet some gun rights advocates have directly attributed the quote to Jefferson.[29]

Gun rights advocates have even edited the Second Amendment itself. For many years the NRA placed at the entrance to its headquarters the supposed wording of the Second Amendment, "the right of the people to keep and bear arms, shall not be infringed," deleting the amendment's first, explanatory phrase. "The National Rifle Association is the only lobbying organization in America with half of a constitutional amendment emblazoning across the front of its headquarters," wrote pro-gun-control attorney Kristen Rand in 1992.[30]

One figure, Pennsylvania Federalist Tench Coxe, seems to have stood alone among contemporaries in saying plainly that the Second Amendment guaranteed an individual right to keep and bear private arms. "The people are confirmed by the article in their right to keep and bear their private arms," he said in 1789. Coxe did not serve in Congress, opposed adding a bill of rights to the Constitution, and had no role in drafting the amendment. Moreover, Coxe made his claim before Congress adopted the final version of the Second Amendment. Yet he is so pivotal to gun rights advocates that two of the most prominent, Stephen P. Halbrook and David B. Kopel, wrote a fifty-three-page article about Coxe. However, they fail to connect the dots between his Second Amendment advocacy and his financial interests as one of America's most prolific merchants of arms.[31]

Like the players in today's gun industry, Coxe profited both from private arms sales and government contracts. In a 1787 paper he urged the government to promote a domestic arms industry and continued this advocacy as an official in the administrations of Washington and Jefferson. Under legislation enacted in 1808 for arming the militia, Coxe won contracts worth more than $400,000, equivalent to over $8 million today. Coxe rises from history not as an independent authority, but as the earliest exemplar of the bond between an individualist interpretation of the Second Amendment and the lucrative business of making and selling arms.[32]

4

A Century of Gun Controls

Firearms are an unmitigated nuisance and should only be in the hands of officers of the law or guardians of trust funds. If there were not so many firearms in the hands of irresponsible persons, there would be many less homicides and cases of deadly assault.

—NEW YORK CRIMINAL COURT JUDGE
JOHN J. DOBLER, 1898[1]

Americans in the nineteenth century shared Judge Dobler's concern about how firearms imperiled public safety. The Second Amendment was a dead letter for its first century. It did not figure in formative policy debates on armaments, and it did not restrict state and local governments from prolifically adopting gun control laws that were rarely struck down or even challenged in the courts. The US Supreme Court declined to apply the Second Amendment to the states or to affirm that it protected an individual right to private arms apart from maintaining a well-regulated militia. Only one state constitution replicated the wording of the federal amendment without qualification, and only one state protected by statute an individual right to keep arms. During Reconstruction, the proliferation of firearms, not discriminatory gun controls, enabled white supremacists to terrorize African Americans.

In the year after ratification of the Second Amendment, the Militia Act of 1792 required all able-bodied white males between the ages of eighteen and forty-five, with certain exemptions, to provide their own stands of arms (a musket, cartridge box, cap box, bayonet, and belt), but left enforcement to states, which typically balked at imposing this costly burden on their citizens. During the debates over the Act, no member of Congress mentioned the newly ratified Second Amendment or addressed the bearing of arms in any context beyond the support of a well-regulated militia under the auspices of government.[2]

Two years later, President George Washington deployed the militia to suppress the Whiskey Rebellion of 1794, an insurrection of Pennsylvania farmers aggrieved by an excise tax on whiskey. Any yielding to internal insurrections, Washington said, would "violate the fundamental principal of our constitution, which enjoins that the will of the majority shall prevail." The gun lobby's favorite source, Tench Coxe, then the federal commissioner of revenue, agreed. Elections, he said, "without fraud or violence," create "an obligation to obedience." Armed opposition to a legitimately enacted law was a "sin against the political gospel." If dissidents continue to "desert this great Commandment of freedom" then righteous Americans should condone any such "strong measures."[3]

Still, the militia was so poorly equipped in 1794 that the federal War Department had to provide ten thousand firearms to the fifteen thousand militiamen summoned in response to the Whiskey Rebellion. In 1799, President John Adams called upon militia forces to suppress another internal insurrection, the Fries Rebellion, in which predominantly German American settlers—led by Pennsylvania auctioneer John Fries—resisted the federal government's new tax on their homes and lands.[4]

In 1807, Congress put the emphatic stamp of law on its fear of internal rebellion with the Insurrection Act. The Act established the wide umbrella of "all cases of insurrection, or obstruction to the laws." It said, "where it is lawful for the President of the United States to call forth the militia for the purpose of suppressing such insurrection, or of causing the laws to be duly executed, it shall be lawful for him to employ, for the same purposes, such part of the land or naval force of the United States." Congress passed the Act without debate; no commentator at the time raised an objection based on an alleged Second Amendment right to keep and bear private arms as a check on government. Since the 1827 US Supreme Court case of *Martin v. Mott*, the authority to decide on intervention "is exclusively vested in the President, and his decision is conclusive upon all other persons."[5]

From the 1790s through 1900, the provisions in the nation's forty-five state constitutions contradict the claim that nineteenth-century Americans commonly believed the Second Amendment conferred a right to keep and bear private arms. All of the constitutions included declarations of rights that closely tracked the federal Bill of Rights, with the *notable exception of the Second Amendment.*

Just four of forty-five states, all from the South—Georgia, Louisiana, North Carolina, and South Carolina—replicated the Second Amendment's wording in their constitutions. However, three of these states added qualifiers that provided for at least some control over private arms. Only South Carolina adopted the Second Amendment's language without emendation. Fifteen other states omitted any references to a right to bear arms, whether for individual or collective defense, and four limited this right to militia service or the common defense. Another four states had ambiguous provisions that referred to defense and security, two of which established the state's authority to regulate firearms. Eighteen states followed the Pennsylvania model or a close facsimile, but seven of them provided for firearm regulations, leaving only eleven of forty-five states with seemingly an unqualified right to keep and bear private arms.[6]

Only a single state, Oregon, in 1868, adopted a law to protect an individual right to bear arms. Still, two decades later, Oregon demonstrated the limited scope of this right when it adopted a law prohibiting the concealed carry of firearms.

Neither the Second Amendment nor even the state

constitutions with the broadest of gun rights impeded the enactment of gun control laws. In the century after enactment of the Second Amendment, guided by the English precedent of the Statute of Northampton, most states forbade the carrying of concealed weapons and nearly half the states adopted regulations that included the registration and taxation of firearms and prohibitions on the brandishing of firearms and the sale or transfer of firearms to minors and persons deemed dangerous. A third of the states embraced especially strict gun control laws that prohibited any public bearing of arms, whether concealed or open.

Arkansas 1881: Prohibited the wearing or carrying "in any manner whatever, as a weapon, any dirk or bowie knife, or a sword, or a spear in a cane, brass or metal knucks, razor, or any pistol of any kind whatever, except such pistols as are used in the army or navy of the United States."

Delaware 1852: "Any justice of the peace may also cause to be arrested . . . all who go armed offensively to the terror of the people."

Kansas 1881: "The Council shall prohibit and punish the carrying of firearms, or other dangerous or deadly weapons, concealed or otherwise."

Massachusetts 1836, Maine 1840, Michigan 1846, Virginia 1847, Wisconsin 1849, Oregon 1853, Minnesota 1873, Pennsylvania 1860: Prohibited "any person, [from] going armed with any dirk, dagger, sword, pistol, or other offensive and dangerous weapon, without a reasonable cause to fear an assault on himself, or any of his family or property."

Tennessee 1879: Prohibited the carrying "publicly or privately, any . . . belt or pocket pistol, revolver, or any kind of pistol, except the army or navy pistol."

Texas 1871: Prohibited any person from "carrying on or about his person, saddle, or in his saddle bags, any pistol," or other dangerous weapon, "unless he had reasonable grounds for fearing an unlawful attack on his person, and that such ground of attack shall be immediate and pressing."

West Virginia 1870: Prohibited persons from going "armed with a deadly or dangerous weapon, without reasonable cause to fear violence to his person, family, or property."

Wyoming 1876: Prohibited persons from bearing "concealed or openly, any fire-arm or other deadly weapon, within the limit of any city, town or village."

The similar provisions in these laws speak to the diffusion of gun control ideology across the nation. Michigan, Pennsylvania, and Wyoming adopted their stringent laws despite boasting constitutions that declared with emendation a right "to bear arms for the defense of himself and the state." Courts did not strike down any of these laws either under state constitutions or the Second Amendment.[7]

Legendary towns of America's Wild West, such as Tombstone, Arizona, Dodge City and Leavenworth, Kansas, and Deadwood, South Dakota, banned the possession of firearms within city limits. The enforcement of Tombstone's gun control law was what led to the iconic shoot-out of America's frontier, the Gunfight at the O.K. Corral, which took place at a storefront near the corral. On October 26, 1881, four Tombstone lawmen—Wyatt, Virgil, and Morgan Earp and "Doc" Holliday—confronted members of the outlaw Cochise County Cowboys gang to demand the surrender of their illegally possessed guns. For reasons undocumented, the encounter quickly turned violent, with both sides firing a total of thirty shots at point-blank range. In less than a minute, three of the outlaws lay dead or dying, and all the lawmen but Wyatt Earp suffered nonfatal wounds.

Despite this bloodshed, when outlaws defied the law, gun control worked well on the frontier to limit firearms violence. Only two other gun deaths occurred in Tombstone for the entire year of 1881, and generally Western towns that banned firearms had fewer gun murders and assaults than gun-open towns. In Kansas's five largest cattle town from 1870 to 1885 murders average only 0.6 annually per town.[8]

State courts struck down only a handful of gun control laws during the nineteenth century, and federal courts played no role in firearms litigation. In the 1833 case of *Barron v. Baltimore*, a unanimous US Supreme Court ruled that the Bill of Rights applied only to the national government, not to the states. The Court reaffirmed this limitation in 1876.[9]

No such limitation on the Second Amendment's coverage applied to a strict gun control bill that Congress enacted for the federally controlled District of Columbia in 1892. The legislation prohibited the concealed carry of handguns and their open carry with unlawful intent. It banned the sale or transfer of handguns to persons under twenty-one years of age. Upon proof of necessity, an individual could obtain from a judge a one-month permit to carry a handgun. The bill passed the House with no debate, and only a single senator, Democrat Roger Q. Mills of Texas, a former Confederate army officer and ardent white supremacist, raised an objection based on the Second Amendment. Other senators sought only to tighten the bill by eliminating the permit exception. No exponent of the Second Amendment challenged in court this legislation nor any other DC gun law until the twenty-first century.[10]

The federal government meanwhile continued the colonial practice of taking censuses of firearms by men eligible for militia service. After conducting an arms tally in 1793, Secretary of War Henry Knox determined that privately possessed guns were insufficient "for security against enemies, internal and external." The federal government "should always possess one-hundred thousand arms placed in their respective arsenals." The arms should "be fabricated among ourselves," to keep America from depending on foreign sources.[11]

Government backing gave rise to a new and tightly regulated arms industry that advanced America's nascent industrial revolution. In 1798, the War Department contracted with Eli Whitney, the inventor of the cotton gin, for ten thousand stands of arms within two years. Whitney could not deliver so many arms with gunsmiths handcrafting each firearm. After years of trial and error, he pioneered the mass production of guns through interchangeable parts assembled by workers without special skills. His innovations inextricably linked domestic arms manufacturers with the needs of the state and inspired mass production in other industries.

In 1808, with America locked in a trade war with Britain, the state militias were so poorly supplied with usable firearms that Congress adopted an "Act making provision for the arming and equipping the whole body of the militia of the United States." As in 1792, during heated debates over the act no member of Congress mentioned the Second Amendment or an individual right to keep and bear arms as a restraint on government. As presciently noted by Representative George Michael Troup of the Committee on Military Affairs, Congress did not vote to arm state militias as a check on the national government. Rather, members worried that arms supplied to state forces could be used for "the rebellion of a state against the authority of the United States," thus "bringing about the very state of things which cannot be thought of without horror."[12]

A slow-moving bureaucracy delayed delivery of the arms. During the War of 1812, militia forces typically proved to be poorly armed, undermanned, and ill trained. Despite the legend of the sharpshooting pioneer, usable guns were especially scarce in frontier regions remote from industrial centers. David Holmes, the territorial governor of Mississippi, reported that "heretofore it has been, and still is, impracticable to procure arms suitable for actual service in this part of the United States." Future president William Henry Harrison, the governor of the less far-flung territory of Indiana, complained that guns "are not to be had in the Western country."[13]

After the War of 1812, the organized, enrolled militia fell into disuse, with the government relying on the regular military supplemented by conscripts and volunteers for militia service. "By the 1840s the militia system envisioned in the early days of the republic was a dead letter," wrote Professor Stephen Skowronek of Yale University. In 1862, both the United States and the Confederacy began drafting soldiers, and the US Congress modified its militia laws to authorize service by African Americans.[14]

During the Civil War, the federal government raced to provision its massively expanding armed forces by importing weapons from Europe, increasing production at federal armories, and contracting for small arms from private American firms. When the military demand for firearms abruptly collapsed at war's end, some gunmakers exited the arms market, but companies such as Colt, Whitney, Sharps, Remington, and Winchester continued to make and sell guns.

During the late nineteenth century, a new kind of volunteer militia, called the national guard, but not equivalent to the modern guard, replaced the traditional enrolled militia. Guard forces did not challenge but served government by crushing internal dissent again, which in this era took the form of strikes by American workers. From 1871 to 1900 governments called out militias and regular army troops to quell many dozens of strikes, although some ill-trained and poorly disciplined militiamen resisted firing upon strikers. During the nationwide railroad strike of 1877 more than a hundred people died in confrontations between strikers and guard members, federal troops, and police forces.[15]

In 1871, former military officers formed the National Rifle Association, not to defend the Second Amendment or protect Americans from the tyranny of government, but to sharpen Americans' marksmanship skills, especially for those serving in national guard forces. Drawing on the example of the British National Rifle Association, Colonel William C. Church proposed in the *Army and Navy Journal* that retired military should form a new organization to bolster the national defense through an effort to "promote and encourage rifle shooting on a scientific basis." Most members of the NRA's organizing committee had fought in the Civil War, and retired Union general Ambrose Burnside served as its first president; former general and former US president Ulysses S. Grant became its eighth president. Although the NRA struggled for financing and membership in its first three decades, the association's military orientation foreshadowed a saving partnership with the American defense establishment.[16]

Controversy over gun control arose in the post–Civil War South, where Black Codes imposed onerous burdens on freed slaves, including restrictions on their access to firearms. Yet states quickly repealed the Black Codes under federal pressure. It was not gun controls but rather the unchecked availability of firearms that enabled private white militias such as the Ku Klux Klan, the White League, and unnamed bands of vigilantes to murder and terrorize African Americans as a strategy to restore white supremacy to the South.

Newly freed and largely impoverished slaves, with their shotguns and a few war-surplus firearms, could hardly win an arms race against well-armed and organized bands of white men, many of them veterans of the war. Blacks were economically dependent on white landowners and outnumbered by white men with military training. Through controlling the black population by force of arms, the white private militias replicated social controls of the slave era.

In 1873, for example, in Colfax, Louisiana, heavily armed whites massacred some one hundred and fifty black people, while losing only three of their own. "All the Negroes ask is to be let alone," Republican senator Oliver P. Morton of Indiana said. "They know that they cannot cope with the whites in any struggle for arms." J. R. Beckwith, the US attorney for Louisiana, said that without the protection of law "there is no adequate remedy for the killing of Negroes in this State."[17]

In their study of Reconstruction, Joshua Horwitz

and Casey Anderson explode the "facile arguments" of gun rights advocates who "assume that an armed populace best protects liberty and that a weak government is less capable of becoming tyrannical." Reconstruction "showed something else entirely: a well-armed populace is capable of enforcing its will at the expense of the rights of minorities if the federal government lacks the political or military strength to intervene." They concluded that "the crime of Reconstruction, therefore, is not enactment of a few gun control statutes but the fact that under the camouflage of states' rights, Southern Democrats were permitted to turn the clock back on freedom and civil rights."[18]

In 1871, to quell antiblack violence, the surviving Republican Reconstruction government of Texas enacted a tight gun control law. In 1872, the state supreme court upheld the act under the Second Amendment, even if it were applied to the states. It said that the amendment covers only "the arms of a militiaman or soldier." It found, "To refer the deadly devices . . . to the proper or necessary arms of a 'well-regulated militia,' is simply ridiculous. No kind of travesty, however subtle or ingenious, could so misconstrue this provision of the constitution of the United States, as to make it cover and protect that pernicious vice, from which so many murders, assassinations, and deadly assaults have sprung."[19]

Consistent with the Texas decision, the US Supreme Court ruled in 1886 that the Second Amendment did not protect privately armed militias that imperiled public safety. Private militia leader Herman Presser had challenged under the Second Amendment his arrest for violating an Illinois law that prohibited armed persons from associating as a military force or "drilling and parading" without a license from the governor. The Court reaffirmed that the Second Amendment did not apply to state law. It affirmed the state's authority to regulate the bearing of arms in the public interest. The Court ruled that even if the Second Amendment covered the states, the Illinois law did not "infringe the right of the people to keep and bear arms" because the law was "necessary to the public peace, safety, and good order." The Second Amendment did not protect armed private militias, which governments could lawfully "disperse" and "suppress."[20]

5

Enter the Federal Government

The sooner we get to the point where we are prepared to recognize the fact that the possession of deadly weapons must be regulated and checked, the better off we are going to be as a people.

—US ATTORNEY GENERAL HOMER S. CUMMINGS, 1934[1]

On January 23, 1911, Fitzhugh Coyle Goldsborough fired six fatal pistol shots at novelist David Graham Phillips, in broad daylight outside the Princeton Club at Gramercy Park North in Manhattan. Goldsborough then killed himself with the same handgun. An outraged George Petit le Brun, who worked in New York City's coroner's office, decided that "the time had come to have legislation passed that would prevent the sale of pistols to irresponsible persons." His lobbying, along with rising crime in the state, prompted the legislature to override objections from the state's gun industry and enact the landmark Sullivan Act, one of America's strictest gun control laws, named after its sponsor, state senator Timothy Sullivan.[2]

The Sullivan Act required discretionary licenses for the possession of handguns and became a model for strict handgun controls in other states and localities. It withstood a constitutional challenge in 1913 when the New York State Court of Appeals ruled that the act represented a legitimate "exercise of the police power" to protect "the safety of the public" and "the preservation of the public peace." The court ruled that in the Constitution "the right to keep and bear arms is coupled with the statement why the right is preserved and protected, viz., that 'a well regulated militia being necessary to the security of a free State,'" and that the Sullivan Act therefore does not violate the Second Amendment.[3]

Similar concern for public safety prompted the federal government to enact the first national gun controls. In 1919, Congress adopted a 10 percent excise tax on the manufacture of firearms as an amendment to the War Revenue Act. Its sponsor, Democratic representative Thomas U. Sisson of Mississippi, said that the tax would raise revenue to defray the costs of the World War and protect public safety, making it, in effect, the first federal gun control law.[4]

In 1927, amid a wave of revulsion against the gang violence that followed the enactment of national prohibition, Congress adopted the first federal law that directly controlled people's access to firearms. By prohibiting the mail order sale of concealable firearms in the Mailing of Firearms Act of 1927, Congress hoped to stop firearms from crossing state lines and nullifying state and local gun controls. This effort failed because pro-business legislators balked at covering private common carriers such as United Parcel Service.[5]

In 1927 testimony before the National Crime Commission, police chiefs from sixteen cities called for the strict federal regulation of handguns. The chiefs unanimously agreed that the possession of a handgun put law-abiding citizens in danger, without affording effective self-defense. The chiefs could not cite any cases "of laymen who have really helped themselves by using pistols for self-protection" in their jurisdictions. "The idea that they do help themselves is a popular fallacy," said Chief William P. Rutledge of Detroit. NRA president Karl T. Frederick, representing the association, claimed to have collected "scads of newspaper clippings showing citizens have helped themselves with arms," but could not provide any reliable data or verifiable examples.[6]

In 1932, voters overwhelmingly elected a Democratic Congress and Franklin Delano Roosevelt, who had served on the National Crime Commission in the 1920s, as the first Democratic president in twelve years. Roosevelt narrowly escaped death or injury by gunfire when Giuseppe Zangara fired five shots toward him during a speech on February 15, 1933, between his election and his March 4 inauguration. Zangara missed Roosevelt but fatally shot Chicago mayor Anton Cermak and wounded four others.

Roosevelt's administration, led by Attorney General Homer Cummings, presented a comprehensive roster of anticrime legislation to Congress, including proposals to tax the manufacture or sale of machine guns, sawed-off shotguns, pistols, and revolvers. Cummings would require the registration of these firearms and restrict their importation, their transport across state lines, and their transfer of ownership from one person to another. Roosevelt's advisers believed that taxing and licensing firearms rather than imposing an outright weapons ban would pass constitutional muster. They worried not about the moribund Second Amendment, but about restrictions on the federal government's power to regulate interstate commerce.[7]

In 1934, Dr. Frederick L. Hoffman, the former president of the American Statistical Association, testified before Congress that the United States far exceeded the rest of the democratic world in gun violence. "It is your belief that the ease with which guns can be had in the United States is a tremendous factor in the high rate," asked Democratic Senator Royal S. Copeland. Dr. Hoffman responded, "The sole factor." This testimony in support of gun control shows how little has changed in nearly a century.[8]

After its founding in 1871, the NRA had avoided political entanglement until a revived association began lobbying against the Roosevelt administration's proposed gun control measures. Contrary to much popular belief, the NRA was never pro–gun control and began its campaign against firearms regulations in the 1930s, although it did not yet cloak its opposition in a defense of the Second Amendment.

In 1903, during the administration of President Theodore Roosevelt, the 1903 Dick Act (and later amendments) reorganized the militia as the National Guard, a military reserve force that the government trained, disciplined, and paid to meet army standards. Government provided military arms to the guardsmen, who did not provision themselves for duty with their private pistols and rifles. Although organized by state and headed by an adjutant general in each state, the federal government held final authority over the National Guard.

This military reform breathed new life into a dying NRA, which had lacked members and resources. In 1907, all but one member of the thirty-seven-person NRA board of directors had a military title, mostly with the National Guard. James A. Drain, Sr., the adjutant general of the State of Washington, who had lobbied for the Dick Act, served as the NRA's president early in the century and in the 1920s. Milton A. Reckord, the adjutant general of Maryland, became the association's CEO. Both leaders divided their time equally between the National Guard and the NRA.[9]

To train members of the new National Guard, Congress set up the National Board for the Promotion of Rifle Practice, which married the defense establishment and the NRA. The board resolved in 1904 that "rifle practice will be greatly promoted by the formation in each state of state rifle associations, to be affiliated with the National Rifle Association," whose members controlled more than a third of the board. Congress eventually appropriated funds to provide surplus firearms and ammunition, at a discount or for free, only to members of the NRA and affiliated rifle clubs, including contingents in schools and colleges. This special arrangement, which cost the government tens of millions of dollars, continued into the 1970s. In 1976, the General Accounting Office reported that, since keeping track in 1958, the military had sold to NRA members at discounted prices 519,093 rifles and carbines, 159,353 pistols and revolvers, and 8,708 shotguns. It had granted NRA-affiliated rifle clubs privileged access to government shooting ranges and loaned the clubs 16,478 long guns. The military distributed free of charge to the clubs many millions of rounds of ammunition.[10]

President Roosevelt cheered on the NRA's merger into the American military establishment. In a letter dated February 16, 1907, Drain asked for Roosevelt to "become a member of the National Rifle Association, together with a letter, suitable for publication, in which you endorse the objects and purposes of the Association." Roosevelt replied, "I am so heartily interested in the success of the National Rifle Association and its work done in cooperation with the National Board for the Promotion of Rifle Practice, that I take pleasure in sending you herewith my check for $25 for life membership therein." With Roosevelt's blessing, Drain copied the letter "for recruiting material in my campaign to build the National Rifle Association into a truly national institution."[11]

Despite the NRA's later raging against socialism and big government, the federal government built the modern association and gave it the clout needed for its lobbying campaigns. The NRA gained renewed life as an adjunct of the American military establishment, subsidized by government appropriations. But for this alliance with government, the NRA would likely have withered and died in the twentieth century. As later explained by NRA president Harold W. Glassen, prior to 1903 "the NRA literally folded and for a decade the Association was in limbo." Then with government backing, the association grew and prospered.[12]

C. B. Lister, the executive director of the NRA, wrote in an internal memo on January 3, 1950, that the association had come to thrive as "a quasi-governmental institution." It benefited from government funds "for the issue of rifles, ammunition, and target range materials" for NRA-affiliated clubs. Through its marksmanship programs, the NRA was "a part of our national defense picture," and for crime control had "initiated the program of police pistol training and gun standardization which is now so generally accepted by up-to-date law enforcement agencies." The "small arms training" that the NRA uniquely provided to the army and the police "is still the primary element in the basic training of the warrior." Socialism, NRA-style.[13]

By the early twentieth century, the NRA was already

supplementing its government support by forging partnerships with the gun industry. Its 1905 report listed eleven industry "trade members," which included such preeminent firms as Smith & Wesson, Winchester, Remington, and du Pont. The gun industry had begun providing modest financial support for the NRA through advertising in its annual report. In 1907, the NRA raised just $6,038, 10 percent of it from gun industry advertising.[14]

In becoming in the 1930s a de facto lobby group that opposed proposals to regulate firearms, the NRA formed a Legislative Affairs Division, although without formally registering as a lobbying group. The NRA relied on practical, not constitutional, opposition to gun controls, which it claimed would burden only law-abiding citizens, leaving them soft prey for hardened criminals. It slammed proposed regulations in press releases, in testimony before Congress, and in its new official magazine, *American Rifleman*. It coordinated opposition with hunting and shooting clubs and mobilized its members and "friends" through a mailer warning that proposed legislation from the Roosevelt administration "is objectionable in almost every respect and should be killed. . . . Personally communicate with your Congressman asking him to oppose the measure."[15]

Knowing that the Democratic Congress would pass some version of gun control, CEO Reckord said that the NRA supports regulation "if it is reasonable and proper, and not a subterfuge." Despite this declaration, the NRA sought to kill administration proposals by misdirection.

"I think our difference may turn entirely upon what is reasonable," President Frederick told members of Congress, emulating the strategy that the National Association of Manufacturers (NAM) deployed against FDR's popular pro-worker initiatives. An internal memo advised that the NAM would be "branded as a selfish reactionary unworthy of any consideration" if it obstinately opposed in principle collective-bargaining rights and unemployment insurance. Instead business should pay lip service to workers' rights, but with enough qualifiers to defeat or enfeeble specific proposals. "Assault every working plan proposed, for they are all vulnerable."[16]

NRA spokespersons assaulted details of the Roosevelt administration's working plans, especially gun registration and the regulation of handguns. Representatives of arms manufacturers that did not produce machine guns for private sale chimed in, warning that handgun regulation would shutter their businesses, imperiling the economy and the national security of the United States. This strategy of death by small cuts worked as planned.

The final, watered-down version of the National Firearms Act of 1934 omitted pistols and revolvers, covering only machine guns and sawed-off shotguns, the so-called gangster weapons. It weakened controls over the transport and sales of weapons and eliminated registration requirements. The NRA and the gunmakers backed this toothless legislation as the best outcome they could have hoped for at the time. As Reckord later explained, "The key point on that bill was that everything pertaining to registration was eliminated from that bill. You see that was the reason why we supported it." The NRA similarly acquiesced to the Federal Firearms Act of 1938, which slightly strengthened the 1934 regulations.[17]

Despite its rise from the ashes in the early twentieth century, the NRA was, by the 1930s, still a little-known organization with fewer than fifty thousand members and a budget of about $250,000. Yet it had achieved a near miracle by gutting the gun control proposals of the mighty President Roosevelt and his Democratic Congress. Beyond its strategy of misdirection, the NRA had mobilized its members and thousands of locally affiliated clubs and traded on its service to America's national defense and law enforcement. A 1938 Gallup Poll found that 79 percent of Americans generally backed gun control measures, but gun control advocates lacked pressure groups of their own.

The Second Amendment as yet played no part in the NRA's lobbying. In a 1932 article, President Frederick denounced the regulation of handguns but conceded, "We must recognize the fact that constitutional provisions which set forth the right of citizens to keep and to bear arms will not protect us against vicious and undesirable statutes affecting pistols. Protection lies in an enlightened public sentiment and in intelligent legislative action. It is not to be found in the Constitution." When asked during a 1934 congressional hearing on whether he believed that the proposed gun control legislation violated "any constitutional provision," Frederick offered a dismissive response that would be unthinkable for today's NRA: "I have not given it any study from that point of view."[18]

The US Supreme Court did study the Second Amendment when it upheld the National Firearms Act in the 1939 case of *U.S. v. Miller*. In 1934, police arrested Jack Miller, a lookout for the notorious O'Malley gang that had perpetrated brazen, armed bank robberies across the Southwest. Prosecutors granted Miller immunity to turn state's evidence against his accomplices. The presiding judge warned him, "You had a narrow escape this time . . . and you won't be so lucky again. Get into something honest."[19]

Miller heard the judge but did not listen. On April 18, 1938, police officers stopped Miller and another thug, Frank Layton, apparently en route to a robbery. The officers found an unregistered sawed-off shotgun in their car, and federal prosecutors charged the men with the rare crime of violating the National Firearms Act of 1934.

Both Miller and Layton pleaded guilty to one count of violating the act, but US District Court judge Hiram Heartsill Ragon rejected their plea and ordered the case to trial. Miller and Layton challenged the indictment, claiming that the National Firearms Act violated the Second and Tenth Amendments to the Constitution. Ragon issued a bare-bones opinion that struck down the act under the Second Amendment. Judge Ragon, a proponent of gun control, had likely issued his ruling as a setup to get the case to the US Supreme Court, where he expected a reversal.

Before the Supreme Court could hear the accused's case, though, Miller was dead, and Layton had disappeared. A day after again arming himself with a shotgun and teaming with another thug, Robert Drake "Major" Taylor, to rob the Route 66 Club in Miami, Oklahoma, a farmhand found Miller's body in a dry creek bed. He had been shot four times, perhaps by his accomplice in a dispute over the $80 they'd netted from the robbery. Layton, meanwhile, had absconded to parts unknown. Neither the defendants nor their attorneys defended their case before the Supreme Court.

The *Miller* opinion, penned by the conservative justice James Clark McReynolds for a unanimous court on May 15, 1939, upheld the constitutionality of the Firearms Act and ruled that the Second Amendment guaranteed a right to possess and bear arms, but only for the common defense through service in a well-regulated militia. McReynolds wrote, "In the absence of any evidence tending to show that possession or use of a 'shotgun having a barrel of less than eighteen inches in length' at this time has some reasonable relationship to the preservation or efficiency of a well regulated militia, we cannot say that the Second Amendment guarantees the right to keep and bear such an instrument." He added, "With obvious purpose to assure the continuation and render possible the effectiveness of such [militia] forces the declaration and guarantee of the Second Amendment were made. It must be interpreted and applied with that end in view."[20]

This decision was so predictable and uncontroversial that it failed to register at the time. The NRA paid it no heed, and a search of ProQuest's archive of major newspapers uncovered just one article devoted solely to the *Miller* case in 1939, on page fifteen of *The New York Times*. Gun control had long been an accepted fact of life for judges, legislators, and the public. After *Miller,* the Second Amendment remained irrelevant to the lives of the American people and even to the NRA.[21]

6

Assassinations and Debates over Gun Control

It is just tragic that in all of Western civilization the United States is the one country with an insane gun policy.

—SENATOR JOSEPH TYDINGS (D–MARYLAND), 1968[1]

In 1963, the following ad appeared in the NRA's *American Rifleman* magazine:

LATE ISSUE! 6.5 ITALIAN CARBINE. Only 36″ overall, weighs only 5 1/2 pounds. Shows only slight use, lightly oiled, test fired and head spaced, ready for shooting. Turned down bolt, thumb safety, 6-shot, clip fed. Rear down sight. Fast loading and fast firing.

Among those who responded was Lee Harvey Oswald. In March 1963, Oswald mailed the ad's coupon and a money order for $21.45 to Klein's Sporting Goods Company in Chicago. He promptly received his weapon via common carrier. No questions asked. No government forms to submit. On November 22, 1963, Oswald fired the shots from this rifle that killed President John F. Kennedy. Less than an hour later, Oswald murdered Dallas police officer J. D. Tippit with another mail-order firearm, a .38-caliber Smith & Wesson revolver.

Even before the assassination, Congress had pondered legislation to tighten its lax firearms regulations. Anyone could so easily evade the National Firearms Act that, through 1962, federal officials had gained not a single conviction under its prohibitions on the interstate shipment of firearms. Members of Congress led by Democratic senator Thomas J. Dodd of Connecticut considered new legislation to close the loopholes in federal law by banning all mail-order handgun sales from private carriers. Broader proposals that Dodd eventually embraced included licensing gun dealers, keeping dangerous and irresponsible persons from possessing firearms, and controlling the importation of firearms that were not used for sporting competition.[2]

The president's assassination gave new urgency to the quest for tightened gun control. "The assassination of President Kennedy has raised again what to many Is [*sic*] the burning issue of some form of national regulation on the sale and use of firearms," wrote Al Bolin in *The Indianapolis Times*. The Senate Committee on Commerce held hearings on amending Dodd's bill by adding rifles and shotguns to the list of weapons banned from interstate shipment.[3]

In support of the fortified Dodd bill, James V. Bennett, director of the Federal Bureau of Prisons, warned, "There are more Oswalds walking the street, more such suggestive persons, more Oswalds stroking their weapons in furtive secrecy, more Oswalds who, with their distressed minds, diseased minds, who would like to focus national attention upon themselves by heinous acts of violence."[4]

The initial Dodd bill on limiting interstate shipments of handguns at first gained reluctant NRA backing as it was preferable to expanded coverage for rifles and shotguns and proposals for registering firearms and licensing gun owners. However, Franklin L. Orth, the NRA's executive vice president and CEO, told members of Congress, "In the form introduced this morning, the association supports the bill of Senator Dodd." However, "I would like to add, parenthetically, that normally we are opposed to legislation relative to guns of any kind because we don't think that they reach the criminal. We think the criminal gets the gun anyway."[5]

Two weeks after the assassination, Orth wrote to Republican senator Hugh Scott of Pennsylvania that the NRA "is most emphatically and unalterably opposed to amendments made by Senator Dodd to his bill," which "has been immeasurably broadened and made more restrictive." Orth warned that "to act hastily on these serious matters in the existing climate of high emotional concern can result in very great injustice to the law-abiding citizenry of the United States."[6]

Hunting and sports shooting groups affiliated with the NRA, many association officials, and grassroots members mobilized against strengthened gun control legislation. A. A. De Carriere, chairman of the NRA's Legislative Committee, wrote to the Senate Commerce Committee in January 1964 that "further amending" of the firearms acts "is not advisable." The laws "are already much too restrictive." In an April 1965 newsletter, the NRA officially retreated from even the appearance of co-operation. It charged that the reinforced Dodd bill could lead to enforcement decisions so onerous "as to totally discourage, and thus to eliminate, the private owner-ship of all guns." Columnist Marquis Childs wrote that the NRA "is the principal force holding back legislation on weapons. While gun manufacturers are not allowed under Association rules to be members, officers of the big weapons companies are active in the group. The NRA denies that it is a lobbyist organization, but by most stan-dards it qualifies."[7]

Gun industry companies hired professional lobbyists to oppose gun controls, and the industry's trade associa-tion, the National Shooting Sports Foundation (NSSF), formed in 1961, added weight to the opposition. Its rep-resentative, John G. Williams of the Remington Arms Company, told Congress that new firearms regulations should exempt guns used for sporting purposes and cover only heavy military weapons, which the government had already regulated in the 1930s.[8]

By the 1960s, the NRA had begun its ongoing clandestine practice of planting favorable ghostwritten materials in the press. In its 1968 report, the NRA Public Relations Committee noted, "A newspaper editorial service were [*sic*] retained to prepare and distribute favorable editorials to more than 11,000 dailies and weeklies in the nation." It said that "pickup of these editorials has been especially good," but that this "quiet 'planting'" of press materials "cannot be reported, itemized, or cost accounted."[9]

Firearms regulation remained moribund until a gunman assassinated Martin Luther King on April 4, 1968, and urban riots followed. Congress quickly enacted a stripped-down version of the Dodd bill that banned only the interstate shipment of handguns. Then, the fatal shooting of Robert F. Kennedy on June 5, 1968—a third assassination in less than five years—revived proposals for amending the law to register guns and license owners. President Lyndon B. Johnson quickly endorsed the amendment, and Democratic senator Joseph Tydings of Maryland sponsored it in the Senate.[10]

NRA president Harold W. Glassen called upon "the sportsmen of America" to lay down a barrage of opposition to the Tydings bill. "The right of sportsmen to obtain, own, and use firearms for proper lawful purposes is in the greatest jeopardy in the history of the country," Glassen wrote in a letter to NRA members, which he claimed were now some eight hundred thousand to nine hundred thousand strong. "Some proponents of restrictive gun legislation," he said, "are clear that their goal is complete abolition of civilian ownership of firearms."[11]

Congress responded with an amendment that slightly tightened the earlier legislation, including the addition of long guns. It limited the interstate shipments of firearms to or from only those licensed by the federal government as dealers, manufacturers, importers, or collectors. Only federally licensed dealers (with fees hiked from $1 to $10) could engage in the commercial dealing of firearms. The law prohibited any sale or distribution of firearms in interstate or foreign commerce to fugitives from justice, drug addicts, proven "mental defectives," persons under indictment or convicted of a crime punishable by more than a year in prison, undocumented immigrants, persons under restraining orders or convicted of domestic violence, dishonorably discharged military personnel, and persons under twenty-one for handguns and under eighteen for long guns. No verification of the buyers' status by government officials was required for dealers, although they had to keep records of transactions. The act banned the importation of surplus military weapons and guns not certified as sporting firearms or collector's items.

Under pressure from the NRA and the gun industry, Congress rejected the Johnson administration's core proposals for registering and licensing firearms. "The measure as a whole appears to be one that the sportsmen can live with," the NRA's president wrote in *American Rifleman*. But for President Johnson "this bill—as big as this bill is—still falls short. . . . If guns are to be kept out of the hands of the criminal, out of the hands of the insane, and out of the hands of the irresponsible, then we just must have licensing. If the criminal with a gun is to be tracked down quickly, then we must have registration in this country." He charged, "The voices that blocked these safeguards were not the voices of an aroused nation. They were the voices of a powerful gun lobby that has prevailed for the moment in an election year."[12]

Johnson was right. The Gun Control Act of 1968, which capped decades of weak federal gun legislation, wouldn't keep guns from the hands of nearly anyone intent upon acquiring a firearm. Anyone could still purchase a handgun, shotgun, or rifle, including semiautomatic weapons, at a local gun dealer with nothing more than proof of residence and age and the buyer's own word that he or she wasn't crazy or a criminal. Dealers had no incentive to verify buyer claims because the law did not hold them liable for selling to prohibited persons, even if the buyer lied. In addition, the military's sale and loan of guns to NRA members bypassed all firearms regulations. "The United States still does not have an effective national firearms policy," the National Commission on the Causes and Prevention of Violence concluded in 1969.[13]

Once again, the NRA had achieved an improbable victory, thwarting the will of another president, blunting the momentum of three stunning assassinations, and defying a public, including gun owners, that favored strict gun control regulations. A September 1966 Gallup Poll found that 68 percent of respondents favored requiring police permits for buying guns. A Harris Poll from September 1967 found that 66 percent of white gun owners backed the registration of firearms. The gun lobby has consistently rejected all such poll findings for neglecting the kind of questions it asked of members and backers, such as "Do you believe that private citizens have the right to own firearms to defend themselves and their families from violent criminal attack?" or "Do you think that owning a handgun could save your life, if you were attacked by a drug-crazed criminal?"[14]

Enforcement of the federal acts by the Bureau of Alcohol, Tobacco and Firearms (ATF) resulted in few prosecutions or convictions relative to the number of likely violations. "Audits of firearms transaction records" revealed that there "may be as many as half a million violations of the Gun Control Act of 1968 each year." Yet in 1973, federal records disclosed only 2,257 indictments for gun law violations and 1,719 convictions.[15]

Disappointed gun control advocates cobbled together an Emergency Committee for Gun Control headed by former astronaut John H. Glenn, Jr., but the committee did not match the power and resources of the NRA and the gun industry, and it soon faded away. "It seems plain now that the National Rifle Association is a little too powerful for the Congress of the United States to cope with all by itself," said a *Washington Post* editorial entitled "Wanted: Anti-Gun Lobby." "Congress is going to have to have help," the editors said, "if it is to put across really effective firearms control with registration, licensing and all that jazz."[16]

After Congress enacted the Gun Control Act of 1968, the FBI investigated the National Rifle Association for failing to register as a federal lobbying organization, a crime punishable by fines and imprisonment. Critics claimed that the NRA was a lobbying group disguised as a charitable and educational organization to avoid taxes and reporting requirements, and to secure subsidies from the government. To gain the power wielded by the NRA, *The Washington Post* editorialized:

> First, you must get yourself chartered as a
> nonprofit organization dedicated to education,
> social welfare and the promotion of public safety.
> [Then] with the facade to protect you from
> taxation, and from any obligation to register as
> a lobby, you can begin to lobby to your heart's
> content in the interest of an industry which will,
> of course, advertise lavishly . . . in the slick-
> paper magazine which you will distribute to your
> 800,000 members. And on top of all that if you'll
> just get yourself a steady, solid subsidy from the
> Government, you'll have it made, man; you'll have
> it made.[17]

The NRA disputed such charges, but rather than risk a criminal prosecution, its CEO registered personally as a federal lobbyist. Still, the NRA insisted that it was an "educational organization" dedicated to marksmanship and shooting sports. As an organization, it remained free of taxation, the disclosure of donors, and lobbying-reporting regulations.[18]

During the debates of the 1960s, the gun lobby and its allies in Congress from both parties raised a variety of objections to firearms regulations with memorable pitch lines that foreshadowed the next half century of controversy over gun controls.

"Now Is Not the Time"

Congress should not be making policy in the emotional aftermath of high-profile assassinations, said William Beers, on behalf of hunting and shooting groups in Arizona. "At the present time our country is caught in the grip of a hysteria brought about by the tragic events that occurred during the black weekend at Dallas, Texas. Emotions have taken the place of common sense and clear thinking on the part of a large segment of our population."[19]

Democratic senator Birch Bayh of Indiana responded that the time for action was not premature, but overdue. Remedial legislation, Bayh said, had been "before the Congress of the United States prior to President Kennedy's death." Thus, "the need for this legislation is not as a result of the death of President Kennedy, but President Kennedy's death, I feel, did focus public attention on one of the loopholes which presently exists in our law."[20]

"Guns Don't Kill People; People Kill People"

If controls deprived criminals of guns, they would resort to other forms of violence, said Democratic representative Robert L. F. Sikes of Florida, a gun-lobby ally and owner of stock in the military contractor Fairchild Industries. If we control guns, he said, "It is reasonable to assume that these [other] weapons should be dealt with and eliminated . . . all knives, ice picks, scissors, et cetera, should be registered. . . . Then naturally rocks, hammers, baseball bats, rolling pins, sticks, et cetera, should be serialized and registered."[21]

Firearms are themselves neutral and only become dangerous when wielded by criminals, said Franklin Foote of the Nebraska Game, Forestation, and Parks Commission. "Where there is a problem in this field, the commission strongly feels that what is involved is a 'people problem' and not a firearm problem. Firearms, in and of themselves, are not in any way inherently criminal or dangerous." He then delivered what became an iconic slogan of the gun lobby: "Guns don't kill people; people kill people."[22]

Authorities on gun violence explained that firearms in their hands makes criminals, juveniles, persons inclined to suicide, or just angry and negligent Americans much more dangerous to others and themselves. FBI director J. Edgar Hoover said, "Those who claim that the availability of firearms is not a factor in murders in this country are not facing reality. Guns are by far the most lethal weapons used to kill—seven times more deadly than all other weapons combined. . . . A readily accessible gun enables the perpetrator to kill on impulse." An FBI study found that "of the 112 law enforcement officers who died from criminal action during the past three years, 108 were killed by guns." Hoover concluded, "The spotlight of public attention should be focused on the easy accessibility of firearms and its influence on willful killings."[23]

"Gun Control Doesn't Work and Hurts Only Law-Abiding Citizens"

Representative Sikes said, "The only people really affected by gun restrictions are the honest people. A man who needs a gun to commit a crime will get one by some method or other. . . . If anyone is convinced that antigun laws will reduce crime and be a guarantee against violence and murder, then he is worse off than the ostrich. New York State has the toughest gun laws in America and probably the highest crime rate."[24]

Leonard E. Reisman, the deputy police commissioner of New York City, stressed that gun control laws, if not infallible, do keep firearms from the hands of criminals and dangerous persons. Although his city's strict Sullivan Act, he said, "has not eliminated the illegal traffic in pistols and revolvers," it "has had a great effect in reducing such illegal traffic" and in preventing "many crimes of violence."[25]

Prison director James V. Bennett testified that New

York City, with its strict gun controls, had one of the lowest urban murder rates in the nation: 5.4 per 100,000 compared to 13.4 in Dallas and 8.1 in Phoenix, both cities that lacked gun controls. In addition, Chicago, Los Angeles, Philadelphia, and Detroit also had lower homicide rates than Dallas or Phoenix. He added that "in states with bare minimum controls over firearms, sixty-five percent of the murders are committed with guns," compared to 32 percent in the states with the "most stringent" controls.[26]

"Self-Defense: Only a Good Guy with a Gun Stops a Bad Guy with a Gun"

Irvine C. Porter, past president of the NRA, testified, "When you get into the question of bank robberies and things of that sort on which some of the statistics have been indicated, a good many of those bank robberies do not occur if the perpetrators understand when they go into a given area they are likely to get shot at. It is like the old saying that there wouldn't be so many duck hunters if the ducks could shoot back."[27]

Journalist Albin Krebs, writing in *The New York Times*, disputed the claim that a proliferation of guns for alleged self-defense made Americans safer. "Each year in this country guns are involved in more than 6,500 murders," he wrote. This compares to 30 in England, 99 in Canada, 68 in West Germany, and 37 in Japan, all nations "where firearms are subject to strict regulations." The National Commission on the Causes and Prevention of Violence concluded in its 1969 report that rather than making Americans safer through self-defense, "the availability of guns contributes substantially to violence in American society. Firearms, particularly handguns, facilitate the commission and increase the danger of the most violent crimes: assassination, murder, robbery and assault." It said, "From the standpoint of the individual householder, then, the self-defense firearm appears to be a dangerous investment" and recommended limiting the possession of handguns to "police officers and security guards, small businesses in high crime areas, and others with a special need for self-protection."[28]

"The Federal Government Should Keep Its Hands off Our Guns"

"The federal government cannot impinge upon the police powers which our Constitution so wisely reserved for the states," said Republican senator Bourke Hickenlooper of Iowa. "Should it do so in this matter of firearms control, or attempt to do so, there is no end to the legislation involving criminal acts to which such a precedent would lead. We would, in effect, be establishing a police state."[29]

Federal legislation was needed, explained Deputy Commissioner Reisman, because "as long as criminals can obtain weapons more easily in other states both through the mail and by personal purchase, the effort to eradicate the illegal traffic in small arms in the State of New York can never be completely successful." Sergeant K. T. Carpenter of the Los Angeles Police Department said, "Mail-order traffic in concealable weapons from the Los Angeles area is virtually uncontrolled." Its strict "existing laws have been circumvented easily by unscrupulous dealers" who "advertise their wares in nationally circulated pulp magazines, the contents of which are designed to tempt the juvenile reader, as well as others not legally entitled to possess a firearm." Richard R. Caples, the Massachusetts Commissioner of Public Safety, said that "approximately eighty-seven percent of all crime guns used in Massachusetts come from outside the commonwealth."[30]

Senator Dodd cited the example of a fourteen-year-old killed "with a mail-order gun by a sixteen-year-old friend who, in ordering the gun, falsified his age. No inquiry was made by the mail-order dealer as to the boy's age, and the law doesn't require one to be made." Senator Dodd pointed to a murderer in Pittsburgh who used a mail-order firearm "from Klein's in Chicago, which had supplied Lee Oswald the weapon he used to assassinate President Kennedy."[31]

"Don't Slide down the Slippery Slope"

Democratic representative John Dingell of Michigan, a member of the NRA's board, testified, "A step of the type embodied in the legislation pending before this committee will do nothing more or less, Mr. Chairman, than be a further step toward ultimate elimination of the right of citizens to possess and enjoy firearms. . . . The evil of the bill is that it is a step in that direction."[32]

Senator Dodd noted that this scare tactic had no merit and that he and other legislators had no intention of sliding down the slippery slope toward the confiscation of firearms. "Let me make clear right away that we do not intend to ban firearms altogether," he said, "for there are many thousands of law-abiding citizens who own firearms. Most use them responsibly in recreational activities. But I repeat, it is to the irresponsible element of our citizenry that attention is directed."[33]

"Gun Control Equals Dictatorship"

Propaganda from the National Rifle Association tied gun control to dictatorship. The association claimed that dictators disarmed the people to seize power in Germany and Italy during the 1930s. Americans are "parroting nonsense and begging their federal government to take from them by force of law one of their basic rights," said NRA president Glassen. "It is reminiscent of the 1930's before and after World War II when the Goebel's [sic] propaganda machine worked so well on the German people using the principle of the Big Lie."[34]

When gun rights advocates failed to prove that gun controls enable dictatorship, Senator Tydings retorted that this is the argument "used by extremists, Minutemen, your Ku Klux Klan. . . . I find it unacceptable in view of the facts as I know them to be." He cited a study by the Library of Congress's Legislative Reference Service that concluded, "We can make no positive correlation between gun laws and dictatorship."[35]

"Gun Controllers Are Commies"

The *American Rifleman*, conservative politicians, and pro-gun members of Congress peddled a fraudulent document termed "Communist Rules for Revolution" to link gun controllers with communist tyranny, atheism, and depravity. Representative John Saylor of Pennsylvania told fellow members, "I call your particular attention to the three communist rules for revolution: first, corrupt the young; second, get control of all means of publication; and third, cause the registration of all firearms." George A. Brautigam, a state attorney in Florida, first introduced the rules to public debate in 1954, with a mailer that displayed a US citizen lying prostrate before a copy of the rules. "In the darkness of night thieves prowl," Brautigam warned. "Thieves who only steal money are petty thieves compared with those who steal our right to live as free Americans."[36]

Democratic senator Lee Metcalf of Montana debunked the "Communist Rules for Revolution" as a right-wing forgery, citing the results of inquiries he made to the FBI, the Library of Congress's Legislative Reference Service, and the chair of the Senate's Internal Security Subcommittee. Gun control advocates, he said, had nothing to do with such "Rules" and "the extreme right wing in America also follows rules, and one of these rules is to make maximum use of false, misleading, and fear-inspiring quotations." Remarkably, the "Rules" still circulate among gun rights advocates.[37]

"Gun Controllers Are Out-of-Touch Elites"

Glassen complained that the "do-gooder" elites who want to control people's lives had mounted "a well-organized and well-financed campaign, including movie stars, prominent figures, and other public relations devices . . . to discredit the NRA" and gun rights.[38]

Republican representative John Lindsay of New York affirmed that it was ordinary citizens, not the elite, who demanded gun controls. "We need to plug the loopholes and bolster up our firearms law," he said, "and provide uniform regulations for all the states. The public recognizes this need. In a recent Gallup Poll, a clear majority of the voters favored stricter firearms control."[39]

"The Culprit Is Culture and Mental Health, Not Guns"

NRA spokesperson Gordon S. Craig said, "I don't know how many hours a day we drench our children with television in which we must kill at least two or three in every half-hour program to have it profitable to the advertiser, and apparently passing the approval of society." Congress should focus not "on the weapon, but the criminal who would use it. . . . It was incongruous that the president, who had showed the most interest in mental health of any to my knowledge, became the victim of one demented—one who at the age of eleven was diagnosed a schizophrenic with paranoid tendencies."[40]

Gun control advocates responded by citing the 1968 study "Firearms, Violence, and Civil Disorders," by the Stanford Research Institute, which debunked the notion that culture and mental health accounted for America's excessive firearms violence. The authors noted, "The United States is far and away the leader among the free industrial countries of the world in both the absolute number and the rate of homicides, suicides, and accidental deaths by firearms." The rate of firearms murder in the United States is "35 times the rate of England," although "many of our citizens are descendants of England, from which we derive much of our common law and culture." England and other peer nations "have strong and effective firearms control laws, and that is precisely where one may find the difference."[41]

"Our Guns Protect Us from Subversives and Rioters"

Thomas L. Kimball, director of the National Wildlife Federation, insisted that restrictions on the possession of firearms is "the most effective and convenient way of disarming the private citizens should a subversive power infiltrate our police system or our enemy occupy our country." In the wake of riots in the 1960s, an editorial in the *American Rifleman* declared that only armed bands of citizens could curb future riots. It warned, "The best police on earth, alone, cannot stem the kind of mob violence that has swept America's cities." Instead, it is "the armed citizen" who "represents a potential community stabilizer." NRA president Glassen said, "I personally do not subscribe to 'Call police.'"[42]

The authors of the Stanford Research Institute study warned that such armed vigilantism did not protect but endangered Americans: "Private paramilitary groups are urging their followers to buy arms and join shooting clubs to defend family, home, and community. Many decent citizens are caught up in the fear of further civil strife and join in the domestic arms race." The danger is that "an environment of a great many guns in private hands" heightens "their potential use for violence in further disorders, crime, impulse killings, suicides, and other undesirable behavior."[43]

Undaunted by these responses, the gun lobby and their supporters in Congress and state legislators have recycled the same arguments ever since. Change the dates and the gun lobby's arguments of the 1960s are indistinguishable from the same bogus claims today.

Second Amendment advocacy figured more prominently in the 1960s than in the 1930s, but it was still far from becoming the icon of gun rights. Senator Bayh noted in hearings that some opponents of the Dodd bill claimed that it violated "the Second Amendment of the Constitution." Bayh admitted, "I do not know how deeply this criticism has penetrated," but he referenced the *Miller* case and lower-court follow-up rulings to prove that "the right to bear arms is granted to a well-regulated militia," and that "the Second Amendment was adopted not as an individual right, per se, but as a protection for the states."[44]

Earlier, in June 1955, the National Rifle Association had examined the history of the Second Amendment and court decisions on firearms regulation, reaching the same conclusion as Senator Bayh. Contrary to the NRA's later claims, Jack Basil, the association's authority on constitutional law and subsequently the director of the NRA's legislative information service, concluded that the amendment protected only a collective, not an individual, right to keep and bear arms. In an internal memo to NRA CEO Merritt A. Edson, until now undiscovered in Edson's files, Basil wrote, "From all the direct and indirect evidence, the Second Amendment appears to apply to a collective, not an individual, right to bear arms. So have the courts, Federal and State, held. Further, the courts have generally upheld various regulatory statutes of the States to be within the proper province of their police power to protect and promote the health, welfare, and morals of their inhabitants."[45]

Reflecting the NRA's slightly changed thinking, its president, Bartlett Rummel, offered a mild rebuttal to Bayh. He said that *Miller* stood for the proposition that "this was an individual thing, that the militia were individuals, and the right to have and bear arms was an individual right at the time." Yet, he did not claim that the Second Amendment precluded adoption of the Dodd bill or any other legislation short of confiscation, and he agreed that the Second Amendment applied only to the federal government. In a 1968 interview with WABC radio, Glassen said that "he and his organization do not now contend that the Second Amendment to the US Constitution precludes 'reasonable' gun controls."[46]

The gun control debates of the 1960s mirrored the social turmoil of the decade. Urban riots devastated major American cities. The nation remained mired in the Vietnam War, and the number of violent crimes more than doubled from 1960 to 1968. Native Americans, African Americans, and Latinos fought against discrimination and inequality. Women demanded sexual freedom, and a new black power movement touted racial pride and sought liberation from dominance by whites. The movement seemed to take a frightening turn for many white Americans with the formation of the Black Panther Party for Self-Defense in 1966.

Conservatives worried about the erosion of America's traditional values and threats to law and order. They backed the war in Vietnam and warned that scruffy, drug-taking, and promiscuous hippies, not clean-cut conservative Americans, could become America's future. To allegedly curb riots and violent crime, conservatives mimicked the gun lobby's all-purpose solution to every ill: more guns. In the wake of riots in 1968, California governor Ronald Reagan said that "law-abiding citizens" were increasingly buying guns "because they have lost faith in government's ability to protect them."[47]

Conservatives linked their opposition to firearms regulation with a defense of the traditional American values of self-reliance, individualism, and the God-given right to protect oneself and one's family. In speech notes, Glassen wrote that the "Communists," "some timid people," and "generally the 'do-gooder'—the man who doesn't believe that there is a 'bad boy'—that no [one] should go to prison except for treatment"—backed gun control. The singular gun control exception for the NRA and its conservative allies was a California law that Governor Reagan sponsored, and the NRA supported, to check the gun-toting Black Panthers in the state. So much for the claim that gun rights advocates were antiracist.[48]

When Maryland senator Tydings ran for reelection in 1970, he faced a cultural cross fire, with "cannon to the right of him, cannon to the left of him," wrote columnist Marquis Childs. "On the one hand he is the sponsor of the District of Columbia crime bill with its no-knock and preventive arrest provisions so odious to liberals. On the other he is under intensive fire from the gun lobby, determined to defeat him in November for sponsoring a registration proposal."[49]

Fire from the left wounded the senator, but bombardment from the right killed his reelection hopes. To maintain its tax exemption, which prohibited the NRA from participating in political campaigns, it joined with gun manufacturers in a front group called Citizens Against

Tydings. The group mobilized hunters and sportsmen against Tydings and flooded the state with bumper stickers reading GUN REGISTRATION MEANS GUN CONFISCATION, IF TYDINGS WINS—YOU LOSE, and PLAYBOY JOE HAS GOT TO GO, referring to a 1969 *Playboy* article in which Tydings charged, "The radical right's philosophy, fears and militant racism pervade the gun lobby." Tydings counterpunched, but to no avail. In 1964 he had thrashed Republican J. Glenn Beall, Jr., with 63 percent of the vote; in 1970 he lost to Beall with only 48 percent. His support for gun control was not the sole reason for Tydings's defeat. Still, "The defeat of Joe Tydings [was] when pols learned to fear the NRA," wrote Jack Limpert, former editor of *Washingtonian* magazine.[50]

Republican Senate minority leader Hugh Scott, who voted for the Gun Control Act of 1968, escaped the gun lobby's wrath. In 1968, the lobby had helped defeat Pennsylvania's Democratic senator, Joseph S. Clark, with ads that equated shooting game with shooting down gun controllers: "HUNTERS! TOMORROW IS OPEN SEASON ON JOE CLARK.... Clark Says Hunters Pull Triggers on Election Day. Let's Prove We Pull Voting Machine Handles. GOOD HUNTING!" Gun rights advocates warned Senator Scott, "We are busily engaged in reloading the old muzzle loaders and preparing for the day when open season is declared on Senator Scott. If Joe Clark thought he got shot out of the saddle . . . wait until we take on Senator Scott."[51]

After meeting with the advocates who called themselves "sportsmen," an aide to Senator Scott explained their single-minded passion: "Gun legislation is by far their most important issue—it's their 'must' issue. It's what makes them decide how to vote. To many actually it is the biggest issue in decades, bigger than Vietnam, taxes, inflation, etc. They see it threatening their way of life." If Sen. Scott votes against their position, to them it won't matter a damn what he has been doing on conservation or in anything else. To them another 'gun control stand' would be unforgiveable."[52]

Senator Scott responding by confessing that he had made a "mistake" in voting for "some provisions" of the law. He called for the repeal of key provisions and launched the "Hugh Scott Championship Trophy" for Pennsylvania shooters. "I don't think gun control is going to be the big issue here that it was," said Gene Shaw of the Pennsylvania Federation of Sportsmen's Clubs two months before the election, which Scott won handily.[53]

Outside the electoral process, federal appeals courts unanimously disposed of gun rights challenges to the Gun Control Act of 1968, rejecting an individual construction of the Second Amendment. In a typical decision, the Eight Circuit Court of Appeals ruled in *U.S. v. Synnes* (1971), "While the Court in *Miller* dealt with the prohibited possession of a sawed-off shotgun, the reasoning and conclusion of that case has carried forward to other federal gun legislation. . . . We think it is also applicable here." Although the Gun Control Act "is the broadest federal gun legislation to date, we see no conflict between it and the Second Amendment since there is no showing that prohibiting possession of firearms by felons obstructs the maintenance of a 'well regulated militia.'"[54]

7

The NRA Reinvents the Second Amendment

The idea that the Second Amendment gives individuals a right to bear arms was advocated so forcefully, so broadly, and so persuasively that Democrats gave up on fighting the issue.

—JEFFREY TOOBIN, LAWYER AND POLITICAL ANALYST, 2012[1]

In 1972, George Wallace, the segregationist governor of Alabama and a "law and order" candidate for the Democratic presidential nomination, won five Southern primaries before Arthur Herman Bremer pumped five bullets into his body at a shopping center in Laurel, Maryland, on May 15 of that year. Wallace survived, but his wounds left him paralyzed from the waist down and ended his campaign. This attempted assassination revived interest in banning the manufacture and sale of the cheap handgun known as the Saturday night special, Bremer's weapon of choice.[2]

The National Rifle Association backed in theory legislation regulating Saturday night specials but followed its strategy of misdirection by shredding the details of proposed laws. CEO Maxwell E. Rich told members of a US House subcommittee in 1972 that the NRA "supported the principle of getting rid of . . . what is called the Saturday night special," but opposed pending bills because such weapons could supposedly not be distinguished from legitimate firearms.[3]

The NRA's position on handguns followed the lead of the gun industry, which had become the association's leading paymaster. In 1971, the NRA reaped $1.7 million in revenue from advertising in its publication, mostly from makers and dealers in guns, ammunition, and accessories. The ad income accounted for more than 22 percent of the NRA's budget, with the rest coming mainly from members' dues and merchandise sales.[4]

However, the NRA did not yet oppose gun control on Second Amendment grounds, as indicated by Rich's dialogue with the subcommittee chair, Representative Emanuel Celler, of New York:

CHAIRMAN CELLER: Has the National Rifle Association come to a conclusion as to whether the bills before us are constitutional or unconstitutional?

MR. RICH: No, we have not.

CHAIRMAN CELLER: Has the National Rifle Association considered the question recently?

MR. RICH: Yes.

CHAIRMAN CELLER: And came to no conclusion?

MR. RICH: On that point, sir, there has been no conclusion.[5]

In its 1975 *Fact Book on Firearms Control Handbook*, the NRA denigrated the Second Amendment as of "limited practical utility" in combating gun control. "While NRA takes the firm stand that law-abiding Americans are constitutionally entitled to the legal ownership and use of firearms, the Second Amendment has not prevented firearms regulation on national and state levels. Also, *the few federal court decisions involving the Second Amendment have largely given the Amendment a collective, militia interpretation and have limited the application of the Amendment to the Federal Government*" (emphasis added). That approach would soon change.[6]

Gun rights advocates had again kicked up enough dust, without much concern about the Second Amendment, to stall new handgun regulation. Still, Rich's seemingly conciliatory testimony outraged hard-core members of the NRA's board, especially as the movement for handgun regulation gained momentum.

In the 1970s, gun control advocates finally countered the gun lobby by forming two enduring national organizations, most significantly the National Council to Control Handguns (renamed Handgun Control, Inc.), and also the National Coalition to Ban Handguns (NCBH), both dedicated to the banning of handguns. Despite a lack of progress in Congress, the city council of the District of

Columbia required the registration of existing handguns in 1976 and barred future private sales and possession of such guns, even though the Second Amendment covered the federally controlled District, unlike the states.[7]

New militant pro-gun organizations matched the rise of a gun control lobby. In 1971, Alan Gottlieb and John M. Snyder cofounded the political action group the Citizens Committee for the Right to Keep and Bear Arms. Three years later, Gottlieb formed the Second Amendment Foundation, which promotes gun rights education and lawsuits to crush gun control laws.

In 1975, California state senator H. L. Richardson founded the Gun Owners of America, dedicated to "never compromising" on gun rights. "I got together with a lot of gun people I know across the United States and talked about going on the attack instead of staying so defensive," Richardson explained. Richardson's gun people included industry executives and members of the far-right extremist group the John Birch Society. Two Birch Society leaders, congressional representatives John H. Rousselot of California and Lawrence P. McDonald of Georgia, served on the Gun Owners board. In 1976, Larry Pratt, another far-right figure, became the executive director and public face of the Gun Owners.[8]

The nation is "flooded with proposed laws that are aimed at total confiscation of firearms from law-abiding citizens," the Gun Owners warned in a solicitation letter. Crime would "double" if gun controllers had their way, and so patriotic Americans must oppose the "radical," "gun grabbing," "soft on crime" politicians who would "destroy our constitution and unleash what could well be the most terrifying crime wave in modern history." The Gun Owners Political Action Committee (PAC) donated some $150,000 to congressional campaigns in 1976. Libertarian Republican Ron Paul of Texas, a leading recipient of the PAC's money, called the Gun Owners "the only no-compromise gun lobby in Washington," a label that the group now proudly displays on its website.[9]

These pro-gun organizations were part of a "new right" network of conservative groups in the 1970s, such as the Heritage Foundation, the Moral Majority, the Eagle Forum, and the National Conservative Political Action Committee. The new right aimed to restore authority to traditional institutions, seize the moral high ground from liberals, and liberate the nation from un-American "elites" who scorned traditional values, embraced foreign ideologies, banished God from the public square, and kept minorities and the poor dependent on government. "It is elitist denigration of tradition, habit and custom that has weakened the bonds of authority," said new right leader Pat Buchanan. "It has been elitist assaults on traditional morality and traditional patriotism that have helped to weaken and destroy the ties between the young and the Church, and the young and the government. . . . To the central crisis—the crisis of authority—they offer less than nothing."[10]

New right conservatives avowed that only a no-compromise defense of citizens' sacred, God-given right to keep and bear arms would protect families at a time of rampant crime and immorality. For the Gun Owners' Larry Pratt, the gun rights and the antiabortion movements equally upheld the Christian reverence for life, making self-defense through firearms ownership no less godly than saving so-called unborn children. Firearms, he said, "are very much part of the administration of justice in God's economy of protecting life," not only "at the corporate level through the state," but also "at the individual level, which Christ spoke to. . . . To say that weapons are inherently antilife is to misunderstand the nature of man and what God has ordained that we do in this fallen world."[11]

John Snyder, of the Citizens Committee for the Right to Keep and Bear Arms, sought to co-opt for America's gun lobby the benign image of Santa Claus and the blessing of a Catholic saint. Beginning in the late 1970s, Snyder sent out Christmas cards with the message "For a safe Christmas and a crime-free New Year." One card showed Santa Claus carrying a sack packed full not with dolls, teddy bears, and toy trucks, but with revolvers. Another shows Santa in his sleigh blasting away with a firearm at a Soviet jet. Yet another showed Santa standing next to a Christmas tree in a homey living room while pointing a huge .57 Magnum revolver at an apparent burglar.[12]

In 1987, Snyder's card featured a cassocked Catholic priest shooting a lizard between the eyes with a handgun, while two fierce-looking thugs cower before him. Snyder hoped this card would help persuade the Vatican to declare the nineteenth-century saint Father Gabriel Possenti the "patron of hand gunners." Snyder claimed that Possenti had wielded a brace of pistols to stop bandits from looting his town. But the saint's holy order, the Passionist Fathers, rejected Snyder's plea. The saint was no gunman, the Fathers said, and the tale of his defending his village with firearms was "inaccurate and untrue." The Vatican disregarded Snyder's request rather than giving it any publicity. Pope Benedict XV, when he canonized Possenti in 1920, had dedicated him as the patron saint of Catholic youth, not of handgunners. Undeterred, Snyder unilaterally declared Saint Gabriel Possenti as the gun lobby's Patron Saint. He founded the St. Gabriel Possenti Society and declared February 27 as his feast day. The myth of the Patron Saint of Handgunners has spread far and wide among gun rights advocates.[13]

In 1975, the NRA began merging into the new right orbit when the leader of its hard-core faction, Harlon Carter, became head of the association's new lobbying arm, the Institute for Legislative Action (ILA). The following year, Carter established the NRA's first PAC, the Political Victory Fund. Like the Gun Owners, the NRA raised the specter of confiscation in its fund-raising appeal: the gun controllers "are not talking of 'Control'; they want complete and total 'Confiscation.'" We need "your financial support . . . to defend Americans' right to protect their homes from criminals." Testifying before Congress in 1975, Carter said that the "National Rifle Association is unalterably opposed" to any "bill that would outlaw any handguns on the grounds that they cause crime." He warned of "civil disobedience" if

Congress continued on its path of declaring "all firearms contraband. . . . The people out west of the Potomac are rising in resentment."[14]

Carter forthrightly opposed continuing efforts to ban Saturday night specials: "It makes no sense to me why possession of a finely made two-hundred-dollar handgun owned by a decent law-abiding man of means should be legal, but ownership of a forty-dollar handgun [Saturday night special] by an equally law-abiding resident of the inner city who can't afford anything better to protect his home and his family should be a felony." Carter's testimony prompted humorist Art Buchwald to propose satirically "gun stamps" for the firearms-deprived poor. Like using food stamps at groceries, poor people could redeem their gun stamps at friendly gun shops so they wouldn't have to "go to bed every night without a gun under their pillow" or "settle family arguments" with "knives and hammers" rather than more efficient and lethal firearms.[15]

Even Carter did not yet embrace an emphatic defense of the Second Amendment. During congressional hearings in 1975, Democratic representative George E. Danielson of California asked Carter whether the amendment "prohibits government to, by legislation, infringe the right of the people to keep and bear arms." Carter responded diffidently "but we do admit to our opponents, as I say, the last word has not been said by the Court. That is about, so far as I know, but maybe my general counsel would like to talk about the Second Amendment, but usually I do not because I feel like that should be the province of the Supreme Court. . . . I have always felt that way."[16]

In early May 1975, the NRA convened a "summit conference" that included "approximately forty" attendees, including representatives of at least thirteen gun or ammunition manufacturers. The conference agreed in principle to mount a public relations campaign against gun control, backed by contributions from participating gun companies and organizations.[17]

The NRA's deepening involvement in conservative politics worried the old-guard leadership, who feared a public backlash that would weaken the association's ability to preserve hunting and sports shooting. The conflict between old and new guard leaders threatened to explode at the 1977 NRA convention in Cincinnati. Disputes within the association became so bitter that board member Gene Crum, associate editor of *Gun Week* magazine, questioned "whether there will even be an organization called the National Rifle Association by 1978."[18]

NRA president Merrill W. Wright responded that insinuations about the association's abandoning gun rights were "ludicrous." He said that "a few vocal members persist in voicing and publishing unwarranted criticism . . . and impute dishonorable motives wholly without reasons." The NRA's "highest priority is safeguarding the right of gun ownership and the future of shooting sports." He did not mention the Second Amendment.[19]

At the NRA's national convention in late May of 1977, the old and new guard clashed during a business meeting that dragged on until nearly 4:00 A.M. The meeting began with the old-guard leadership shutting off the air-conditioning to discourage attendance. This did not work; the heat did not discourage participation by the motivated and well-prepared militants. They armed themselves with walkie-talkies for communication in the tumultuous meeting hall, studied parliamentary tactics, and distributed orange hats for the identification of their loyalists. They rallied some one thousand members to vote for the expulsion of the NRA's management and to install the new guard leader Harlon Carter as CEO. Within a year of this "revolt in Cincinnati," Carter appointed his loyalist Neal Knox as head of the ILA and expanded its tiny staff by hiring nearly fifty lobbyists, lawyers, and researchers.

The revamped NRA joined the new right in supporting Republican candidate Ronald Reagan for president in 1980. For the first time in an election cycle, the NRA opened its purses for pro-gun politicians, through a recently formed political action committee (PAC), the NRA Victory Fund. Led by the NRA, pro-gun groups in 1980 outspent gun control organizations by thirteen to one. The NRA further mobilized its passionate members and backers to go to the polls and vote for candidate Reagan. After Reagan's election, Democratic House majority leader Jim Wright of Texas said, "Every member of Congress tells the same story. There are hundreds of people, in some cases literally thousands, who never write to them on any other subject but become irate and paranoid and very frightened at any suggestion of gun control."[20]

During the Reagan years the NRA made the Second Amendment politically relevant for the first time in US history. After the attempted assassination of President Reagan by John Hinckley, Jr., in March 1981 prompted new interest in gun control, the NRA's office of general counsel submitted to the Senate Committee on the Judiciary a twenty-seven-page, single-spaced brief on the Second Amendment. Disregarding the findings of the NRA's Jack Basil in 1955, Harlon Carter's earlier testimony before Congress, and the NRA's 1975 *Fact Book*, the brief claimed that the amendment "clearly recognized the right, and moreover the duty, to keep and bear arms in an individual capacity."[21]

Ironically, the NRA submitted its brief shortly after the US Supreme Court, in the 1980 case of *Lewis v. United States*, unmistakably rejected an individual-rights interpretation of the Second Amendment. Justice Harry Blackmun ruled for the Court that restrictions on the possession of firearms by convicted felons "are neither based upon constitutionally suspect criteria, nor do they trench upon any constitutionally protected liberties." Citing *Miller*, he ruled, "The Second Amendment guarantees no right to keep and bear a firearm that does not have 'some reasonable relationship to the preservation or efficiency of a well regulated militia.'" Three justices dissented, but not on Second Amendment grounds.[22]

The NRA's revamped Second Amendment strategy resonated with Republicans in Congress. The Senate Subcommittee on the Constitution, headed by conservative

Republican Orrin Hatch of Utah, proclaimed in a 1982 report that it had uncovered "clear—and long lost—proof that the second amendment to our Constitution was intended as an individual right of the American citizen to keep and carry arms in a peaceful manner, for protection of himself, his family, and his freedoms." Rather than "long lost" facts, the report contained only material cribbed from the NRA's memo, which it reprinted. The NRA purchased copies of Hatch's report, which it mailed "to every federal legislator and to key state legislators."[23]

To the dismay of the gun lobby, however, in 1981 the small Chicago suburb of Morton Grove, Illinois, had adopted an ordinance that prohibited the sale and possession of handguns within its jurisdiction. Fearing that Morton Grove could inspire other localities to bypass state legislators and adopt similar gun bans, the NRA and other pro-gun groups challenged its ordinance in federal court as a violation of the Second Amendment and the Illinois constitution.

Like many other states, Illinois qualified the right to keep and bear arms as "subject only to the police power." The circuit court ruled that constitutional gun rights in the state are "so limited by the police power that a ban on handguns does not violate that right." The Morton Grove handgun ban would survive, even if the Second Amendment covered the states and localities, because "construing [its] language according to its plain meaning, it seems clear that the right to bear arms is inextricably tied to the preservation of a militia. This is precisely the manner in which the Supreme Court interpreted the second amendment in *United States v. Miller*." The US Supreme Court turned down an appeal of this ruling.[24]

Stymied before the bar, the gun lobby pressured most states to adopt preemption laws that prohibit local governments from enacting firearms regulations that are more stringent than the laws enacted by the state legislature. Although the NRA typically upholds the right of local people to control their destiny, gun controls are an exception. "There are lots of areas where home rule certainly applies," said Kansas State Rifle Association president Patricia Stoneking, "but this is not one of them. Not when it comes to an unalienable, natural, God-given right for people to protect themselves."[25]

By the end of Harlon Carter's tenure as CEO in 1985, the reinvigorated, militant NRA had tripled its membership to an estimated 3 million and comparably expanded its budget. In speeches, press releases, media appearances, ads, and articles in its publication, it began elevating the Second Amendment to a sacred text, blessed by the founders and ordained by God. "For us the fundamental is, do you believe in the Second Amendment?" explained NRA lobbyist Tanya Metaksa.[26]

Beyond propaganda, the NRA worked its way into the world of legal scholarship to displace the prevailing collective rights interpretation of the Second Amendment. Data compiled for law journal articles from 1912 to 1959 found that consistent with Basil's NRA memo, all eleven articles embraced the collective rather than the individual rights interpretation of the amendment. From 1960 to 1969 eleven articles upheld the collective and only three the individual interpretation of the amendment. From 1970 to 1979 a majority of articles, eight to six, upheld the collective view. Then the balanced shifted dramatically. From 1980 to 1999, after the revolution at Cincinnati, and despite the *Lewis* ruling, Second Amendment scholarship soared in volume and reversed prior trends; forty-six articles took the collective and seventy-nine the individual position. Nearly all the individualist scholarship came from lawyers, many of whom worked for the NRA in litigation or received NRA grants and other support. Stephen P. Halbrook, the NRA's most prominent litigator, who the ILA features on its website, contributed twelve of the pro-individualist articles, by himself tipping the balance of writings since 1912 toward the NRA position. However, the contribution of respected, liberal law professor Sanford Levinson of the University of Texas gave credibility to the NRA-backed work.[27]

Carl T. Bogus, a professor at Roger Williams University School of Law and a supporter of gun control, admitted that the NRA-backed "law office scholarship" constituted "one of the most successful attempts to change the law and to change a legal paradigm in history." He said, "They were thinking strategically. I don't think the NRA funds scholarship out of academic interest. I think the NRA funds something because it has a political objective." Bogus was right. Through its "law office scholarship," the NRA had executed one of the most extraordinary political and intellectual coups in the history of the United States.[28]

After Reagan's narrow escape from death, James Brady, Reagan's press secretary, who had suffered a grievous head wound during the shooting, and his wife, Sarah, gave fresh inspiration for Handgun Control, Inc., and moved the organization toward incremental goals rather than an absolute ban on handguns. In 1989, Sarah Brady became the group's chair, and in 2001 it changed its name to the Brady Campaign to Prevent Gun Violence, with the affiliated Brady Center to Prevent Gun Violence, dedicated to research and litigation. That same year the National Coalition to Ban Handguns became the Coalition to Stop Gun Violence, with a broadened mission to control assault weapons as well as handguns.

Nonetheless, through the 1980s, the gun lobby halted momentum for firearms regulation. Polls showing public support for gun control did not matter to members of Congress, who say, "If they [the gun lobby] only control two or three percent of the vote in my district, that's enough" to turn an election. Sanford D. Horwitt, a gun control consultant, conceded, "The NRA, unlike any other group in the country, has just made mincemeat of the legislative process." Opposition groups lacked grassroots members, financial resources, and constitutional cover. If the NRA could control 2 to 3 percent of the vote in congressional districts, gun control groups could not muster even 1 percent.[29]

The NRA's increasingly robust promotion of the

Second Amendment led to the first rollback of federal gun controls through the Firearm Owners Protection Act of 1986, although with some exceptions. The act aimed to curb alleged abuses by the Bureau of Alcohol, Tobacco and Firearms (ATF) in enforcing federal gun controls and eased restrictions on gun sales and transportation. It legalized the shipment of ammunition through the mail, but in a compromise with gun control advocates it also banned the sale to civilians of machine guns manufactured after 1986. Congress also banned the manufacture, sale, or import of armor-piercing bullets for handguns, with limited exceptions.[30]

Then in the late 1980s, the NRA hit a roadblock; on top of internal dissension in the post-Carter era, it faced a public backlash against its opposition to the banning of armor-piercing bullets, termed cop killers, and semiautomatic pistols. By 1991, the Association's membership had fallen from a peak of 3 million to 2.3 million.[31]

The NRA took some solace from the US Supreme Court's 1990 decision in *United States v. Verdugo-Urquidez*. The Court ruled that Fourth Amendment protections against searches and seizures did not cover "aliens outside the U.S." and that that term *the people* as written into both the Fourth and Second Amendments, "refers to a class of persons who are part of a national community." The gun lobby claimed that this construction of *the people* means that the Second Amendment guarantees an individual right to keep and bear arms. However, the decision did not define Second Amendment guarantees.[32]

Four years later, the American Bar Association (ABA) advised that despite much misinformation about the Second Amendment, "the United States Supreme Court and lower federal courts have consistently, uniformly held that the Second Amendment to the United States Constitution right to bear arms is related to 'a well-regulated militia' and that there are no federal constitutional decisions which preclude regulation of firearms in private hands." The ABA backed national legislation as the only effective gun controls and urged that "leaders of the legal profession join and work with our counterparts in the medical, teaching, religious, civic, law enforcement and other professions, to prevent and reduce gun violence." It pledged to "educate the public and lawmakers regarding the meaning of the Second Amendment."[33]

After the election of Democrat Bill Clinton in 1992, a weakened NRA failed to stop Congress from enacting the Brady Handgun Violence Prevention Act of 1993, named after James Brady. The "Brady Bill" required background checks before an individual could purchase a handgun and later any firearm from a federally licensed dealer, manufacturer, or importer. Under the FBI's National Instant Criminal Background Check System (NICS), established five years later, a firearm sale from a federally licensed dealer could be completed if the purchaser passed the check or the FBI reached no verdict after three days. Banned purchasers included felons, fugitives, domestic abusers, and the dangerously mentally ill. Former presidents Jimmy Carter, Gerald Ford, and Ronald

Reagan supported the Brady Bill. In 1994, Congress followed up the Brady Bill by imposing a ten-year ban on the manufacture, sale, and possession of certain semiautomatic firearms that were defined as assault weapons. It also banned the possession and transfer of "large capacity" ammunition magazines.

The NRA's public standing plummeted again in April 1995 after Timothy McVeigh bombed the Alfred P. Murrah Federal Building in Oklahoma City, which housed the officers of the ATF as well as a children's daycare center. McVeigh's bomb killed 168 people, including 19 children, and injured many hundreds of others. McVeigh had ties to the armed right-wing militia movement and had been an NRA member from 1990 until 1994, when he became disillusioned with the association's failure to block national gun controls. To the envelope of an anti-gun-control diatribe he mailed to his congressional representative in 1992, McVeigh attached a decal reading I'M THE NRA.[34]

A year after McVeigh joined the NRA, Wayne LaPierre, then the head of the ILA, became the association's CEO. With his master's degree in government from Boston University, his history as a lobbyist, his Beverly Hills suits, designer glasses, and coiffed hair, LaPierre was more a city slicker than a rugged outdoorsman. But he brought to the job an intensity that escalated the NRA's message to a new level of aggression.

In a fund-raising letter less than a week before the bombing, LaPierre echoed the inflammatory claims of far-right militias. He called ATF agents "jack-booted government thugs." He warned of the ATF's "power to take away our Constitutional rights, break in our doors, seize our guns, destroy our property, and even injure or kill us." Whether "intentionally or not," wrote Charles M. Sennott in *The Boston Globe* on August 13, 1995, "the NRA has found itself the establishment player at the confluence of a broader coalition of pro-gun activists, paramilitarists and hate groups—all of whom see gun control as a burning constitutional threat, and the federal government as an avowed enemy."[35]

In protest, former president George H. W. Bush ripped up his NRA life-membership card. "Your [LaPierre's] broadside against Federal agents deeply offends my own sense of decency and honor," Bush wrote in an open letter. "It offends my concept of service to country. It indirectly slanders a wide array of government law enforcement officials, who are out there, day and night, laying their lives on the line for all of us." The NRA's president, Thomas L. Washington, fired back by asserting that his association had documented examples of "black-suited, masked, massively armed mobs of screaming, swearing [federal] agents invading the homes of innocents."[36]

Even a wounded NRA still had some clout in Congress. It failed in its campaign to abolish the CDC's National Center for Injury Prevention after center-funded research by Professor Arthur Kellermann found that firearms in the home led to a significantly increased risk of gun deaths and injuries. But in practice the gun lobby quashed government-sponsored research on gun violence when Republican representative Jay Dickey of Arkansas, the self-proclaimed "point man" for the NRA, inserted into the 1996 budget an amendment saying, "None of the funds made available for injury prevention and control at the Centers for Disease Control and Prevention may be used to advocate or promote gun control." Congress also cut $2.6 million from the CDC budget for research on gun violence. Although the amendment did not explicitly prohibit all gun-related research, it deterred federal employees from risking their careers by conducting or funding such research.[37]

Despite winning the Dickey Amendment, the NRA seemed sufficiently in decline at the beginning of 1997 for Josh Sugarmann, founder of the gun control group the Violence Policy Center, to confidently predict, "In the light of the NRA's political and financial woes in the wake of the 1995 Oklahoma City bombing . . . like the 'evil empire' of the Soviet past, today's NRA is a virtual nation-state fast approaching moral and financial bankruptcy." Sugarmann was an optimist.[38]

In 1997, the NRA heeded the advice of former Senate minority leader Republican Bob Dole of Kansas for an "image repair job" by promoting NRA member Charlton Heston as its public face. Heston was a revered actor who had played Moses in Cecil B. DeMille's epic drama *The Ten Commandments*. Heston had impeccable civil rights credentials, having stood with Martin Luther King, Jr., during the 1963 March on Washington. Even in his seventies Heston still had the craggy good looks and down-to-earth charisma that LaPierre lacked.

Under Heston, the NRA reenergized by championing Second Amendment rights, which it linked to the conservatives' culture war against a left that threatened America's traditional moral values, common heritage, and personal freedoms. Heston's NRA upheld manly patriotism, self-reliance, and faith in God's will, virtues threatened by the effete, bohemian "adversary culture" of gun controllers. In a February 1997 speech at the National Press Club, Heston said, "The Second Amendment must be considered more essential than the First Amendment." It was "America's First Freedom, the one right that protects all the others." The NRA followed up Heston's speech with a "Help Me Save the Second Amendment" public relations campaign. It featured an ad emblazoned with Heston's face and the message "Politicians scorn it. Media pervert it. Regulators defile it. Movies disgrace it. Publishers censor it. Teachers misrepresent it. And kids don't get it. Unless we act, our Second Amendment is in grave peril." In February 1999, in his delivery of a Harvard University Law School speech entitled "Winning the Cultural War," Heston said, "Firearms are—are not the only issue. No, it's much, much bigger than that. I've come to understand that a cultural war is raging across our land."[39]

Through service in the culture war, the NRA bolstered its alliance with the Republican Party. In 2000, the association abandoned any lingering pretext of nonpartisanship and deployed nearly all its money and influence on behalf of Republicans. Heston embarked upon a sixteen-state tour to pump up gun-owner turnout for Republican presidential candidate George W. Bush, and 85 percent of the NRA's contributions flowed to Republicans. The GOP responded by invoking the Second Amendment by name for the first time in its party platform. At the 2000 NRA convention, Heston held aloft a replica of a flintlock long gun and uttered what became his signature battle cry for gun rights: "From my cold dead hands!"—which the NRA's public relations consultant, Ackerman McQueen, had written for him.[40]

President Heston's leadership, the restored Second Amendment, the linking of gun rights to cultural restoration, and the NRA's success in electing Bush led *Fortune* magazine in 2001 to recognize it as "the top political lobbying organization in the United States." At the NRA's 2002 annual meeting, CEO LaPierre told forty-five hundred delegates, "You are why Al Gore isn't in the White House." He slammed advocates of gun control for engaging in a "political terrorism" that posed "a far greater threat to freedom than any foreign force."[41]

In 2003, the NRA cashed in on its political advocacy when Congress enacted new restrictions on the ATF, named after their sponsor, Republican representative William Todd Tiahrt of Kansas. As later modified, the Tiahrt amendments prohibited ATF from making available to the public, including researchers, its internal information on the tracing of firearms, other than aggregate statistical reports. They required the FBI to destroy all approved background check data within twenty-four hours, making it impossible to catch or rectify errors. The amendments also blocked ATF from requiring gun dealers to submit inventories, relieving lax and corrupt dealers from accountability.

The gun control movement had no counter to the NRA's deification of the Second Amendment, responding instead with the self-defeating strategy of "We, too, support the Second Amendment, but . . ." During his campaign for the 2004 Democratic presidential nomination, Massachusetts senator John Kerry, a hunter and sportsman, said with a shotgun in hand on a duck hunting trip, "I believe in the Second Amendment in this country. *But* I don't believe that assault weapons ought to be sold in the streets of America. . . . I want to prove to people that you can be responsible about guns, and you're not anti–Second Amendment, *but* you can still vote for common sense in this country" (emphasis added).[42]

Wrong, said LaPierre. Kerry thinks he can "con American gun owners and get away with it. . . . The American people will see through the deceit" and recognize that "John Kerry is the most rabidly antigun nominee for president in the history of our nation. . . . The worst thing that could happen to the Second Amendment and to our freedoms is for John Kerry to be elected president." In a campaign ad, LaPierre asked, "Senator Kerry, how can you talk out of both sides of your mouth and keep a straight face?" Kerry and the gun control movement had no persuasive answer.[43]

In 2004, Congress proved the futility of the "yes, but"

strategy when it let the 1994 assault weapons ban expire. The following year, President Bush signed the Protection of Lawful Commerce in Arms Act (PLCAA) that, with narrow exceptions, restricted victims of gun crimes from naming firearms manufacturers in federal or state civil suits. The law's chief sponsor, Republican senator Larry Craig of Idaho, claimed that it would "stop junk lawsuits that attempt to pin the blame and the cost of criminal behavior on businesspeople who are following the law and selling a legal product." It would not "bar the courthouse doors to victims who have been harmed by the negligence or misdeeds of anyone in the gun industry."[44]

However, the law's protections are so broad and its exceptions so narrow that it has killed off virtually every lawsuit against the gun industry, no matter the grounds. That's why the NRA, which lobbied strenuously for this law, hailed it as a "historic" victory for freedom and "the most significant piece of pro-gun legislation in twenty years." Still, no federal court had in more than two hundred years struck down a single gun control law under the Second Amendment. In many scores of decisions, only a single federal court, the Fifth Circuit in 2001, had upheld the NRA's individual-rights interpretation of the amendment's meaning. Yet, that court still declined to strike down the federal regulation under challenge, which prohibited persons subject to a restraining order for domestic violence from possessing firearms shipped in interstate or foreign commerce.[45]

8

The Original Sin of Justice Scalia's Originalism: *D.C. v. Heller*

There is already a large sleeper terrorist army inside the U.S. . . . *"We the people," armed, are TRULY what the Writers of the Constitution intended for us to be and that is the CITIZEN MILITIA. If suicide terrorists DO attack our city, ARMED CITIZENS could be the First to counter these hostilities in our individual neighborhoods.*

—DICK HELLER, PLAINTIFF IN *D.C. V. HELLER*, 2008[1]

In 2002, Clark Neily III and Steve Simpson, two young unknown lawyers who worked for the libertarian Institute for Justice, set in motion a lawsuit that made the Second Amendment constitutionally relevant for the first time in 220 years. These activists, with financial support from wealthy libertarian Robert A. Levy, decided to challenge the District of Columbia's stringent gun control law that prohibited the private possession of a handgun, as a violation of the Second Amendment, despite the contrary *Miller* and *Lewis* rulings on the right to keep and bear private arms. Neily and Simpson targeted the federally controlled District to circumvent Supreme Court rulings that the Second Amendment did not cover state or local law.

Neily persuaded Alan Gura, a thirty-one-year-old, small-time lawyer to litigate the case. The NRA responded by trying to smack down the libertarians. NRA attorneys feared that a Supreme Court that was evenly divided between conservative and liberal justices, with moderate justice Sandra Day O'Connor as the swing vote, could follow precedent and reject their individual-rights interpretation of the Second Amendment. Some speculated that the NRA wanted to avoid a favorable verdict so that it could keep agitating its gun-owner base.

The libertarians persevered and chose as their lead plaintiff the appealing Shelly Parker, an elderly African American woman who lived in a dangerous neighborhood. The NRA then filed a competing case, *Seegers v. District of Columbia*, with "trapdoors" that would let the courts rule without reaching the constitutional question. An attempt by NRA attorneys to consolidate the cases failed when the DC Court of Appeals dismissed its lawsuit by ruling that its plaintiffs lacked standing to sue because they could not prove any personal harm from the challenged gun controls. The David of gun rights had defeated its Goliath, or more aptly, Goliath had defeated himself.[2]

Gura had protected his lawsuit by recruiting five plaintiffs in addition to Ms. Parker. Plaintiff Dick Heller carried a handgun as a security guard at the Thurgood Marshall Federal Judiciary Building, but the DC government had turned down his application to bring the firearm home to his dangerous neighborhood. The court ruled that only Heller had standing to sue because his rejected handgun application amounted to a personal injury. So, *Parker v. District of Columbia* became *Heller v. District of Columbia*. Dick Heller was no Shelly Parker. He was a white male who wanted firearms not for self-defense, but to battle alleged terrorists and "the insanity of it, the overreach of government relegating all of us to second-class citizenship." Still, he had salvaged the lawsuit.

In July 2005, Justice O'Connor changed the course of American history by announcing her retirement from the Supreme Court. After President George W. Bush elevated the reliable conservative Samuel Alito as O'Connor's successor in 2006, the Court's balance shifted to a five-justice conservative majority.

Advocates on either side of the gun control divide snapped to attention after the Court agreed to review the 2–1 ruling of the DC Court of Appeals that the District's law violated the Second Amendment. Sixty-seven groups filed amicus curiae (friend of the court) briefs, with forty-seven urging the Supreme Court to affirm the lower court's rule and twenty urging it to remand the case to the DC District Court. Most Republicans in Congress, joined by George W. Bush's vice president, Dick Cheney, as president of the Senate, and a majority of state attorneys general filed briefs urging affirmation. The Texas solicitor general, Ted Cruz, wrote the attorneys general brief. The US Department of Justice, the attorneys general of several other states, and many police chiefs and law enforcement agencies filled opposing briefs.[3]

Justice Antonin Scalia, the intellectual leader of judicial conservatives, wrote the opinion for a 5–4 Court majority, with Alito casting the deciding vote. But Scalia faced a dilemma in justifying the ruling. Scalia was the nation's foremost advocate of the judicial philosophy of originalism, which purports to recover the framers' intent in adopting constitutional provisions. This approach, originalists claimed, captures the original, fixed meaning of the Constitution without regard to "current social values" or the political leanings of judges. However, because not a single figure involved in the original crafting, adoption, or ratification of the Second Amendment said that it protected an individual right to keep and bear private arms, Scalia pivoted away from originalism and instead claimed to recover the "original plain meaning" of the amendment, citing many sources from before and after its adoption.[4]

Scalia had thus adopted a jurisprudence that he had previously scorned, the "living constitutionalism" that interprets the Constitution as a document that adapts to current conditions. Conservative legal scholar Nelson Lund wrote that *Heller* "was a near perfect opportunity for the Court to demonstrate that original meaning jurisprudence is not just 'living constitutionalism for conservatives.'" Instead, "Justice Scalia flunked his own test." His "majority opinion makes a great show of being committed to the Constitution's original meaning but fails to carry through on that commitment."[5]

Justice Scalia claimed that his approach properly relied on "a variety of legal and other sources to determine *the public understanding* of a legal text in the period after its enactment or ratification. That sort of inquiry is a critical tool of constitutional interpretation." Scalia's sources ranged from the English jurist William Blackstone's commentary in 1769 to a 1998 US Supreme Court opinion by Justice Ruth Bader Ginsburg, but it excluded copious material from when framers drafted and adopted the amendment.

Scalia's methodology read history backward from his present-day views, rather than reading history forward impartially. Similarly, Scalia read the Second Amendment backward. He began with the operative clause of the amendment at its end, then proceeded to the first justifying phrase. Scalia reinterpreted the *Miller* ruling that construed the Second Amendment as applicable only to the protection of a well-regulated militia. Yet he only briefly considered this same construction in the Court's more recent ruling in the 1980 *Lewis* case. He admitted that the *Lewis* Court contradicted his individualist interpretation, but said that a Second Amendment claim was not raised by plaintiffs and "it is inconceivable that we would rest our interpretation of the basic meaning of any guarantee of the Bill of Rights upon such a footnoted dictum in a case where the point was not at issue and was not argued."

The Court issued its landmark ruling on June 26, 2008, in the waning days of the term and during a presidential election campaign. Another intellectual giant of the Court, Justice John Paul Stevens, broke with usual practice and summarized his dissenting opinion directly from the bench. Although a registered Republican nominated by Republican president Gerald Ford in 1975, Stevens emerged as a maverick on the Court who voted often, but not always, with its liberal wing. In 2008, at the age of eighty-eight, he was then the longest-serving justice on the Court.

In his dissent, Justice Stevens took seriously, not dismissively, the first phrase of the amendment. He said that it "identifies the preservation of the militia as the Amendment's purpose; it explains that the militia is necessary to the security of a free State; and it recognizes that the militia must be 'well regulated.'" There is no statement "related to the right to use firearms for hunting or personal self-defense," which was present in the constitutions of Pennsylvania and Vermont at the time. He drew on the history of colonial America and the early republic to indicate that "the contrast between those two declarations and the Second Amendment . . . confirms that the Framers' single-minded focus in crafting the constitutional guarantee 'to keep and bear arms' was on military uses of firearms, which they viewed in the context of service in state militias."

Stevens, unlike Scalia, cited debates at the Constitutional Convention and the ratifying conventions to show that they focused not on individual rights, but on the dangers of a large standing army and the need to prevent the federal government from disarming the state militias. He argued that James Madison, in framing the Second Amendment, adopted explicitly military wording, not the individual-rights wording of the Pennsylvania constitution.

Citing Court precedents, Stevens wrote, "Since our decision in *Miller*, hundreds of judges have relied on the view of the Amendment we endorsed there; we ourselves affirmed it in 1980." He said, "No new evidence has surfaced since 1980 supporting the view that the Amendment was intended to curtail the power of Congress to regulate civilian use or misuse of weapons." Regardless of what plaintiffs may have argued, the 1980 *Lewis* case clearly affirmed that "the Second Amendment guarantees no right to keep and bear a firearm that does not have 'some reasonable relationship to the preservation or efficiency of a well regulated militia.'"

Stevens later said that he persuaded Scalia to add a clause to the decision that left a door open for gun control. Scalia ruled:

> Like most rights, the Second Amendment right is not unlimited. It is not a right to keep and carry any weapon whatsoever in any manner whatsoever and for whatever purpose: For example, concealed

weapons prohibitions have been upheld under the Amendment or state analogues. The Court's opinion should not be taken to cast doubt on longstanding prohibitions on the possession of firearms by felons and the mentally ill, or laws forbidding the carrying of firearms in sensitive places such as schools and government buildings, or laws imposing conditions and qualifications on the commercial sale of arms.

The interpretation of such exceptions remains disputed, and the Court may yet resolve it in future cases. Nonetheless, Stevens said in 2019 that *Heller* was "unquestionably the most clearly incorrect decision" during his thirty-five-year tenure as an associate justice.[6]

Republican presidential candidate John McCain hailed the *Heller* ruling as a "landmark victory for Second Amendment freedom in the United States.... Unlike the elitist view that believes Americans cling to guns out of bitterness, today's ruling recognizes that gun ownership is a fundamental right—sacred, just as the right to free speech and assembly." He said, "The Supreme Court ended forever the specious argument that the Second Amendment did not confer an individual right to keep and bear arms."[7]

The less forthright response by his Democratic opponent, Barack Obama, echoed the failed "we support the Second Amendment, but ..." strategy. "I have always believed that the Second Amendment protects the right of individuals to bear arms," Obama said, "but I also identify with the need for crime-ravaged communities to save their children from the violence that plagues our streets through commonsense, effective safety measures. . . . Today's decision reinforces that if we act responsibly, we can both protect the constitutional right to bear arms and keep our communities and our children safe." Even the brilliant and eloquent Obama could not reconcile support for the Second Amendment with the quest for effective gun control.[8]

Among scholars, liberals predictably disparaged Scalia's opinion, but so did prominent conservatives, who agreed that he had abandoned originalism for judicial activism, the sin that liberals had committed in the 1973 *Roe v. Wade* decision on abortion rights. A conservative judge of the Fourth Circuit Court of Appeals, J. Harvie Wilkinson, whom President Bush had considered as O'Connor's replacement, wrote, "*Heller* encourages Americans to do what conservative jurists warned for years they should not do: bypass the ballot and seek to press their political agenda in the courts." Both "the *Roe* and *Heller* Courts," Wilkinson said, "are guilty of the same sins" of "judicial aggrandizement: a transfer of power to judges from the political branches of government—and thus, ultimately, from the people themselves."[9]

Another conservative jurist, Richard A. Posner of the Seventh Circuit Court of Appeals, whom *The Journal of Legal Studies* recognized as the most cited legal scholar of the twentieth century, noted that the "irony" of Justice

Scalia's opinion is that "the 'originalist' method would have yielded the opposite result." Posner noted, "For more than two centuries, the 'right' to private possession of guns, supposedly created by the Second Amendment, had lain dormant." This was because "the text of the amendment, whether viewed alone or in light of the concerns that actuated its adoption, creates no right to the private possession of guns for hunting or other sport, or for the defense of person or property." Posner further scored Scalia for adopting the approach of "law office histories" sponsored by the NRA. Two years after *Heller,* in *McDonald v. Chicago,* the US Supreme Court, by a 5–4 vote, for the first time incorporated the Second Amendment under the Due Process Clause of the Fourteenth Amendment as applying to the states, not just the federal government.[10]

In moments such as this the full weight of the *Heller* decision comes home to roost. As Warren Burger, the former solidly conservative chief justice of the US Supreme Court, explained in 1990, "The gun lobby's interpretation of the Second Amendment is one of the greatest pieces of fraud, I repeat the word *fraud,* on the American people by special interest groups that I have ever seen in my lifetime. The real purpose of the Second Amendment was to ensure that state armies—the militia—would be maintained for the defense of the state. The very language of the Second Amendment refutes any argument that it was intended to guarantee every citizen an unfettered right to any kind of weapon he or she desires."[11]

9

Iron Triangle: The Gun Lobby, Gun Industry, and Politicians

You have to be in cahoots with the manufacturer in order to make the publication appeal to the readership. . . . We are locked in a struggle with powerful forces in this country who will do anything to destroy the Second Amendment. The time for ceding some rational points is gone.

—RICHARD VENOLA, FORMER *GUNS & AMMO* EDITOR, 2014[1]

In his 1961 farewell address, President Dwight David Eisenhower, a former general, warned of the threat to the nation from the emergence of a "military-industrial complex." He said that the "conjunction of an immense military establishment and a large arms industry is new in the American experience. . . . The potential for the disastrous rise of misplaced power exists and will persist. We must never let the weight of this combination endanger our liberties or democratic processes." Peering into the future, Eisenhower said, "America knows that this world of ours, ever growing smaller, must avoid becoming a community of dreadful fear and hate and be, instead, a proud confederation of mutual trust and respect."[2]

Six decades later, some sixty-six thousand Americans have died of all causes in foreign wars, while nearly 2 million have perished in our homeland from firearm homicides, suicides, and accidents. A new complex that conjoins the arms industry, a dynamic gun lobby, and dependent politicians now threatens the nation. The Second Amendment is the weld that holds the iron triangle together. It is a marketing tool for the gun industry, a rallying cry for the gun lobby, and a cover for do-nothing politicians on firearms control. The mythology of the Second Amendment has resonated with the American public and is now entrenched in American jurisprudence.

A splashy online presentation, by an arms merchant that grandly called itself the American Historical Foundation, unabashedly connected gun industry profits and the Second Amendment. For a price of $3,995, Second Amendment loyalists could purchase its "Second Amendment Tribute .50 Cal. Revolver . . . the BIGGEST" and the "Most-Powerful" of handguns, adorned with a "hand-engraved" Second Amendment tribute. The weapon "honors our powerful Right to Keep and Bear Arms! And powerful this revolver is, with about three times the punch of a .44 Magnum, and 10X the punch of a .38 Special!"

Scrubbing away the Second Amendment's first clause, the ad says that engraved on the revolver's "underlug" are "the words of the Second Amendment, 'The Right of the People to Keep and Bear Arms.'" The company urges potential customers to "be one of the few people in the world who can own the first biggest, most-powerful, hand-engraved handgun in the world!" The .50-caliber bullets fired by this "most-powerful" handgun could penetrate much of the body armor used by police officers.[3]

In celebration of the Second Amendment, the Patriot Ordnance Factory–USA offers "A FACTORY FREE-DOM TOUR," which promises to explain to visitors "what the Second Amendment means to them." On the Factory's website, the proprietors wield military-style-looking assault rifles fitted with high-capacity magazines. For "fire-breathing patriots," the Factory advertises "the ultimate fighting machines . . . the tools of freedom," including five semiautomatic pistol versions of the AR-15 assault rifle. GunsInternational.com advertises a full line of more than forty NRA-themed rifles, with prices from $250 to $7,650. Its website includes an ad for a discounted NRA membership.[4]

If you're uncomfortable with shopping online, no problem. America now has some fifty thousand brick-and-mortar gun stores, close to double the number of McDonald's restaurants and Starbucks coffee shops combined. Weapons emporiums across the land operate under the banner of the Second Amendment, with titles such as the Second Amendment Armory, the Second Amendment Emporium, or the Second Amendment Gun Shop.[5]

To line the pockets of the gunmakers and dealers, the

gun lobby upholds as a Second Amendment freedom the keeping and bearing of semiautomatic assault weapons, the most dangerous and expensive of firearms. With each trigger pull, these weapons, which were initially designed for warfare, self-load a new bullet—no manual loading required. Assault weapons feature easily reloadable, high-capacity magazines that facilitate mass killing by firing some forty to fifty rounds per minute. Anyone can buy on-line magazines with capacities of up to 100 rounds. Armed with a semiautomatic firearm and a 100-round magazine, a gunman killed nine victims and wounded fifteen in just 32 seconds on August 4, 2019, in Dayton, Ohio.

The gunmakers often enhance assault weapons with other military features, such as pistol grips and slings, flash suppressors to keep the shooter free of blinding muzzle flashes, folding stocks that shorten and conceal the weapons, muzzle brakes to dampen recoil, and barrel designs to prevent overheating with rapid-firing of dozens of rounds. The industry also offers noise suppressors that make it difficult for victims and first responders in mass shootings to recognize the firing. SilencerCo, which dominates with some 70 percent of the market, sells about eighteen thousand suppressors per month. Pro-gun magazines promote such assault firearms and provide what amounts to free advertising for their makers. Per the NRA, "semi-automatics account for over half of the 10–15 million new firearms bought annually."[6]

The NRA claims to protect "everyday Americans" in "their fundamental right to self-defense." But the costly assault weapons they hawk benefit gunmakers, not your everyday American. People fixate on many things, comic books, watches, cars, even garden gnomes. But nothing matches the thrill of domination and control that comes with owning firearms, the bigger and deadlier the better. In December 2018, the NRA alerted readers of *American Rifleman* to "2019's new guns," which cost anywhere from $450 to $3,000. For maximum firepower you can shell out $2,971 for the Windham Weaponry RMCS-4 Multi-Caliber rifle, with a thirty-round detachable magazine that can hold four calibers of bullets, and a pistol grip and a sling for ease of firing dozens of rounds per minute. To get around Congress's ban on sawed-off shotguns, you can purchase the $915 SKO Mini 12-gauge semiautomatic shotgun, with up to a twenty-five-round magazine, which evades federal law by having a pistol grip rather than a rifle stock.[7]

The gun lobby celebrates every variant of assault weaponry. In late 2017 and 2018, the NRA's *American Rifleman* and the independently published pro-gun magazine *Guns & Ammo* featured stories honoring the AK-47, the deadly Russian-made assault rifle that has killed more than 8 million people worldwide. The publications guided readers to purchasing off-the-shelf variants of the AK-47 from American gun dealers, one of which a white nationalist used to murder twenty-two primarily Hispanic persons in El Paso, Texas, on August 3, 2019.

In 2018, *Firearms News,* a premier pro-gun magazine, featured an assault weapon on the cover of nearly all of its bimonthly editions. In November 2018, the magazine showcased a notorious weapon of war, the "Semi-Auto FG 42, A Modern Reproduction of Germany's Green Devil's Rifle," fitted with a high-capacity magazine and military-grade large-caliber bullets. Nazi paratroopers in World War II used this firearm or facsimiles to kill Allied soldiers and quite possibly to murder Jewish men, women, and children. The maker of the reproduced weapon gushed, "The thinking is very German and out of the box. . . . Simply handling it transports you back in time and puts a smile on your face."

In fact, if "you have $100,000 laying around," you can buy a genuine machine-gun version: "a full-auto, transferable, Type II, FG 42 machine gun, as according to one of the top 'class 3' dealers in the USA, Frank Goepfert of Midwest Tactical." Contrary to common belief, you can buy a machine gun in America today. Machine guns are regulated and taxed under the federal firearms laws of the 1930s. These costly weapons must be registered with the federal government but are not banned outright so long as they were made before 1986. Only about a dozen states ban machine guns within their jurisdictions.[8]

If you are a convicted felon or a violent domestic abuser who can't pass a firearm background test, the NRA says that you're covered with "easy build AR 15 components" that let you assemble your assault weapon conveniently at home. Just consult the "80% Lowers" website "brought to you by your Second Amendment!" for instructions on "How to Build Your Own AR 15—Legally and Unregistered."[9]

Kevin Janson Neal's history of violence barred him from legally buying guns, but he still murdered by gunshot five people and injured eighteen in Tehama, California, in 2017. Neal massacred his victims with two AR-15 assault rifles—illegal in California—that he had assembled at home from legally purchased components. "He can get parts through a number of variety of sources, and they come together and they can build them in their shop or they can build them in their garage," said Phil Johnston, Tehama County's assistant sheriff. "It's really not hard. Anybody can build their own gun," added a gun dealer. In 2019, the arsenal found in the home of arrested domestic terrorist Christopher P. Hasson had components for making an untraceable AR-15 assault rifle.[10]

In merchandising assault weapons, the gun lobby overlooks how these firearms shred human bodies. This includes the NRA's favored AR-15, which it calls "the contemporary equivalent of the musket—an everyday gun for everyday citizens. Fundamentally, the AR-15 is democratic. It is the yeoman's gun; the people's gun; the Brown Bess of our era." The weapon "does not represent some bizarre over-extension of the right to keep and bear arms. It is the very core of that right," assuring "that the Second Amendment can be enjoyed by everybody." It is "so smartly designed it can be handled without trouble," even "by children."[11]

Trauma surgeon Dr. Jeremy Cannon, a veteran of the Iraq and Afghanistan wars, explained why the AR-15 is not a child's gun or even a "people's gun." He wrote, "The tissue destruction is almost unimaginable. Bones are exploded, soft tissue is absolutely destroyed. The injuries to the chest or abdomen—it's like a bomb went off. . . . Bystanders are traumatized just seeing the victims. It's awful, terrible. It's just a ghastly thing to see."[12]

A 2018 study found that "semiautomatic rifles are designed for easy use, can accept large magazines, and fire high velocity bullets, enabling active shooters to wound and kill more people per incident" than non-semiautomatic weapons. From 2000 to 2017, the killed and wounded from mass-shooting incidents averaged 9.72 with semiautomatic weapons, 78 percent higher than the 5.47 average with other firearms.[13]

For the first three hundred years of European settlement in America, outside of warfare, there is not a single recorded instance of anyone using the Brown Bess musket to murder multiple victims in a mass shooting. In just 2017 through 2019 combined, killers wielding AR-15s or their equivalent murdered more than several hundred Americans in more than twenty such mass shootings.

Adam Lanza, the twenty-year-old who killed twenty-six children and adults at Sandy Hook Elementary School, fired at least 154 rounds from his unmodified AR-15 in less than four and half minutes. A shooter using a Brown Bess musket could likely have fired only some nine to twelve rounds of highly dubious accuracy in this brief period, and that's if the firearm did not jam or misfire, as often happened. A test-firing of smoothbore muskets, like the Brown Bess, from a fixed platform found that the physics of the weapon, even without human error, "scattered their bullets so badly that they effectively hit their intended target solely by random variation." The musket shooter would have stopped to reload for fifteen to twenty seconds after each shot, giving his targets time to flee or counterattack.[14]

Major companies that make or sell firearms and accessories donate a portion of their sales to the NRA. The gun manufacturers and dealers buy the bulk of the more than $25 million worth of advertising in NRA publications and contribute directly to the organization's lobbying arm, the ILA. An accounting of industry funding is difficult because the ILA, as an independent "issue-advocacy" group that does not endorse or contribute to political candidates, exists in the realm of "dark money," without any requirement to disclose the identity of its contributors. In the election year of 2016, the NRA reported $105 million in grants and contributions from unrelated organizations, without disclosing their origin.[15]

Nonetheless, the NRA's "Golden Ring of Freedom," which recognizes major donors, provides a glimpse of gun industry contributions. The Violence Policy Center found that, as of 2013, MidwayUSA, a maker of ammunition and gun parts, reached the highest level of recognition within the Ring of Freedom, by contributing between $5 million and $10 million. The gun manufacturers Beretta, Smith & Wesson, Springfield Armory, and Ruger held down the second level with contributions of between $1 million and $5 million. The Freedom Group, a conglomerate of arms makers; Brownells, a manufacturer of ammunition and gun accessories; and Pierce Bullet Seal Target Systems, a vendor of gun accessories, also reached the second level. Some thirty other gun industry concerns round out a list of major donors. A separate compilation by the Issue One Database of Dark Money Donors lists $12.1 million in contributions from Sturm, Ruger & Co. from 2011 to 2016.[16]

As a testament to its value for the American right, preeminent conservative financiers the billionaire Koch brothers funneled millions of dollars into the NRA through organizations such as the American Encore, which donated $3.15 million between 2011 and 2016, and the American Future Fund, which donated $3 million. Among other right-wing donors, the Freedom Partners Chamber of Commerce donated $8.36 million, American Action Network, $2.68 million, Judicial Crisis Network, $1 million, and Crossroads Strategies $725,000.[17]

The gun lobby's dependence on the gun industry locks it into the military-industrial complex. The NRA has partnered with the military establishment since the early twentieth century. In 2018, retired lieutenant colonel Oliver North, of Iran/Contra notoriety, held the NRA's presidency, and twenty-one of its seventy-six board members were retired military. The NRA claims to follow in the tradition of the founders who upheld a right to private arms as an alternative to a permanent military establishment that they abhorred as a threat to liberty. Yet, the association has cheered on the creation of the world's largest military in the United States and backed conservative politicians who support an ever-expanding defense budget that pads the profits of the NRA's financiers in the firearms industry. A comparison between the NRA's rating of US Senate and House members and the rating of the pro-military American Security Council shows a powerful correlation between the ratings, even when controlling for party. While it touts a right to private arms as a check on government, the gun lobby promotes a massive military establishment that renders irrelevant any such counterforce.

As the military budget grows, so do funds for arms contracts that benefit the NRA's financiers. Although these gunmakers do not manufacture missiles and jet planes, they continue in Eli Whitney's tradition of supplying small arms to the military. With contracts worth $1.4 billion from 2001 to 2016, Colt led the way. In 2017, the American base of the arms manufacturer Sig Sauer won a $580 million contract to supply sidearms to the US Army.[18]

The gun lobby reaches beyond America's borders to sustain the international arms trade that profits its financiers and upholds its version of Second Amendment rights. "When guns are being confiscated in Australia and Britain . . . NRA members must stand shoulder to shoulder to defend the Second Amendment," said the NRA's lobbyist Tanya Metaksa two decades ago. American makers of light arms—rifles, handguns, and shotguns—primarily market their products within the United States, but they increasingly sell arms abroad. In 2017, US gunmakers exported 488,300 light arms to foreign nations, up 70 percent since 2012. The U.S. accounts for more than a third of the worldwide exports of light arms; top exporters include NRA donors and advertisers such as Ruger, Colt, Smith & Wesson, and Henry. Legally exported firearms arm criminal gangs and drug cartels, genocidal regimes, terrorist cells, guerrilla warriors, and armies of child soldiers.[19]

German prosecutors in 2019 criminally charged Ron Cohen, the CEO of the American arm of Sig Sauer, with conspiracy to illegally sell many thousands of pistols to the National Police in Colombia during a time of civil conflict, when Colombian government forces were complicit in murders, assaults, kidnapping, and rapes. Prosecutors charged that the German arm of Sig Sauer manufactured some thirty-eight thousand pistols from 2009 to 2011, which it shipped to Sig Sauer's American facility in New Hampshire, which then sent the arms to Colombia to evade German laws prohibiting exports to that nation. The United States had no such prohibition. Prosecutors further charged that Sig Sauer had covered up the transaction by submitting to German officials documents that falsely claimed that the arms were solely for sale in the United States. In early 2019, Ron Cohen pleaded guilty in German court to violating the country's export laws. Although facing substantial prison time if found guilty, his plea deal called for a suspended sentence and a fine of $675,000.[20]

Export data omits the trade in parts, ammunition, and accessories, which in value worldwide equals the sales of light arms. The Small Arms Survey of the Graduate Institute of International and Development Studies, Geneva, reported that the parts and accessories are "used in the illicit production of small arms and light weapons by armed groups and arms traffickers. . . . These weapons are then illicitly re-exported to criminals in other countries."[21]

The United States imports far more rifles, handguns, and shotguns—4,492,256, in 2017, accounting for about one in three US arm sales—than it exports. Foreign sellers have generously contributed to the NRA. A major exporter, Brazil's Forjas Taurus, bestows a free NRA membership on buyers. Italian gunmaker Beretta has donated $1 million to the NRA, and another Italian manufacturer, Benelli, between $500,000 and $1 million. The Austrian gunmaker Glock has donated between $250,000 and $500,000.[22]

To curb the violence perpetrated by arms exports, the United Nations in 2013 adopted by a vote of 154 to 3 the Arms Trade Treaty (ATT), which prohibits any nation from the transfer of conventional arms "if it has knowledge at the time of authorization that the arms or items would be used in the commission of genocide, crimes against humanity, grave breaches of the Geneva Conventions of 1949, attacks directed against civilian objects or civilians protected as such, or other war crimes." The treaty has no impact on domestic gun policies. It reaffirms "the sovereign right of each country to decide for itself, pursuant to its own constitutional and legal system, how to deal with conventional arms that are traded exclusively within its borders."[23]

The American gun lobby stood with Iran, North Korea, and Syria in opposing the ATT, cloaking its obstruction in the Second Amendment. NRA CEO LaPierre said, "The cornerstone of our freedom is the Second Amendment. Neither the United Nations, nor any other foreign influence, has the authority to meddle with the freedoms guaranteed by our Bill of Rights, endowed by our Creator, and due to all humankind." If "you ignore the right of good people to own firearms to protect their freedom, you become the enablers of future tyrants whose regimes will destroy millions and millions of defenseless lives." LaPierre's answer to violence in unstable nations abroad was more, not fewer, guns: "If every family on the planet owned a good-quality rifle, genocide would be on the path to extinction."[24]

Equally inflammatory was an unsigned email, circulated among gun rights groups, that headlined in capital letters the warning that through the ATT "OBAMA FINDS LEGAL WAY AROUND SECOND AMENDMENT. AND USES IT. IF THIS PASSES, THERE COULD BE WAR." Larry Pratt of the Gun Owners of America suggested that the 2012 massacre of twelve persons at a theater in Aurora, Colorado, might have been an inside job by the government to win support for the treaty.[25]

The gun lobby and industry convinced the US Senate to adopt an amendment to prevent the United States from signing the ATT. The amendment's sponsor, Republican senator James Inhofe of Oklahoma, whom the NRA rated A+, said, "This is probably the last time this year that you'll be able to vote for your Second Amendment rights." His proposed amendment never became law, and the United States signed the Arms Trade Treaty in September 2013, joining more than a hundred other nations. The Senate, however, has not ratified the treaty, and the NRA has lobbied the Trump administration for withdrawal. President Donald Trump has eased export controls on light arms and shifted enforcement from the Department of State to the pro-business Department of Commerce. The NRA's Institute for Legislative Action hailed these initiatives as a "win-win for America's firearms industry."[26]

Then, in the midst of a rousing anti-gun-control speech at the NRA's annual convention on April 26, 2019, President Trump countermanded America's signing of the treaty, in effect withdrawing the United States. "We're taking our signature back," Trump said. After signing the withdrawal order, Trump flung his pen into the cheering crowd. "The United States will now lock arms with Iran, North Korea, and Syria as nonsignatories to this historic treaty whose sole purpose is to protect innocent people from deadly weapons," said Abby Maxman, president of Oxfam America, which is part of an international antipoverty movement.[27]

The day after Trump's speech, a gunman wielding an AR-15-style assault rifle burst into a synagogue in Poway,

California, during Passover services, killing one person and wounding three, including the rabbi. It was the second synagogue massacre with an assault weapon in just six months. President Trump again offered his "thoughts and prayers," but nothing more to control gun violence. "Thoughts and prayers without policy change are useless," responded the Reverend Robert Lee IV, a descendant of the Confederate general. "God didn't tell Noah to send thoughts and prayers to save him from doom. . . . God didn't tell Moses to send thoughts and prayers to save the Israelites from bondage."[28]

The NRA does not fund gun lobbies globally, but it still intervenes against firearms controls in foreign lands. It has been pushing Canada to adopt the American model of lax gun controls even as far more Americans than Canadians per capita die from gun violence. Tony Bernardo, the executive director of the pro-gun lobby the Canadian Institute for Legislative Action (CILA), said that he "coordinates with the NRA, relying on their expertise." NRA executive vice president Wayne LaPierre has urged "all Canadian firearms owners to become CILA-supporting members." The NRA helped gun rights advocates in Brazil defeat a gun control referendum. Today, absent the gun ban, Brazil has by far the most firearms homicides and deaths of any country in the world.[29]

In Australia, where there were just 27 gun murders in 2018, pro-gun rights senator David Leyonhjelm said, "We love the NRA here in Australia amongst us gun owners." The Shooting Industry Foundation of Australia

(SIFA), which lobbies politicians to unwind gun control, "has learnt from this American example, and its methods emulate it," the Australian Broadcasting Corporation reported in November 2018. "Expect to see more from SIFA in the lead-up to other elections in the future—Australia's very own NRA." Like the NRA, the gun industry backs and funds SIFA.[30]

In 2015, former NRA president David Keene, future president Pete Brownell, and other NRA leaders and donors traveled to Moscow with Russian citizen Maria Butina, a lifetime NRA member and the founder of a so-called Russian pro-gun group named Right to Bear Arms. A federal judge later sentenced Butina to eighteen months in prison for acting as a covert agent of the Kremlin in the United States.

The NRA delegation met with Foreign Minister Sergei Lavrov and Deputy Prime Minister Dmitry Rogozin, whom the Obama administration had sanctioned after Russia's invasion of Crimea. They met, too, with oligarch and Putin ally Alexander Torshin, a lifetime NRA member and financier of the Right to Bear Arms, whom the United States sanctioned in 2018. The delegation visited the maker of the T-5000M sniper rifle, which the US military says poses a deadly threat to Russia's adversaries. At the time, Brownell was working to establish a Russian distribution network for the accessories and ammunition sold by his company, Brownells, Inc.[31]

A US intelligence report has revealed that Torshin "spent years aggressively courting NRA leaders, briefed the Kremlin on his efforts and recommended they participate." Steven L. Hall, a retired CIA agent with expertise on Russia, said, "My assessment of what was happening with Torshin and Butina and the NRA was that the Russians decided, a good period of time before 2016, to run an influence operation here in the US." Their goals were "to help Donald Trump win" and "to create as much chaos in our democracy as possible." The NRA's ties to the dictatorial, anti-American Russian regime exposes as a lie the NRA's claim to be the patriotic defender of America's liberties and freedoms.[32]

10

Follow the Money

This PROUD member of the "unwashed masses" that the [NRA] Old Guard looks down on and feels deserve secrecy from the inner workings has had enough and will no longer tolerate the foxes keeping watch over the hen house.

—STEVE HOBACK, FORMER NRA STAFFER AND
LIFE MEMBER, 2019[1]

Internal dissension has racked today's NRA, similar to the clash between its old and new guard in the 1970s. At the NRA's April 2019 convention, association president Oliver North charged that CEO LaPierre had billed the NRA lavishly for a Beverly Hills wardrobe and luxury travel, and other perquisites, and squandered association funds by paying nearly $100,000 a day to the law firm of outside counsel Bill Brewer during the past year.[2]

LaPierre fired back by charging that North was extorting him to resign and that one of the NRA's outside public relations vendors had paid North exorbitant sums for little work on a documentary. LaPierre survived the conflict and pushed North out of the presidency in favor of the compliant eighty-year-old Carolyn D. Meadows, who had worked closely with LaPierre since the late 1980s. Unlike the leadership changes from the 1977 "revolt in Cincinnati," the ratification of LaPierre's four decades of leadership means that the foxes will continue to keep watch over the henhouse of the NRA.[3]

In 1973, "Deep Throat"—since revealed as associate FBI director Mark Felt—advised reporters Bob Woodward and Carl Bernstein to uncover the sins of Watergate by tracing the source of President Richard Nixon's illegal campaign cash. The movie *All the President's Men* memorably shortened this advice to "follow the money." The opaque and byzantine financial arrangements of the NRA rival the operations of Nixon's reelection campaign. But persistence pays off to disclose a racket that enriches the NRA's leaders rather than serving loyal members such as Steve Hoback.

There is plenty of NRA money to follow; hundreds of millions of dollars flow into and out of the association each year. But the money actually flows through four separate parts of the organization. The first component is the National Rifle Association, the parent organization that directly or indirectly controls all other components. It accounted for about half of its $413 million budget in the election year of 2016, funded primarily from membership dues, advertising fees, product sales, donations from conservative political organizations, gun industry, ads, and subsidies from its affiliated charities.

Under America's tax laws, the NRA operates as a 501(c)(4) nonprofit organization. It is exempt from federal taxes, but its donors cannot deduct their contributions to the NRA on their federal tax returns. In return for forgoing tax-deductible contributions, the tax laws authorize the association to engage in legislative lobbying and in political activity to support or oppose candidates. However, it operates in the realm of dark money, without having to disclose the sources of its donations. In 2017, when NRA revenue plummeted by $55 million and its two-year deficit reached $64 million, dark money contributions of $18.8 million from one person, and $1 million or more from six others, all unidentified, kept the association from sinking more deeply into debt.[4]

The NRA controls four affiliated charitable foundations: the NRA Civil Rights Defense Fund, the NRA Special Contribution Fund, the NRA Freedom Action Foundation, and the NRA Foundation. Like the NRA proper, its foundations do not need to disclose their donors. However, the foundations are distinct 501(c)(3) charitable organizations. Unlike contributors to the NRA, donors to such charities can deduct contributions on their federal tax returns. In return for this fund-raising privilege, the charitable foundations cannot engage in more than insubstantial lobbying and cannot "participate in or intervene in (including publishing or distributing of statements), any political campaign on behalf of (or in opposition to) any candidate for political office." The NRA exercises effective control over these foundations through overlapping officers and the appointment of trustees. This tight relationship between parent NRA and these affiliated charitable foundations invites self-dealing.[5]

The NRA Civil Rights Defense Fund provides financial aid for research and litigation in support of Second Amendment rights. The NRA Special Contribution Fund promotes firearms training and education. However, the NRA Freedom Action Foundation, despite reaping the benefit of a charity, is a political operation dressed in charitable clothes. Its mission is to "reach out" to pro–Second Amendment citizens and "teach the importance of exercising their precious voting rights." The NRA Foundation, by far the largest of the parent organization's charitable arms, also has a nearly unlimited mandate to "support of a wide range of firearm-related public interest activities of the National Rifle Association of America and other organizations that defend and foster the Second Amendment rights of all law-abiding Americans."

Although a charity cannot front for a political and lobbying organization, the NRA Foundation operates a money machine for the parent NRA. The NRA's Board of Directors appoints the trustees of the foundation, more than half of whom double as NRA board members. According to 2017 tax filings, the foundation's president, William H. Satterfield, is an NRA board member and ironically the head of its Ethics Committee. The foundation's vice president, Carolyn D. Meadows, is a former vice president of the NRA and, as of 2019, its president.

The foundation's treasurer and CEO, Wilson H. Phillips, Jr., is also treasurer of the NRA, and the foundation's executive director, H. Wayne Sheets, is a former board member.[6]

In 2017, the NRA Foundation gave the parent NRA a grant of $18.8 million; no other grant topped $425,000. From 2013 to 2017, the foundation dished out $87.4 million in grants to the NRA, about 57 percent of all grant allocations for these five years.[7]

Although the foundation broadly lists "2nd Amendment protection" as one purpose of its NRA grants, it claims to review these grants so that they are "used only for charitable program purposes." Whether this professed self-policing is real or pro forma for the IRS, segregation is difficult if not impossible for the profoundly political NRA. Lobbying and partisan politics infuse the NRA's publications, its television broadcasts, its ads, its website and social media presence, its sponsored interviews and writings, its alerts to members and firearms owners on gun control legislation, its advice on contacting lawmakers, and its mobilization of members for elections. According to a Common Cause report, even the NRA's firearms instructors and coaches "are constantly recruited to take leadership roles, as well as join in political activities supporting the NRA leadership's positions."[8]

The NRA Foundation provides no disclaimer for three other subsidies to the parent association that are buried within its tax filings. The foundation's 2017 filings list no payments to its own employees or to employees of a "related organization." It reports only an estimated twelve thousand "volunteers." Yet, on the next to last page of its voluminous filings, the foundation reported a $5 million transfer to the NRA for the "sharing of paid employees with related organization(s)."[9]

From 2013 to 2017, the foundation shelled out $245 million in compensation for NRA employees, for an average of $4.9 million per year. Yet association officials and other employees routinely engage in political advocacy and lobbying.

In 2017, the NRA Foundation additionally loaned the NRA $5 million and paid it more than $1 million for miscellaneous expenses. In sum, the foundation made $30 million in payments and loans to the NRA during 2017, equal to two-thirds of the foundation's budget. From 2013 to 2017 the foundation shelled out $129 million to the NRA, for an average of $25.8 million per year, equal to three-fifths percent of the foundation's budgets.

The Special Contribution Fund, a much smaller charitable operation, also transfers tax-deductible dollars to the NRA. For the five-year period from 2013 to 2017, the Special Contribution Fund transferred $8.6 million to the NRA, equal to 44 percent of the fund's budgets. Taken together, over five years, the two foundations poured $138 million into the NRA.

Tens of millions of dollars in subsidies each year from its affiliated charities enables the association's officers to enrich themselves with exorbitant payouts for a nonprofit, social-welfare organization. In 2017, despite falling revenue and a $64 million two-year deficit, the association paid LaPierre $1.4 million, Cox $1.2 million, and seven other officials more than $650,000—far exceeding what other nonprofits with much larger budgets paid their officials. In 2017, the NRA further paid $710,000 to executive director Sheets of the NRA Foundation. According to the foundation's tax filing, Sheets worked only one hour of work per week for the foundation and conducted no work for any related organization. The NRA said that Sheets also functioned as an independent fund-raising consultant. LaPierre, Sheets, and perhaps other officials reportedly reaped additional perquisites, through billings of many hundreds of thousands of dollars for Beverly Hills clothing, luxurious travel, and other expenditures that they passed through outside vendors and that the NRA did not separately tally in its IRS reports.[10]

"Wayne LaPierre, the CEO of the NRA, along with fellow executives and outside contractors (in particular advertising agency Ackerman McQueen), has been recklessly shoveling money out of NRA coffers for decades—to the tune of possibly hundreds of millions of dollars," wrote gun rights advocate Jeff Knox, the son of the late Neal Knox, Harlon Carter's chief lieutenant in the NRA's militant 1977 "revolt in Cincinnati." "Continuing to deny and circling the wagons to protect against outside assaults will not save the NRA. The destroyer is inside the circle. Only decisive action to root out the corruption and return to the core values and principles of the organization can save it."[11]

The lavish salaries and benefits reaped by NRA leaders do not trickle down to rank-and-file employees. Association workers told National Public Radio (NPR) of low salaries and poor working conditions. "People at the bottom were not making a lot of money. Fundraising people made some money, but not much compared to a typical D.C. nonprofit," said Aaron Davis, who worked on NRA fund-raising from 2005 to 2015. "We were horribly underpaid," added Steve Hoback, who worked as an NRA trainer from 2009 to 2012. He said that he said he started out at $28,000 per year and advanced to $32,000 per year after three years of work. "There was a culture of fear," at the NRA said Vanessa Ross, who managed the group's disabled shooting services from 2008 to 2011. "The moment you poked your head up and started asking questions, that's when I felt everything turn—then it was like I was the pariah." She said that the NRA fired her when she questioned cutbacks in the disabled shooting program.[12]

NPR discovered that despite the $3.8 million in retirement benefits accorded CEO LaPierre, its pension obligations for ordinary employees are woefully underfunded. According to Brian Mittendorf, chair of Accounting Department at Ohio State University, "the organization's financial trouble puts these rank-and-file employees' future at risk . . . The people at the top are going to be financially secure. It's the rank-and-file employees that are at risk."[13]

The NRA claims to stand without compromise for law

and order. Yet by exploiting its charitable foundation for its own purposes, the NRA has at best pushed the tax laws to the edge and at worst violated the laws. New York State charters the association, and the office of the state attorney general, which shuttered the Trump Foundation, is investigating its finances.[14]

President Donald Trump quickly assailed the state's investigation. "The NRA is under siege by Cuomo and the New York State A.G., who are illegally using the State's legal apparatus to take down and destroy this very important organization, & others." "74,600 Americans have died from gun violence since you were elected. You have done nothing but tweet about it," Governor Cuomo fired back. "Unlike you, NY is not afraid to stand up to the NRA. As for the NRA, we'll remember them in our thoughts and prayers." Soon after, Washington, D.C.'s attorney general launched another investigation of the NRA's finances.[15]

The NRA also controls the NRA Victory Fund, a political action committee (PAC) that supports and opposes candidates and contributes to campaigns. Targeted to Republicans, the fund's contributions reward the loyalty of politicians. More important, though, is the fourth NRA component, the Institute for Legislative Action (ILA), which lobbies and advocates for "Second Amendment Rights." Unlike the Victory Fund, the ILA does not make political contributions, although it engages in lobbying and in independent campaign spending. In the 2012 presidential election cycle, the NRA PAC made

$11.2 million in contributions, and the ILA spent $8.6 million on independent expenditures, almost entirely for Republicans.

The NRA's political spending soared four years later, with PAC spending rising by 71 percent to $19.2 million, and ILA spending quadrupling to $35.2 million. The NRA devoted more than $30 million in combined 2016 PAC and ILA funds to elect Republican presidential candidate Donald Trump, and millions more in support of congressional candidates, 98 percent of them Republicans.[16]

In April 2019, the Giffords gun control group filed suit against the Federal Election Commission for failing to act against campaign finance law violations by the NRA. Giffords charged that the NRA "violated the Federal Election Campaign Act by using a complex network of shell corporations to unlawfully coordinate expenditures with the campaigns of at least seven candidates for federal office, thereby making millions of dollars of illegal, unreported, and excessive in-kind contributions, including up to $25 million in illegal contributions to now President Donald J. Trump." The Federal Election Commission is one of the least effective of federal agencies, with decision making stymied by conflicts between Republican and Democratic commissioners.[17]

Spending by the ILA and the Victory PAC underestimate the political resources that the NRA mustered in 2016. Its IRS filling lists $65 million for advertising and promotion and $81 million for "member communication expenses," some of which was likely aimed at political mobilization of the 5 million claimed NRA members. "These field operations," said GOP operative and lobbyist Charlie Black, "may be even more important than the ads, and the field work doesn't have to be reported under campaign finance laws."[18]

The NRA salted its 2016 publications with political advocacy, mixing gun rights with extreme right-wing politics and unabashed Republican partisanship. The NRA's preelection edition of *American Rifleman* featured CEO LaPierre on the cover, with the warning in large all-caps text "THAT ONLY YOUR VOTE CAN SAVE US." Inside, a full-page banner ad said, "MAKE AMERICA FREE AGAIN, VOTE TRUMP/PENCE." LaPierre urged NRA members to "do your part to save your God-given right to defend yourself and your family from the gravest threat it's faced since the founding of our nation." Beneath a photo in which he's brandishing an assault rifle with a fearsomely large magazine, columnist Mark Keefe wrote that only the NRA could stop (Jewish) billionaires Michael Bloomberg and George Soros from "destroying America's first freedom—the Second Amendment. . . . Trump is the clear firearm freedom candidate." ILA director Chris W. Cox warned that the election of Hillary Clinton would threaten "Gun Rights and Our Way of Life."

In 2019, the NRA filed two lawsuits in 2019 against its main vendor, Ackerman McQueen, which along with its affiliates raked in more than $40 million for the NRA in 2017 and has worked with the Association for thirty-eight years. The suits charge that Ackerman McQueen has unlawfully withheld billing information and breached its contract, leaked damaging information about the association to the press, and tried to organize a coup against LaPierre. Ackerman McQueen countered with a $50 million lawsuit against the NRA, which claimed that the firm complied with all financial requirements and that the NRA is attempting to evade paying it "a very substantial amount of money in the form of severance and cancellation fees."[19]

Contrary to its propaganda, the NRA is not a grassroots organization, but an insiders' club run by a seventy-six-member, self-perpetuating board of directors, which chooses the president, the CEO, the head of the ILA, and other officers. A committee, composed primarily of existing board members, nominates candidates for the board. Candidates can self-nominate by petition, but without the committee's imprimatur, petitioners rarely win. Only lifetime NRA members, and annual members with an unbroken five years of loyalty—about a quarter of all members—vote for seventy-five of the seventy-six board positions. The final board member is selected by a vote of those attending the NRA's annual meeting. These insular rules shield the NRA from any hostile takeover.[20]

A shattering study by two political science professors found that wealthy special interests, such as the NRA, largely control the policy making in the United States. After analyzing survey data on 1,779 national policy issues, the authors found that when controlling for the power of economic elites and organized interest groups, the influence of ordinary Americans registers at a "*nonsignificant, near-zero level.*" The influence of the special interests remains dominant even when their policy preferences diverge from those of most Americans.[21]

Still, concerted mass movements of ordinary citizens, such as the civil rights and women's movements of the 1960s, can again challenge wealthy special interests. A movement capable of smashing the NRA and the iron triangle on guns cannot be diffuse and incremental. A lack of imagination, courage, and focus has been a formula for failure by progressive reformers. Gun control advocates need to defy what the conventional wisdom defines as "political reality" and create a new context for change, such as the gun lobby did with its reinvention of the Second Amendment. Liberal activist and Brandeis University professor Robert Kuttner incisively wrote, "The liberal imagination has been stunted by decades of conservative obstruction and has lost its power to inspire. Most of what ails the middle class requires far more robust policies than are currently in mainstream debate. Liberals should say what they are really for. They might even win more followers."[22]

Today's gun control movement has gained piecemeal some firearms regulations in the states, which cannot substitute for the comprehensive national gun control program that would follow from a successful repeal strategy (see chapters 13 and 14) and is the only sure antidote for America's gun violence epidemic. "We've got a crisis here," said Daniel Webster, the director of the Center for Gun Policy and Research at Johns Hopkins University. "And if you're just trying to say, 'Okay, what's the easiest political thing to do?,' you're likely to aim low and have minimal impact. . . . We've got a huge problem, and you don't solve huge problems with tiny changes."[23]

For too long, gun control advocates have fought a losing battle on the Second Amendment turf of the gun lobby. It's past time for reformers to change the terms of engagement and gain "the power to inspire" by forthrightly pursuing what the gun reform movement in its heart is "really for." America lived comfortably without a meaningful Second Amendment for upward of two hundred years. We can do so again.

Debunking the Gun Lobby's Case for Firearms Self-Defense

Most purported self-defense gun uses are gun uses in escalating arguments and are both socially undesirable and illegal.

—DAVID HEMENWAY, DIRECTOR, HARVARD INJURY CONTROL RESEARCH CENTER, 2000[1]

On the night of July 16, 2018, in North Philadelphia, two men fired at least twenty shots into a group of children. Before their clean getaway, the gunmen killed a fourteen-year-boy and struck one adult with a stray bullet. The perpetrators injured three other children, aged eleven, fourteen, and sixteen. The father of the murdered child said that he just happened to be in the wrong place at the wrong time. Earlier that same day, in Palm Beach Gardens, Florida, a single shooter killed two victims, age twenty-one and twenty-two, and wounded four others; in Washington, D.C., gunmen killed a ten-year-old child and wounded four adults.[2]

A week later, the CDC reported a 31 percent increase in gun homicides in just two years, from 2014 to 2016. However, the Dickey Amendment chilled research into the causes behind this upsurge in deaths. The amendment's sponsor, late congressman Jay Dickey, came to regret his role in restricting gun research. In a coauthored op-ed that he published in 2012, Dickey said, "The federal government has invested billions to understand the causes of motor vehicle fatalities and, with that knowledge, has markedly reduced traffic deaths in the United States." However, "it's vital to understand why we know more and spend so much more on preventing traffic fatalities than on preventing gun violence."[3]

In the 2018 budget resolution Congress explained what was already known, that the Dickey Amendment did not explicitly prohibit federal support for gun violence research. However, research remained chilled; Congress did not appropriate any substantial research funds. A 2017 study found that "in relation to mortality rates, gun violence research was the least-researched cause of death." From 1975 to 2012, America experienced four hundred cases of cholera, and the National Institutes of Health (NIH) doled out 212 research awards to study the disease. During this same span, when Americans suffered from several million deaths and injuries from gunfire, the NIH granted just three research awards to study firearms injuries.[4]

Fortunately, we now have a wealth of credible, independent studies that document the undeniable correlation between lax gun controls and the deaths from murder, suicides, and accidents that they facilitate. Still, though, the gun lobby insists that Americans are safest when their access to every type of firearm, allegedly for self-defense, is little controlled.

We know from death records that gunshots killed nearly forty thousand Americans in 2017—a death toll from firearms that is topped only by Brazil's—and per capita only by a few strife-riven less-developed countries—and that gunshots likely injured close to another hundred thousand. The gun lobby argues preposterously that gun violence in America would somehow be lessened with more guns for good guys to stop bad guys with guns. They prop up this myth about firearms self-defense by asserting that law-abiding Americans use guns for defense against criminals millions of times each year, many times more than the total of all gun crimes.

The lobby's claim of such widespread acts of self-protection relies on the same bogus methodology that would project millions of space-alien abductions and encounters taking place across the United States. Absent any hard proof of firearms self-defense, the gun lobby turns to this bogus alien abduction methodology: take a survey, ask a yes-or-no question about some phenomenon, no matter how outlandish, and a few respondents will inevitably say yes. Then project that vanishingly small percentage of positive answers to an adult population of more than 200 million, and you have proof of almost anything for millions of Americans.

In one national, scientifically conducted CNN poll in 2014, 3 percent of respondents—projected to be 7.5 million adult Americans—agreed that missing Malaysia Airlines Flight 370 was very likely snatched by space aliens, time travelers, or beings from another dimension. A Public Policy poll from 2013 found that 4 percent—projected to be 10 million adult Americans—agreed that shapeshifting lizard people control American politics.[5]

National surveys have found that about 2 percent of respondents claim to have been abducted by space aliens or to have experienced a face-to-face encounter with aliens, which projects to some 5 million alien abductions or encounters in the United States. Yet, neither America nor anywhere else in the world has seen a single plausible, much less verified, account of space-alien abductions or encounters. This "alien abduction" methodology proves only that no reliable conclusions can be inferred from meager survey responses.[6]

The percentage of poll respondents indicating an alien abduction or encounter actually tops the percentage in survey data reporting the defensive use of firearms, which hovers at just over 1 percent annually. In a 1993 survey that still grounds the gun lobby's claims about firearms self-defense, gun rights advocate Gary Kleck, assisted by survey researcher Marc Gertz, found that among 4,977 respondents, 1.33 percent—or 66—claimed that they or a family member had used guns for self-defense during the year. These few positive responses projected to up to 2.5 million annual uses of guns for self-defense by adult

Americans. Applied to today's larger population, estimated defensive uses of guns would rise to about 3 million, all based on answers by sixty-six people in a survey interpreted by researchers with an interest in the outcome.[7]

Kleck insists that his defensive gun users described each episode, but so do persons who profess an alien abduction. Psychology professor Michael J. Strube, who studied the psychology behind alien abductions, asked, "Are humans being snatched daily in great numbers by aliens? No—there is simply no evidence to support the claim. Do significant numbers of otherwise normal people believe that they have been the victims of an abduction? Undoubtedly—the evidence seems clear on this point."[8]

Like reports of alien abductions or lizard people ruling America, self-reported claims about defensive gun uses are plagued by obvious response error, so-called false positives. Philip J. Cook and Jens Ludwig, who conducted the 1994 National Survey of Private Ownership of Firearms in the United States (NSPOF), cite half a dozen reasons for false positives, more than enough to explain virtually all of Kleck's positive answers or answers in other surveys with similar methodology. "Respondents may falsely report [defensive gun uses] because they are confused, have a distorted memory, or are simply having fun with the interviewer." Besides, "fighting off a criminal attack is (in most circumstances) a heroic act" that may tempt "some respondents either to make something up or else to change the details of an actual event." Yet another "source of false positives is strategic behavior by gun advocates."[9]

A failure to report a defensive gun use, "false negative responses," the researchers explain, could not offset false positive reports. "There is much greater scope for false positives than false negatives—only a relatively few respondents are logically capable of giving a false negative, whereas anyone who did not use a gun defensively can give a false positive." The researchers conclude that any attempt to project their survey responses to the US adult population would produce results that are "far higher than the underlying reality" because even a handful of false reports are sufficient to greatly magnify the results."[10]

A "more fundamental problem" that these researchers address is that alleged defensive gun uses may represent needless or even illegal violence. They question whether "the number of DGUs [defensive gun uses] serves as a measure of the public benefit of private gun possession, even in principle? When it comes to DGUs, is more better?" They note that "gun use may take the place of other means of avoiding trouble" and that "readiness to use guns in self-defense may lead to fatal mistakes."[11]

Other studies that look behind self-reports prove that alleged defensive gun uses do not benefit the American people. Researchers from Harvard University found that criminal court judges who read accounts of self-reported defensive gun use from surveys "rated a majority as being illegal, even assuming that the respondent had a permit to own and to carry a gun, and that the respondent had described the event honestly from his own perspective."[12]

Claims of self-defense can cynically cover murderous violence. Historically, the armed, private militias of white supremacists who murdered and assaulted African Americans during the post–Civil War Reconstruction invariably claimed self-defense from black criminals and rioters. White terrorists insisted that "the Negroes have conspired and armed themselves to exterminate the whites, and that these murders are committed by the whites in self-defense," explained Republican senator Oliver P. Morton in 1874. A *Chicago Tribune* editorial from 1876 noted "the White-Line justification for the massacre of Negroes—to wit: that invariably in self-defense the White-Liners had to slaughter the blacks."[13]

Today, prisons are filled with violent felons who have professed self-defense with firearms. There's Michael David Dunn, who killed seventeen-year-old Jordan Davis when Dunn fired ten shots into a car of unarmed black teenagers after claiming to have seen something that looked like a weapon. Drug dealer Mark Lorenzo Blake, Jr., shot a police officer five times during a foot chase, allegedly in self-defense because he said that he feared the police would shoot him.[14]

Credible survey research debunks the NRA's alien abduction model and demonstrates that gun crimes and suicides far exceed any defensive uses of guns. From the US Department of Justice's National Crime Victimization

Survey (NCVS), which authorities in the field regard as the gold standard of crime surveys, a report on firearms self-defense that roughly coincides with Kleck's time frame found nothing remotely close to his projected 2.5 million defensive uses of firearms. The NCVS, which includes both crimes reported and not reported to the police, found that from 1987 to 1992, both for personal and property crimes, *fewer than one-half of 1 percent of victims* attempted to use firearms in their defense. Even among these very few armed victims, "only about one in three faced an armed offender." That's equal to about one-tenth of 1 percent of victims.[15] Updated NCVS data confirms this minimal pattern of defensive gun use. From 2007 to 2011, the survey found that about 0.8 percent of victims attempted to use firearms in their defense, which would include off-duty police officers and security guards.[16]

Unlike the Kleck/Gertz survey, the NCVS relies on multiyear averages, with combined responses in the hundreds of thousands, compared to just under 5,000 for Kleck's single survey. Kleck's survey had a response rate of 61 percent, compared to more than 90 percent for the National Crime Victimization Survey, which was conducted not by self-interested researchers, but by the US Bureau of the Census, which has developed techniques for avoiding both false positive and false negative responses. The NCVS surveyed a representative national sample, compared to the biased sample in the Kleck survey, which queried only male heads of households, the persons most likely to own and use guns. Much more comprehensive than Kleck's, the

NCVS study included police officers and adolescents. Survey takers assured respondents that federal law protected their anonymity. The NCVS may well overreport defensive gun uses because it includes police and for the same reasons that produce false positives in any survey approach.

The NCVS queried about defensive measures after verifying a crime, whether completed or just attempted. Pro-gun advocates have claimed that defensive gun users may have prevented even attempted crimes just by brandishing a firearm, although any such reports are subjective, prone to recollection error and embellishment, and impossible to verify. Moreover, 64 percent of Kleck's self-defense respondents "claimed that the incidents had become known to the police," unlikely when a crime was neither attempted nor completed.[17]

Unlike the open-ended NCVS, the Kleck/Gertz survey begins with the suggestive question of whether "you yourself or another member of your household used a gun, even if it was not fired, for self-protection or for the protection of property at home, work, or elsewhere?" Like queries about alien abductions or lizard people, this question openly invites false positive answers, even if only from 1 to 2 percent of respondents. The researchers provide no objective criteria to judge the legitimacy of self-defense reports and no independent verification, which would not be difficult for just sixty-six persons with positive responses. Voting surveys often include independent verification, such as checking registration rolls to validate self-reported responses.

Another survey with 1,906 respondents found that over five years only 2 (.02 percent a year) had ever used a gun for defense in the home, which the gun lobby claims is a typical self-defense scenario. Thirteen had guns brandished against them, mostly directed against women by male family members or intimate partners.[18]

Kleck is a proficient academic who has vehemently defended his work after withering criticism from other researchers. However, reliable verification tests with independent, non-self-reported data contradict his claim of millions of self-defense gun uses each year. Arthur Kellermann of Emory University and coresearchers provided an independent check on the defensive deployment of firearms by studying verified police reports of home invasion crimes in the city of Atlanta during 1994. The gun lobby touts home defense as a preeminent reason for owning guns. Yet, they found that in only 3 of 198 cases (1.5 percent) did a resident ever use a firearm for self-protection. In another independent check, Kellermann reviewed reports from the police, medical examiners, emergency medical providers, and hospital staffers in three cities. Not counting police officers acting in the line of duty, he found that harmful or deadly uses of firearms exceeded gun use for self-defense by about 61 to 1 (610 to 10).[19]

The 64 percent of defensive gun users in the Kleck/Gertz study who said their actions became known to the police should generate about 1.9 million reports based on the current population. The Gun Violence Archive independently checked this supposition by consulting media reports and police records. For 2018, the archive documented only 1,767 reports to the police of defensive gun uses; somehow more than 99.9 percent of Kleck's claimed reports of self-defense with firearms had disappeared. The archive's findings are stable over time. For the five years from 2014 to 2018, the annual number of reported uses of guns for self-defense averaged an identical 1,767. Kleck says defensively that the 64 percent figure "should be interpreted with caution." But even if Kleck's report rate was cut in half, that would still generate nearly 1 million police reports, with more than 99.7 percent unaccounted for. Even if Kleck's report rate were cut in half and the Archive's numbers doubled, more than 99.5 percent of Kleck's police reports would still be missing.[20]

The Kleck/Gertz survey also found that 8.3 percent of defensive gun users shot and wounded or killed offenders. This would project today to about 250,000 injuries or deaths from defensive gun uses alone, far more than the total number of Americans killed or injured by gunfire annually according to the CDC. Even if only one in twenty of the alleged defensive gun users killed their victim, that would nearly equal the total number of gun homicides in America and exceed by nearly forty times the total number of justifiable gun homicides that year (347). Kleck says that the 8.3 percent result should be interpreted with caution, but fails to acknowledge how it challenges the validity of his survey-projection methodology.

Programs that insure people from criminal and civil liability for using guns in self-defense provide more hard facts, with money at stake, that debunk the gun lobby's claims. If millions of Americans used guns in self-defense each year, then waves of policyholders making claims would bankrupt every insurance plan. Rather, gun-liability insurance is a profitable business, in which the NRA's Carry Guard insurance plan competes with outfits such as U.S. Law Shield, which has about 240,000 policyholders and rakes in more than $30 million per year. This self-selected sample of gun owners who shell out hundreds of dollars for insurance should far eclipse in percentage of claims those of the just over 1 percent of defensive gun users that the gun lobby projects to all adult Americans, only about 40 percent of whom have access to guns personally or in the home. Yet U.S. Law Shield says that it handles only between 75 and 160 cases annually, fewer than one-tenth of 1 percent of policyholders. In Washington State, the NRA sold 811 Carry Guard policies from April 2017 through December 2018 without fielding a single claim.[21]

The NRA has aggressively marketed Carry Guard, stoking the same fears that it exploits to build membership, expand revenue, and stifle gun control. "You should never be forced to choose between defending your life . . . and putting yourself and your family in financial ruin," an NRA ad warned. In late 2018, the states of California, New York, and Washington outlawed the sale of the Carry Guard policies. Blowing away the NRA's claims about firearms self-defense, New York's insurance regulators found that Carry Guard "unlawfully provided liability insurance to gun owners for certain acts of intentional wrongdoing," and for acts "beyond the use of reasonable force to protect persons or property."[22]

Resort to firearms for defense may not actually be effective in preventing injury, death, or property loss. After examining all published studies, the RAND Corporation concluded in 2016, "The existing evidence for any causal effect of DGU on reducing harm to individuals or society is inconclusive." It warned "that even if DGUs have a positive causal effect on such outcomes as injuries and property loss, it may still be the case that DGUs do not provide net societal benefits if many or most involve illegal use of firearms."[23]

The gun lobby attempts to bolster its bogus statistics with scattered anecdotes of self-defense with firearms, which prove nothing in a country of 330 million people. When debate revived about banning assault weapons in 2018, for example, gun control advocates churned up eight examples across the nation of alleged self-defense with AR-15 rifles from 2013 to early 2018, even though based on gun lobby claims there should have been more than 15 million defensive gun uses to choose from during this five-year-plus span. Still, three of these eight best cases were less than convincing upon checking the article's references. One involved several men guarding a gas station during the 2017 unrest in Ferguson, Missouri, armed with a variety of weapons, mostly handguns. Another cited an incident in Houston where in the linked story, the police did not confirm the weapon used by the shooter. A third example cited a student who allegedly scared off intruders in his apartment with an AR-15, but the article directs readers to a broken link, and other accounts of this incident indicate that the intruders, who were armed with BB guns, had only seen the barrel of his gun.[24]

Although the gun lobby insists that the defensive use of firearms protects women from rape and violence, the evidence proves that access to guns makes women much less safe. Among the G7 nations plus Australia, the U.S. had 44 percent of the combined populations, but 93 percent of the female murder victims. An eleven-city study of domestic violence that probed causality by controlling for other risk factors found that a woman was five times more likely to be murdered in a violent domestic dispute when the abuser had access to a gun. For women who possessed firearms "there was no clear evidence of protective effects." In 2017, the ratio of murdered women to women who killed offenders in justifiable homicides was forty-nine to one.[25]

Domestic gun violence against women spills into workplace killings and other mass shootings. Relatives or domestic partners murdered 40 percent of the women killed at work in 2016, compared with 2 percent of men killed there. Guns accounted for most of these murders. A study by ABC News of twenty mass shootings in 2018 with at least four fatalities found that seven massacres "involved men fatally shooting either their girlfriend, wife, or ex-partner." In another case, a man killed the four children of his former domestic partner.[26]

"Unlike in years past when they may go into a location and harm that person, instead they're going into a school, a workplace, a house of worship, and they're seeking to address their grievance by shooting a large group of people," said John Cohen, a criminal justice professor and a former Homeland Security official. In November 2017, Devin Kelley entered a church in Sutherland Springs, Texas, with an assault rifle and thirty-capacity magazines to murder his mother-in-law and her relatives. He killed twenty-six, including seven children and an unborn child. In Denton, Texas, in May 2018, Amanda Painter's ex-husband, Justin Painter, shot and killed her boyfriend and her three children, aged four, six, and eight, then killed himself. Amanda said that Justin told her he was sparing her life so that she could live with the pain from her murdered children.[27]

Other studies show that for all Americans the dangers of gun possession far outweigh any value for self-defense. A 2004 national study found that adjusting "for demographic and behavioral" factors, guns in your home did not protect you, but left you at a "significantly greater risk of dying from a firearm homicide and firearm suicide than those without guns in the home." A 2014 compilation of published studies concluded that "all but 1 of the 16 studies . . . reported significantly increased odds of death associated with firearm access." A team of researchers led by Professor Charles Branas, chair of the Department of Epidemiology at the Columbia University School of Public Health, compiled data on 677 individuals who had verifiably "been shot in an assault and 684 population-based control participants within Philadelphia, PA, from 2003 to 2006." They found that after adjusting for "confounding variables . . . individuals in possession of a gun were 4.46 times more likely to be shot in an assault than those not in possession." In situations where victims had a chance to resist, the ratio rose to 5.45 to 1.[28]

Law enforcement agencies documented 347 justifiable civilian homicides with firearms in 2017, compared to 14,542 gun murders, for a ratio of 42 to 1. Counting suicides and fatal accidents with firearms, the ratio rises to 115 to 1. Similar findings on "legal intervention deaths" from the independent Fatal Injury Reports developed from the National Vital Statistics System (NVSS), maintained by the CDC, verify the FBI numbers on justifiable homicides.[29]

Even justifiable gun homicides are not necessarily legitimate acts of self-defense rather than needless gun violence. Although Kleck has claimed that such homicides are underreported, because many murders are unsolved, these are not the types of homicides that involve law-abiding citizens defending themselves with guns. The numbers of justifiable gun homicides are more likely inflated than understated, because nearly 90 percent are from states with stand-your-ground laws. These laws, which the gun lobby has aggressively promoted, allow persons to use deadly force rather than retreat or deescalate the conflict when faced with perceived threats to their persons or property. "Because the stand-your-ground law makes it harder to prove that a homicide wasn't justified, the justified homicides go up," said John Roman, senior fellow in justice policy at the Urban Institute.[30]

In 2006, after Florida and several other states had passed pioneering stand-your-ground laws, the NRA proclaimed that "this train keeps a rollin'—Castle Doctrine Sweeps America." Its stand-your-ground campaign, the Association said, "is turning focus from criminals' rights to those of the law-abiding who are forced to protect themselves." Yet, studies show that these laws increase not decrease homicides and firearm injuries. A 2017 study found, for example, that "after removing justifiable homicides from the overall homicide count, we estimated a 21.7% increase in unlawful homicides" resulting from stand-your-ground laws. Another controlled 2017 study found that "at least 30 individuals are killed each month as a result of Stand Your Ground laws" and that these laws also are associated with an increase in hospitalizations related to firearm-inflicted injuries. In 2017, states with stand-your-ground laws had an average firearms homicide rate of 5.7 per 100,000 and an average total homicide rate of 7.4 per 100,000, far exceeding the rates of 3.9 and 5.8 for other states. The causality is simple. The stand-your-ground law "has an emboldening effect. All of a sudden, you're a tough guy and can be aggressive."[31]

NRA propaganda delivers the stern warning to "rapists and robbers and street gangs and drug dealers" that "law-abiding Americans," led by the NRA, "are banding together to *put you away*." Yet, drug dealers, violent gang members, and other criminals benefit from the NRA-sponsored stand-your-ground laws. A *Tampa Bay Times* study found that nearly 60 percent of persons claiming self-defense under stand your ground in Florida had previously been arrested one or more times. Forty percent had been arrested three times or more. More than a third had had a record of threatening someone with a gun or illegally carrying a firearm. Fifty-nine percent of persons with an arrest record and 45 percent of persons with three or more arrests walked free after invoking stand your ground. "Being a felon in possession of a gun or a drug dealer," the study found, "has not prevented defendants from successfully invoking the law."[32]

"The legislators wrote this law envisioning honest assertions of self-defense, not an immunity being seized mostly by former criminal defendants trying to lie their way out of a murder," said Kendall Coffey, a former US attorney from South Florida. Charlie Rose, a professor of law at Stetson University, agreed that the Florida "statute has a lot to do with the right to bear arms and not a lot to do with self-defense."[33]

Tavarious China Smith, a notorious drug dealer from Manatee County, Florida, with a lengthy rap sheet, twice escaped prosecution, in 2008 and 2010, under stand your ground for fatal shootings in disputes with other dealers.

In 2010, Smith chased down his victim after a gunfight and shot him multiple times in the back. "I agree this was probably not the class of people lawmakers were trying to protect when they wrote this law," said Tony Brown, the assistant state's attorney who declined to prosecute Smith. "But the law provides a larger umbrella than simply the homeowner that's protecting his house."[34]

On the streets of Tallahassee in 2008, rival gang members engaged in a gunfight, firing twenty-five to thirty rounds from assault rifles. Each side blamed the other for starting the violence, which killed one gang member, fifteen-year-old Michael Jackson. A judge ruled that two other gang members charged in the murder, Jeffrey Brown and Andrae Tyler, were immune from prosecution because they were standing their ground in the shoot-out. "The law would appear to allow a person to seek out an individual, provoke him into a confrontation, then shoot and kill him if he goes for his gun," said Leon County circuit judge Terry P. Lewis. He called for repeal or modification of the stand-your-ground law, saying that it "could conceivably result in all persons who exchanged gunfire on a public street being immune from prosecution." Defenders of the law insisted that it wouldn't again excuse gang violence. But it did.[35]

In 2017, a shoot-out in Miami between gang members at a Martin Luther King Day parade left eight bystanders wounded, including six children. Police arrested two gang members involved in the shootings but released them without charges. "A conflict in the evidence" and legal issues surrounding "mutual combatants" and "the implications of Florida's stand-your-ground law precludes the filing of the charges," said a spokesperson for the Miami-Dade State Attorney's Office.[36]

For the five years prior to Florida's enactment of its stand-your-ground law in 2005, justifiable homicides averaged twelve per year, but the numbers tripled in the five years following 2005, to an average of thirty-six per year. In 2016, Florida expanded its stand-your-ground law to shift the burden of proof to prosecutors. The following year, the number of justified homicides reached seventy-eight, including sixty-one by gunfire. For all states, the rate of per capita justifiable homicides in 2017 was about seven times higher in stand-your-ground states than in other states.[37]

Stand-your-ground laws are rife with racial bias. A 2018 study found that stand-your-ground laws lead to nearly five times as many "monthly killings of black Alleged Perpetrators of Crimes" as compared to "white Alleged Perpetrators." In Florida, for 2017, whites killed a black victim in 19.2 percent of civilian justifiable homicides, compared to just 2.5 percent of all nonjustified civilian homicides, a ratio of nearly eight to one. After studying stand-your-ground laws for ten years, the American Bar Association concluded, "Stand your ground laws increase homicides, have no deterrent on serious crimes, result in racial disparities in the criminal justice system and impede law enforcement."[38]

The gun lobby has applied its failed logic of firearms

self-defense to mass shootings, claiming that nearly all shooters chose "gun free zones," supposedly to avoid resistance by armed citizens. Echoing dubious claims by pro-gun advocates, Donald Trump said in a 2018 speech to the NRA, "Ninety-eight percent of mass public shootings have occurred in places where guns are banned, just so you understand."[39]

An FBI study found that 64 percent of mass shooters targeted places with a personal connection, "arriving at a targeted site with a specific person or persons in mind." The other 36 percent of shooters may not have targeted "gun-free zones," but instead chose locations for the availability of victims, such as Stephen Paddock, who killed fifty-eight concertgoers from a high window at a hotel in Las Vegas, Nevada, or Omar Mateen, who massacred forty-nine people in the crowded Pulse nightclub in Orlando, Florida. Or hatred and ideology may have driven the choice of targets, such as with the anti-Semitic white nationalist who murdered eleven worshippers at the Tree of Life synagogue in Pittsburgh or the white nationalist who slaughtered twenty-two victims in El Paso, targeting Hispanics.[40]

Despite insisting that mass shooters invariably target gun-free zones, the gun lobby contradictorily asserts that many such massacres are stopped or interrupted by gun holders. Yet, FBI studies of 250 "active shooter incidents" from 2000 to 2017 found that in only fourteen of these episodes (5.6 percent) was the shooter engaged and stopped by armed resistance before police arrived. In most cases the intervenors were security personnel or off-duty police officers, not armed private citizens. In more than twice as many shootings (29, 11.6 percent) "the situation ended after citizens without firearms safely and successfully restrained the shooter." In shootings at high schools, about half were halted when unarmed school personnel restrained the shooter. Six armed intervenors and twenty-six on-duty police officers died in the shootings studied by the FBI.[41]

As illustrated by two recent tragedies, a good guy who brandishes a gun during a shooting incident risks being shot by police, who make split-second decisions under tense and confusing conditions. A police officer shot and killed Emantic Fitzgerald Bradford, Jr., a licensed firearm carrier who drew his weapon to protect shoppers from a shooter at an Alabama mall in November 2018. That same month, a responding officer killed Jemel Roberson, a security guard and licensed gun owner, after Roberson stopped a shooter at a bar in a Chicago suburb.[42]

While overplaying the few successful interventions by armed citizens, the gun lobby neglects the many more concealed-carry-permit holders who perpetrated mass shootings. Research by the Violence Policy Center, updated for recent crimes, indicates that from 2007 through November 2018, killers with concealed-carry permits perpetrated thirty-three mass shootings of at least three fatalities, resulting in 165 deaths. These findings "likely represent a small fraction of actual events" because "there is no comprehensive recordkeeping of deaths involving concealed handgun permit holders and many states in fact bar the release of such information."[43]

Americans have paid a terrible price for the gun lobby's marketing of its mythologies about the defensive uses of guns. "We're evolving into an increasingly coarse society with no obligation to diffuse a situation and rapidly turn to force," said Professor Dennis Kenney, of the John Jay College of Criminal Justice. "People are literally getting away with murder."[44]

12

"More Guns, Less Crime," Another Gun Lobby Myth

There is really uniform data to support the statement that access to firearms is associated with an increased risk of firearm-related death and injury.

—DR. GAREN WINTEMUTE, PROFESSOR, UNIVERSITY OF CALIFORNIA, DAVIS, HEALTH, 2017[1]

Another pillar of defense for the gun lobby is a 1998 book by John R. Lott, Jr., *More Guns, Less Crime*, which—based on a study of right-to-carry laws in the states—claims that as access to guns goes up, violent crime goes down. Although Lott claims to have conducted surveys similar to the one conducted by Gary Kleck and Marc Gertz, he relies primarily on the statistical analysis of data on crime in the United States.

Lott is the essential all-purpose expert for the gun lobby, which depends on his unrestrained advocacy. The NRA has cited Lott's work hundreds of times, far more than for any other researcher. Dana Loesch, later an

NRA spokesperson, said in 2015, "Without John Lott and his mathematician's mind and love of numbers, we would have to go through a lot more data by ourselves. We don't have anybody else on our side that does what he does."[2]

In numerous media appearances, op-ed articles, legislative testimony, and other forums, Lott has repeated his counterintuitive claims that the proliferation of firearms reduces crime. He is often the face of the gun lobby, appearing on receptive media to exonerate the NRA after mass shootings or other gun tragedies. He has claimed that his research should inform policy decisions to roll back gun control laws and expand access to firearms.[3]

Scholars have so tellingly criticized Lott's work that, to redeem his reputation, he fabricated a fictional online person or "sock puppet" that he named Mary Rosh, who purported to be a former student of his. Rosh aka Lott defended Lott's work, praised his skills as a teacher and researcher, vouched for his independence and objectivity, and assailed his critics. He was "the best professor I ever had. Lott taught me more about analysis than any other professor that I had, and I was not alone. . . . There were a group of us students who would try to take any class that he taught." A review of Lott's book on Amazon .com signed "maryrosh" enthused, "SAVE YOUR LIFE, READ THIS BOOK—GREAT BUY!!!!" She said, "Unlike other studies, Lott used all the data that was available. He did not pick certain cities to include and others to exclude. No previous study had accounted for even a small fraction of the variables that he accounted for."[4]

Only when caught by blogger Julian Sanchez did Lott confess his fraud. "I probably shouldn't have done it—I know I shouldn't have done it—but it's hard to think of any big advantage I got except to be able to comment fictitiously," he said. Conservative commentator Michelle Malkin wasn't buying his excuse. "Lott's invention of Mary Rosh to praise his own research and blast other scholars is beyond creepy," she said. "And it shows his extensive willingness to deceive to protect and promote his work." Lott claimed that he only used Mary Rosh as a pseudonym, but a phony identity is not a pseudonym, as Donald Kennedy, the editor of the respected *Science* magazine pointed out: "Lott cannot dismiss his use of a fictitious ally as a 'pseudonym.' What he did was to construct a false identity for a scholar, whom he then deployed in repeated support of his positions and in repeated attacks on his opponents. In most circles, this goes down as fraud."[5]

The fabrication of Mary Rosh was not the only way in which Lott sought to burnish his reputation. In 2015, Lott, who typically publishes his gun research through his home-brewed if grandiosely named Crime Prevention Research Center, announced an important accomplishment. His website proclaimed the publication of his gun research in a referred journal: "CPRC Has New Refereed Publication in Econ Journal Watch: Explaining a Bias in Recent Studies on Right-to-Carry Laws," Lott headlined. The website featured the impressive banner of the *Econ Watch Journal,* below it, the date, volume, and issue number of publication, "vol 12(3) September 2015," an article below that appeared to be reproduced directly from the journal, and a link for downloading the paper, which turned out to be a manuscript version not a journal reprint. However, Lott's paper was not then or ever published in *Econ Watch Journal,* although a reader would have to track down editions of the journal to prove him wrong. Lott later claimed in August 2016, "I forgot to go back and remove the note that the paper was forthcoming." Yet his post said that the paper was "in" the journal, not that it "was forthcoming." Three years after Lott admitted to this lapsed memory, the publication claim and the faux journal article remained archived on his website.[6]

Lott has continued to misrepresent his alleged peer-reviewed publications. In a September 2017 blog entry on his website, he refers readers to "Dr. John Lott's peer-reviewed research" on murder rates for women. However, a click on the hyperlink that Lott provides discloses not the expected published article in a peer-reviewed journal, but to Amazon.com's page for buying Lott's book, *More Guns, Less Crime.*[7]

Lott also claimed to have conducted a telephonic survey of 2,424 persons "during the first three months of 1997," which purportedly showed that 98 percent of Americans who used guns for self-defense only had to brandish, not fire their weapons. When other researchers asked for the underlying survey data, Lott said that the data had been lost in a computer crash and that paper tally sheets were misplaced when he moved his office. Lott could not produce written documentation of the survey's methodology and questions, phone records, or payment receipts. He could not recall the exact dates of the survey or the name of a single person who had made the many thousands of calls needed for a response of 2,424. Later, Lott claimed to have uncovered two persons who allegedly recalled taking his survey. They are John Hamilton, a retired Tennessee detective, and David Gross, a former board member of the NRA and a leader of the militant gun rights group Minnesota Concealed Carry Reform Now. Lott identifies Gross only as a former prosecutor—as assistant city attorney in Minneapolis he prosecuted misdemeanors— omitting his pro-gun affiliations. He also said that he supplied 1997 tax records to other academics that showed large payments to research assistants, although he admitted that he had not saved itemized records of expenditures. He also submitted communications from colleagues who appeared to confirm a computer crash but could not affirm that the survey data was on the crashed hard disk. None of the respondents cited by Lott had direct personal knowledge of his conducting the survey or provided any documentary evidence of the survey.[8]

Tellingly, in testimony to the Nebraska state legislature, Lott cited the 98 percent finding on February 6, 1997, well *before* his purported three-month study from early 1997 was completed. In his 2000 response to a critic, Lott specifically attributes the 98 percent figure only to his own 1997 survey, not anyone else's research: "However, I also found a significantly higher percentage of them [defensive gun uses] (98 percent) involved simply brandishing a gun. My survey was conducted over 3 months during 1997." In 2003 Lott reaffirmed that regarding "the claim that I have attributed the 98 percent brandishing estimate to others instead of myself . . . the fact is I never attributed this number to anyone else other than myself." John Lott does not mention his Nebraska testimony in any of his several defenses of the survey that I have reviewed. Readers can reach their own conclusions from the critiques and Lott's defenses documented in the Notes section. However, John Wiener, a professor at the University of California, Irvine, devoted a chapter of his book, *Historians in Trouble: Plagiarism, Fraud, and Politics in the Ivory Tower*, to John Lott, even though Lott is not a historian. "The conclusion seemed obvious," Wiener wrote, after reviewing the evidence, "Lott had never done the national survey. He was lying."[9]

Ironically, although Lott has staunchly opposed comprehensive background checks for gun purchases, he testified before President Donald Trump's now-defunct commission on voter fraud that such checks should be required for voting. Shortly after his testimony Lott published an op-ed entitled "Background Checks Are Not the Answer to Gun Violence." Commissioners thought Lott must be joking when he proposed to "apply the background check system for gun purchases to voting," but

Lott insisted that he was serious. Apparently, for John Lott, buying a gun trumps the right to vote.[10]

John Lott's modus operandi is to present such a complex and convoluted analysis that it takes expert review to sift through the chaff. In 2005, members of an expert panel of the National Research Council (NRC) of the preeminent National Academies of Sciences did just that in an independent review of Lott's claim about "more guns, less crime." Fifteen of sixteen panel members concluded that available evidence could not sustain a finding that the passage of right-to-carry laws decreases violent crime.[11]

Since 2005, much new evidence and superior methods have proven that more guns lead to *more*, not less, crime. An October 2017 summary of research in *Scientific American* concluded, "About 30 careful studies show more guns are linked to more crimes: murders, rapes, and others. Far less research shows that guns help." The most comprehensive study of right-to-carry (RTC) laws, by researchers from Stanford University, Columbia University, and the University of California, Berkeley, draws upon "14 additional years of state panel data" since the 2005 NRC review. The study's "major finding" is that RTC laws "are associated with higher aggregate violent crime rates. . . . Our synthetic control approach also strongly confirms that RTC laws are associated with 13 to 15 percent higher aggregate violent crime ten years after adoption." Another study from 2017 that focused on intentional homicides found that "RTC laws increase firearm homicides by at least 8.5% and handgun homicides by perhaps as much as 16% while having no statistically significant impact on nonfirearm homicides." So, there was no substitution effect of homicides with guns for homicides by other means.[12]

Other analyses confirm these findings. A study of state-level data from 1981 to 2010 probes homicide rates "as a function of gun ownership level, controlling for potential confounding factors." The researchers found that firearms possession by state "is significantly associated with firearm and total homicides but not with nonfirearm homicides."[13]

For 2017, on average, the forty-one states with permissive right-to-carry laws had gun murder rates that were 51 percent higher than the nine states with restrictive laws, gun death rates from all causes that were 141 percent higher, and overall homicide rates that were 43 percent higher.[14]

Pro-gun advocates correctly note that based on limited available data, the overall incidence of crime is lower among holders of concealed-carry permits than the general population. This differential is typical of any group of white, middle-aged, and relatively affluent men and women. But the possession of guns does matter for crime. As compared to nonholders, the crimes committed by concealed-carry holders consist more prevalently of firearms assaults and murders as opposed to other typically less violent crimes.[15]

These pro-gun advocates also ignore the effects of stolen firearms, mostly from legal-carry holders in their states or licensed dealers. A 2017 study found that approximately 380,000 guns are stolen each year. "Among gun owners, 2.4% report having one or more guns stolen in the past 5 years." Some stolen guns wind up in the hands of dangerous people. Many more are stolen by criminals who commit firearms murders, assaults, armed robberies, carjackings, and kidnappings. "The impact of gun theft is quite clear," said Frank Occhipinti, deputy chief of the firearms operations division of the ATF. "It is devastating our communities."[16]

A study by the US Department of Justice found that of 256,400 state and federal prisoners who used a firearm in their crimes and reported their source, 16,410 said they had stolen their guns. Another 110,765 prisoners said they obtained their guns "off the street," or from "an underground market," common venues for selling or trading stolen guns. The survey does not include the majority of criminals who were never incarcerated or completed their prison terms.[17]

The most refined study of stolen guns and crime, published in February 2019, found that the use of stolen guns in crime is much more prevalent than previously believed. For the first time, researchers bypassed ATF restrictions to track stolen guns individually through "thousands of public records and more than 50 interviews." After tracking some two hundred guns stolen from firearms dealers in North Carolina during 2014, the researchers found that within three years more than a third (sixty-eight) were recovered in crimes, not just in North Carolina, but also in New Jersey, Maryland, and Pennsylvania. Perpetrators likely used many more of the stolen guns in crimes where they escaped without leaving their firearms behind.[18]

The notion that guns make people safer from crime crashes against the stark differences in gun violence between the United States and peer democracies with much tighter firearms controls. Unable to turn international comparisons to their advantage, pro-gun advocates recycle stale arguments about the influence of culture, environment, and mental health and the "substitution effect" of other weapons for firearms.

Yet other democracies also grapple with drug use, criminal gangs, poverty, racism, and violent video games. The variable factor is guns, as illustrated by a 2018 study of rap music videos in the United States and the United Kingdom. Many of the most popular rap videos in the United States feature guns and gun violence—visuals notably absent from the UK videos. For example, in the music video for Chief Keef's US hit "I Don't Like," the rapper and his companions brandish handguns and insert magazines into the firearms. The music video for 21 Savage's "No Heart" shows a poker game, with pistols and assault rifles casually scattered around the table. Later, 21 shoots a store clerk with a handgun and mows down an associate with a rapid-fire rifle. Not one of the more than two dozen most-viewed music videos by the main distributors of rap in the UK displays a firearm of any kind.[19]

Studies show that mental illness is a poor predictor

of violent crime. Per a 2016 review of relevant findings, "those with mental illness make up a small proportion of violent offenders" and "current evidence is not adequate to suggest that severe mental illness can independently predict violent behavior." This finding "clearly contradicts the general belief that patients with severe mental illness are a threat." A pathbreaking study published in April 2019 found that "counter to public beliefs, the majority of mental health symptoms examined were not related to gun violence. . . . Instead, access to firearms was the primary culprit."[20]

Other nations, like the U.S., also struggle with mental disorders. A recent worldwide study found that 17.3 percent of the US population suffers from some form of mental illness, compared to a closely comparable average of 15.3 for the G7 nations plus Australia. With a per capita gun murder rate of 5 percent of the US rate, Australia has a higher incidence of mental illness at 18.4 percent of its population. "Isn't it strange how mental illness hardly massacres anyone in Canada, Japan, Australia, or the United Kingdom," said Shaun Dakin, an adjunct faculty member at George Mason University.[21]

As part of its mantra that "guns don't kill people, people kill people," the gun lobby would have you believe when guns are regulated, killers just switch to knives. Knives can kill, but not nearly with the deadly efficiency of guns, contrary to what NRA ally President Donald Trump told a cheering crowd at the NRA's 2018 conference. Trump conceded that in Britain, strict gun controls keep firearms from criminals, but countered that predators slaughter with knives instead. "They don't have guns," Trump said. "They have knives, and instead there's blood all over the floors of this hospital. They say it's as bad as a military war-zone hospital. Knives, knives, knives, knives." In fact, there is no "substitution effect" in which murders by knives or other means in the UK just replace gun murders. Per capita, an American in 2017 was twelve times more likely to be murdered by guns, knives, or any other means than a resident of the UK. As compared to all G7 nations plus Australia, an American was more than twenty times per capita more likely to be murdered by gunfire and seven times more likely to be murdered by any means.[22]

"Although one can certainly kill people with other weapons (e.g., knives), one can kill more people much faster with guns than with other weapons," wrote Ohio State University psychology professor Brad J. Bushman, an authority on the causes and consequences of human aggression. "Guns also increase the physical and psychological distance between the killer and the victims, which makes killing much easier. When is the last time you heard of a drive-by stabbing?"[23]

Even the most zealous pro-gun advocates cannot claim that more guns mean fewer suicides. Instead, they would have us just remove from debates about gun violence the self-inflicted deaths by gunfire that far surpass the toll of firearms homicides. Recall that in 2017, 14,542 Americans died in gun homicides, but 64 percent more—23,854—died at their own hand from gunshots. "The exclusion of suicide," wrote Michael Anestis, in his book *Guns and Suicide: An American Epidemic*, "is so absolute that some gun rights advocates have argued vehemently that it is actually disingenuous to include suicide deaths in national gun death statistics. . . . With the national suicide rate climbing annually, continuing to ignore suicide when discussing guns is costing thousands of American lives every year."[24]

The use of firearms enables impulsive suicides and proves fatal far more often than other methods of self-harm. "Time is really key to preventing suicide in a suicidal person," said Jill Harkavy-Friedman, vice president of research for the American Foundation for Suicide Prevention. "First, the crisis won't last, so it will seem less dire and less hopeless with time. Second, it opens the opportunity for someone to help or for the suicidal person to reach out to someone to help. That's why limiting access to lethal means is so powerful."[25]

A study of 153 near-death suicide survivors found that 5 percent reported spending just one second, and 24 percent reported spending less than five minutes, between deciding and then attempting suicide. The Harvard School of Public Health warned that people who attempt suicide with "pills or inhale car exhaust or use razors have time to reconsider their actions or summon help. With a firearm, once the trigger is pulled, there's no turning back." National data for 2017 from the CDC confirms a fatality rate of 82 percent for attempted gun suicides,

2.4 percent for poisoning, and less than 1 percent for cutting and piercing. Firearms accounted for 51 percent of suicides, but only 1 percent of nonfatal attempts.[26]

A 2019 study that controlled for "the effects of demographic, geographic, religious, psychopathological, and suicide-related variables" found "that access to and familiarity with firearms serves as a robust risk factor for suicide." A similarly controlled 2018 study found that household gun ownership accounted for 55 percent of the differences in youth suicide rates across all American states. "For each 10 percentage-point increase in household gun ownership, the youth suicide rate increased by 26.9 percent."[27]

An international comparison confirms the link between firearms access and the prevalence of gun suicides in the United States. Remember that the 2017 per capita rate of firearms suicides in the United States was *seven times higher* than the rate for the other G7 nations plus Australia, compared to a per capita suicide rate by other means that was *40 percent lower* in the United States than in these peer nations.[28]

The debate over firearms access must focus on public safety not national defense, as in earlier times. In the nuclear age, citizens armed with rifles, pistols, and shotguns are no longer viable for defense of the country. The militia of early America has become the government-armed and government-trained National Guard, and the nation is amply protected from foreign adversaries by a dominant military. America funds its military more lavishly than any other eight countries of the world combined. The gun lobby has backed and cheered on this massive military buildup that has made it impossible to uphold their claim that armed citizens could check an oppressive government. The framers of the Second Amendment never intended to arm citizens against their government, and such resistance today would be futile anyway against the American military force. Only dangerous private militias cling to the fantasy of a popular uprising where their private guns are a match for government tanks, planes, missiles, and artillery.[29]

The gun lobby so fears the truth about guns and violence that it would suppress credible research, not only through the Dickey Amendment, which restricted federal funding, but also through efforts to intimidate the work of independent researchers. Just hours before the Thousand Oaks massacre of November 7, 2018, the NRA responded to a physicians' position paper on reducing gun deaths by tweeting that America's "self-important" doctors should "stay in their lane" and not address gun violence or remedies.

The NRA's warning only stiffened the resolve of the doctors, nurses, and paramedics who struggle daily to repair bodies shattered and organs exploded by gunfire. Dr. Joseph Sakran, who at age seventeen was saved by trauma surgeons from a gunshot in the neck and now saves others as a trauma surgeon himself, decided to act. Using the hashtag #ThisIsOurLane, which he originated,

Dr. Sakran launched into the Twittersphere numerous impassioned responses to the NRA:[30]

> DR. DENA GRAYSON: "Gun violence literally *is* our 'lane.' I've had the spilled blood of gunshot victims on my scrubs and shoes. When did the NRA save someone who is shot and dying?"
>
> DR. JAMIE COLEMAN: "If a virus killed 20 children in five minutes . . . If a virus killed 58 people in 15 minutes . . . If a virus killed anywhere, in schools, churches, businesses, concerts . . . If a virus killed more & more over time. They would be SCREAMING at us to do something. THIS IS OUR LANE."[31]

When conservative gun enthusiast Ann Coulter chimed in, tweeting, "Emergency room doctors pull cue balls, vines & gummy bears out of human orifices every week. That doesn't make them experts on pool, horticulture or chewy candy," Dr. Jim Eubanks responded, "When cue balls, vines and gummy bears result in 40K deaths a year and are the #3 cause of death of American children and teens, you better believe we will become experts on them as well."

In an open letter to the NRA, more than twenty-six thousand doctors and medical staff said, "Every medical professional practicing in the United States has seen enough gun violence firsthand to deeply understand the toll that this public health epidemic is taking on our children, families, and entire communities. . . . We are absolutely 'in our lane' when we propose solutions to prevent death and disability from gun violence."[32]

Less than two weeks later, gun violence crashed with horrifying impact into the doctors' lane. With his semiautomatic Glock 17 handgun, Juan Lopez committed mass murder at Mercy Hospital in Chicago. Lopez, who held a concealed-carry permit, murdered armed police officer Samuel Jimenez, pharmacist resident Dr. Dayna Less, and emergency room physician Dr. Tamara O'Neal, Lopez's ex-fiancée. It was the deadliest hospital shooting in nearly twenty-five years.[33]

After the massacre, Dr. Megan Ranney tweeted a picture of her late colleague Dr. O'Neal with the words "This is the face of the amazing emergency physician Dr. Tamara O'Neal, at work today, before she was murdered. Tonight, hold her, her family, & our colleagues at #MercyHospital #UIC in your hearts. And tomorrow, pledge to fight for women like her." Ranney added in an interview, "Gun violence is indisputably an epidemic in the United States, and as doctors, we don't just treat epidemics, we also know how to fix them." Research and advocacy by physicians, for example, had a major impact on improving vehicle safety.[34]

Despite a barrage of gun lobby propaganda, the American people have seen for themselves that more guns make them less safe. In a January 2019 Reuters/Ipsos poll, 55 percent of respondents said that to curb gun violence "they wanted policies that make it tougher to own guns, while 10 percent said making firearm ownership easier would be better." Yet for those "who want tougher gun controls now," only 8 percent felt "very confident" that their elected representatives would do anything about it.[35]

These skeptics are correct. As long as the Second Amendment remains on the books of the Constitution, the iron triangle of the gun lobby, the gun industry, and the mostly Republican pro-gun politicians will continue to hold fast against the move toward necessary, comprehensive national gun control. The American people can disband the triangle, lessen the slaughter, and bring the United States in line with its peer nations only by educating and organizing to repeal the Second Amendment. By playing not to lose, the gun control movement has been losing. It wins only by becoming as bold and uncompromising as the gun lobby. Fortunately, there is a path to repeal.

13

A Path to Repeal

In Prohibition there will be no turning back. The course of the nation is fixed. The Eighteenth Amendment will be honored, not in the breach, but in the keeping.

—JAMES J. BRITT, SENIOR ATTORNEY, PROHIBITION
UNIT, US TREASURY, 1925[1]

For Wayne B. Wheeler of the Anti-Saloon League, the dark clouds of World War I had the silver lining of encouraging moral reform. "America has just two gigantic foes, kaiserism and the liquor traffic," Wheeler said, forecasting victory over both cited evils. Wheeler was right. In January 1919, two months after the Allies defeated the German kaiser, the states ratified the Eighteenth Amendment to the US Constitution, prohibiting the manufacture, sale, and transport of alcohol in the United States. Later that year, Congress overrode a veto from Democratic President Woodrow Wilson and adopted the Volstead Act to enforce the amendment's provisions.[2]

The patriotic fervor of a war billed as a crusade for democracy, the spirit of shared sacrifice, and the linking of German Americans with the brewing industry and the saloon contributed to the passage of the Prohibition Amendment. But no less important was the political activism of the Anti-Saloon League (ASL), which foreshadowed the NRA as the first American advocacy group focused on a single issue with skilled leadership and a passionate grassroots following nationwide. The ASL assiduously pumped out dry propaganda, dispatched lecturers across America, and forged alliances with Protestant church groups, especially evangelicals. It drilled and mobilized its loyalists to reward their dry friends and punish their wet enemies. Just as they would later fear the wrath of the NRA, members of Congress in the early twentieth century worried that their political futures could turn on their approval by the ASL. After dry victories in the congressional elections of 1916, Wheeler said that the league had "laid down such a barrage as candidates for Congress had never seen before. . . . We knew that the Prohibition Amendment would be submitted to the States by the Congress just elected."[3]

The famed preacher Billy Sunday confidently predicted that with a dry America "the reign of tears is over. The slums will soon be a memory. We will turn our prisons into factories and our jails into storehouses and corncribs. Men will walk upright now, women will smile and the children will laugh. Hell will be forever for rent." Three-time Democratic presidential candidate William Jennings

Bryan proclaimed of the liquor interests, "They are dead! They are dead!" Instead, the experiment with Prohibition did not save lives and uplift morality, but rather led to a reign of crime and corruption, which prompted the repeal of the Eighteenth Amendment in 1933, just fourteen years after its adoption. Like the Prohibition Amendment, the Second Amendment has contradicted its promised results. It has made Americans less, not more, safe and merits repeal.[4]

Although drinking declined during Prohibition, a continuing thirst for alcohol gave rise to a thriving underground market operated by organized criminal syndicates that waged bloody street battles for control of lucrative bootlegging and paid off law enforcement officials to look the other way. A low-paying job, law enforcement in the corrupt US Prohibition Unit became a ticket for bribes and payoffs. Murders and suicides spiked during the 1920s, fanning sensational coverage in the tabloid press. Federal prisons swelled with felons convicted of violating the dry laws and collateral crimes, and the cost of federal law enforcement quintupled, while intruding into the everyday lives of Americans. Prohibition-related violence culminated in a shocking mass murder when alleged henchmen of the notorious gangster Al Capone gunned down seven members of a rival bootlegging gang on St. Valentine's Day in 1929.

The scandals that plagued Methodist Episcopal bishop James Cannon, Jr., America's leading dry clergyman, further discredited Prohibition. Prompted by information supplied by one of Cannon's political enemies in his home state of Virginia, Democratic senator Carter Glass, the press reported in 1929 and 1930 that Cannon had engaged in shady stock speculation—condemned as gambling by pious church members—through a crooked brokerage firm and, adding lust to greed, that he had had an affair with his current wife before the death of his former wife. In 1928 Cannon had been "the undisputed boss of the United States," wrote the journalist H. L. Mencken in 1934. "Congress was his troop of Boy Scouts, and Presidents trembled whenever his name was mentioned," but since then "his whole world is in collapse."[5]

The Great Depression, which began in 1929, ignited a new wave of violent crime and underscored the lost tax revenue and jobs from killing the legal liquor industry. Even stalwart drys could only tepidly defend America's "noble experiment." In 1930, Republican president Herbert Hoover appointed a commission on Prohibition headed by a former Republican attorney general, George Wickersham. Although Hoover anticipated a setup to defend Prohibition, the commissioners declined to cooperate. Their January 1931 report did not openly recommend repeal, but of nine signed commissioners, all but one opted for repeal, resubmission of the amendment to the states, or a government monopoly on the manufacturer and sale of alcohol. The commissioners warned of "the injury to our legal and political institutions" from disobedience to an unenforceable law.[6]

On June 6, 1932, during the seemingly interminable

Depression, industrialist John D. Rockefeller, Jr., a tee-totaler who had financed the anti-alcohol movement, changed his mind and published a letter in *The New York Times*, calling for repeal of the Prohibition Amendment. "It is my profound conviction," he wrote, that the benefits of Prohibition "are more than outweighed by the evils that have developed and flourished since its adoption, evils which, unless promptly checked, are likely to lead to conditions unspeakably worse than those which prevailed before." Rockefeller's turnabout, the *Times* reported, "caused the greatest political sensation in the capital in years."[7]

Other leaders of business, led by Pierre du Pont, one of the richest Americans, had already put their prestige and resources behind the counterforce to the ASL, the Association Against the Prohibition Amendment, a single-issue group dedicated to repealing the Eighteenth Amendment and the Volstead Act. Socialite Pauline Sabin formed a complementary grassroots group for women, the Women's Organization for National Prohibition Reform, which by the time of repeal had amassed a membership of more than 1 million.[8]

The final blow to Prohibition came in November 1932 with the election of Franklin Delano Roosevelt, an opponent of Prohibition, and a soaking-wet Democratic Congress. Even before the seating of the new Congress, the lame-duck session acted in February 1933 to adopt a repeal resolution by a two-thirds vote of both chambers. To bypass hostile state legislatures in the South, the resolution mandated ratification by state conventions. In less than a year, on December 5, 1933, three-quarters of the states had ratified the Twenty-First Amendment, which ended national Prohibition. Six of the eleven states of the Confederacy had voted in convention for ratification. For the first and only time in US history to date, the American people had repealed a constitutional amendment.

It will be difficult to win two-thirds of both chambers of Congress and three-quarters of the states for a repeal of the Second Amendment, which is part of the Bill of Rights. "There's not a snowflake's chance in hell we are going to repeal the Second Amendment anytime soon," said pro-gun-control law professor Adam Winkler, reprising what respected political analyst Charles Merz had written in 1931, that it "was practically impossible to repeal any part of the Constitution once it was adopted." Yet, two years later after Merz's pronouncement, Prohibition was history. In her article "The Do-Nothing Strategy," political activist Karyn Strickler said, "Political reality is created" through bold, strategic, grassroots organizing, not fixed in stone. You will be told it's impossible, but even "a small group of committed, passionate people will make political reality anything they say it is." As US Supreme Court justice Louis D. Brandeis said, "Most of the things worth doing in the world had been declared impossible before they were done."[9]

The repeal of the Eighteenth Amendment and the information imparted in this book offer a road map for repealing the Second Amendment. It may seem incongruous to compare repeal of a prohibition amendment to repeal of an amendment that seemingly expands people's rights. Yet, repeal of the Second Amendment, like ending Prohibition, would expand rights to life and liberty, which mean much more than an unrestricted right to possess and carry the deadliest of firearms. It means the freedom to walk the streets, drive a car, or attend schools, concerts, clubs, or places of worship without the fear of injury or death at the barrel of a gun.

No part of the Constitution is immutable. Repeal of the Prohibition Amendment is not the only historical repair of defects in the Constitution. Amendments instituted the ticket system of electing the vice president, abolished slavery, directly elected senators, and progressively taxed incomes. Social movements have also achieved improbable constitutional change through the courts. Two decades ago only 27 percent of Americans backed same-sex marriage according to the Gallup Poll, only slightly higher than current public support for repealing the Second Amendment. Gay activists in the twenty-first century backed what the conventional wisdom said was too extreme for America: full marriage equality across the nation. They worked relentlessly to change public attitudes about their sexualities and the place of universal marriage rights in our constitutional order. Same-sex marriage is today the law of the land, with public approval at 67 percent.[10]

A basic rule of political organizing is to unite supporters before trying to convert waverers or opponents. This book is aimed at convincing gun control advocates that their cause is best served by pursuing repeal of the Second Amendment rather than continuing a strategy of piecemeal reform and relying on the uninspiring claim that "we support the Second Amendment, but . . ." The anti-Prohibition movement succeeded not by chipping away at the Volstead enforcement act but by directly pursuing repeal of the Eighteenth Amendment, even as pundits of their time dismissed this effort as impractical. Today's gun control movement must similarly take on the Second Amendment, which covers the gun lobby's defense of unrestricted access to firearms and gives conservative judges a cudgel to wield against gun control laws.

The incredible survivors of school shootings have galvanized young people behind gun control. Yet, as constitutional scholar and political analyst Jonathan Turley said, "If it is real reform that these students want, they must convince their fellow citizens, as Justice Joseph Story once said, that part of the Constitution 'has become wholly unsuited to the circumstances of the nation.'"[11]

In coalescing behind repeal, one group should be an all-purpose organization, modeled on the Association Against the Prohibition Amendment. Another should be a woman's organization modeled on Sabine's Women's Organization for National Prohibition Reform. The already-robust women's group Moms Demand Action for Gun Sense in America could become the focal point for women dedicated to repeal.[12]

The revamped gun control movement should launch a new campaign of education based on the true history of the Second Amendment and how it contributes to needless deaths and injuries from gun violence today. The movement would reanimate the American tradition of gun control and show how the gun lobby's bogus and absolutist construction of the Second Amendment has made Americans captives of this deadly approach. It would show why only repeal can break the power of the gun lobby and lead to lifesaving gun controls. It would expose the self-dealing of the NRA as an organization, but not demonize gun owners, promote the confiscation of all firearms, or restrict the use of guns for hunting, sports, or legitimate self-defense, through permit laws. Like the gun lobby with Charlton Heston, advocates for repeal should find appealing public figures as the faces of the movement and disseminate its message through social media, the press, public lectures, radio and television, and a grassroots campaign.

Once the repeal movement gains traction, it should look for some gun rights advocates who have changed their minds and recruit them to join the crusade, as Rockefeller, Jr., did for Prohibition repeal. Prime targets are hunters and sportsmen who would be repelled by the NRA's cozy ties to the Russians, its subservience to the gun industry, and the corruption that enriches its leaders at the expense of the rank and file. The movement should also look for prominent victims of gun violence who have changed their minds as a result of this experience. Repeal of the Second Amendment would free the NRA to return to its historic mission of supporting hunting, sports shooting, marksmanship, and firearms safety. Although the absence of fear might dry up the contributions that sustain the bloated compensation of NRA leaders.

In 2013, Adolphus Busch IV, the former CEO of the Anheuser-Busch brewing giant, followed the earlier example of former president George H. W. Bush and renounced his lifetime membership in the NRA. "The NRA I see today has undermined the values upon which it was established," Busch said. "Your current strategic focus places a priority on the needs of gun and ammunition manufacturers while disregarding the opinions of your 4 million individual members." The gun control movement can look for more prominent individuals to renounce their NRA memberships and publicize it widely.[13]

For decades, corporations have partnered with the NRA to provide discounts and deals to members. But after the Parkland massacre, major companies severed their business ties to the association. The list of departed outfits reads like a who's who of service companies, including Delta and United Airlines, MetLife, United Van Lines, Paramount Rx, Symantec, Dick's Sporting Goods, Wyndham and Best Western Hotels, Chubb insurance, and most major rental car companies. Dick's has stopped selling guns in 125 of its stores.[14]

While gun control advocates can look for more corporate partners to cut ties to the NRA, they can also use their buying and persuasive power to convince corporate managers to take the next step and support repeal of the

Second Amendment, like the business leaders in the anti-Prohibition movement. Gun control, like a legal market for alcohol, is good for business. "Above all things, entrepreneurs, CEOs and boards of directors want safe spaces in which to conduct their businesses," wrote business columnist Elizabeth MacBride in late 2018. "If there's a question about that in America, that's a problem." A recent study found that "surges in gun violence reduce the growth rate of new retail and service businesses" and "slow home value appreciation."[15]

Other potential allies are leaders of the faith community who reject the equation of gun rights with religious teachings. Prominent evangelical minister Rob Schenck has said, "You can't be pro-life and pro-gun." Christians must follow the teachings of Jesus and not "jump on a secular bandwagon of fear mongering, contempt and bravado to gin up support for gun rights." The US Conference of Catholic Bishops challenged "the culture of violence" and backed "measures that control the sale and use of firearms and make them safer." It called for a near universal ban on the private possession of handguns. Rabbi Yitz Greenberg, a renowned religious scholar, said flatly, "[t]he right to bear arms should have been repealed long ago. The entrenched insistence on gun possession is overlaid with elements of paranoia and conspiracy thinking, which represent danger to a civil peaceful society."[16]

Repeal organizations need to pursue political action as relentlessly as the gun lobby, to elect members of Congress and a president open to repealing the Second

Amendment. This may seem like an impossibility, but when one looks clearly at the electorate and its feelings about gun control, electing such members of Congress and a sympathetic president isn't unthinkable. A winning potential base vote already exists in the 60 percent of Americans who yearn for stricter regulations to control gun violence. A Fox News poll from May 2019 found that gun control is now a priority issue, with 71 percent of registered voters saying "gun violence is a major problem that needs attention from the government." "The ultimate rulers of our democracy are not a President and senators and congressmen and government officials, but the voters of this country," Franklin Roosevelt said.[17]

The time is now for a movement to repeal the Second Amendment. Youth turnout soared in the 2018 elections, and the voters sent dozens of new gun control proponents to the US House of Representatives. In 2018, for the first time in history, pro-gun-control ads outnumbered pro-gun ads, and gun control groups outspent the gun lobby. Sixty-one percent of 2018 voters backed stricter gun control laws, compared to just 8 percent who wanted controls loosened, according to an Associated Press poll. A March 2018 NBC News/*Wall Street Journal* poll found that the association had a negative favorability rating for the first time in decades.[18]

The NRA is torn by internal conflict, financial woes, and revelations of corrupt self-dealing. The states of New York and Washington have suspended the NRA's insurance program for gun owners and fined its underwriter.

New York governor Andrew Cuomo has urged other companies to reconsider their relationship with the NRA. The association sued Cuomo, charging that he threatens the business ties on which its survival depends. The association is in dueling lawsuits with its primary vendor, Ackerman McQueen. In Hawaii, Democratic state lawmakers introduced a resolution urging Congress to "consider and discuss whether the Second Amendment of the United States Constitution should be repealed or amended to clarify that the right to bear arms is a collective, rather than individual, constitutional right.[19]

Once the American people elect a pro-repeal Congress and president, the momentum would shift against the Second Amendment as it did against Prohibition in 1932. This would be the moment for the president to appoint a commission to study the Second Amendment, with results anticipated as more positive than the Wickersham report on Prohibition. Congress should simultaneously launch its own investigation into gun violence and its remedies through a joint House/Senate select committee, akin to the committee that broke open the Watergate scandal in 1973. After a repeal resolution gains congressional support, Congress should again mandate ratification by state conventions, not legislatures, many of which are dominated by pro-gun politicians. Repeal would not abrogate the common-law right of legitimate self-defense or eliminate people's property right to own guns. But it would open the way for the reforms addressed in the next chapter.

Shakespeare wrote that "there is a tide in the affairs of men. Which when taken at the flood leads on to fortune." The tide has come for America's gun control movement; it can either seize the moment and strive to repeal the Second Amendment or risk being swept into the shallows of history.

14

After Repeal: Gun Control Reforms for a Safer America

Politicians who sit in their gilded House and Senate seats funded by the NRA telling us nothing could have been done to prevent this; we call BS. They say tougher guns laws do not decrease gun violence. We call BS.

—EMMA GONZÁLEZ, MARJORY STONEMAN DOUGLAS HIGH SCHOOL SHOOTING SURVIVOR, 2018[1]

Since the national firearms debates of the 1930s, the gun lobby has argued that gun controls are ineffective and perpetuate gun violence. The lobby claims that controls only keep guns away from law-abiding citizens who need firearms for self-defense against criminals, who will readily evade even the stiffest regulations. These claims are not just false, they are triply false. Guns, we have seen, are rarely used for legitimate defense against crimes or attempted crimes. So-called law-abiding citizens are more likely to be killed by other law-abiding citizens than by hardened criminals. And controls work to curb not just gun violence, but the firearms suicides that the gun lobby would ignore, but that result in 64 percent more deaths than gun homicides.

On October 1, 2017, from his room on the thirty-second floor of the Mandalay Bay Hotel in Las Vegas, Stephen Paddock fired more than eleven hundred bullets into throngs of persons below listening to singer Jason Aldean at a country music concert. Paddock killed 58 concertgoers and injured 851, including more than 400 with gunshot wounds, before committing suicide. Until perpetrating the deadliest mass shooting in the history of the United States, the sixty-four-year-old Paddock had been a model citizen, with no criminal record. He purchased his arsenal of assault weapons legally in states with lax gun laws.

Like Paddock, otherwise law-abiding citizens, not criminals, have typically massacred innocent Americans in mass shootings. Of the seventeen perpetrators of sixteen mass shootings with at least ten slain victims since the lapse of the assault weapons ban in 1994 through mid-2019, fourteen had no criminal record. Three had an arrest record, but one was not prosecuted, and another was convicted only of misdemeanor fraud. Just one of the seventeen killers had been convicted of a violent crime.

What united nearly all of America's worst mass shootings was not habitual criminals evading gun laws, but an everyman's easy access to semiautomatic weapons—the weapon of choice in nearly all postban massacres—and high-capacity magazines. The United States has far more mass shootings per capita than peer nations with strict gun controls, and within America, gun laws and access to guns matter. A study published in 2019 found that "states with more permissive gun laws and greater gun ownership had higher rates of mass shootings, and a growing divide appears to be emerging between restrictive and permissive states."[2]

The gun lobby's distinction between law-abiding citizens and criminals dissolves for all murders, not just mass killings. The gun lobby would have you take up arms for protection from criminal strangers bursting into your home or business or assaulting you on streets. It's another myth. Law-abiding citizens are much more likely to be killed in a domestic dispute or in an argument or brawl that turns deadly than by a criminal during a felony. For 2017, among more than six thousand firearm murders with specific circumstances documented by the FBI, perpetrators killed only 10 percent during a robbery, burglary, larceny, rape, or auto theft, and an additional 8 percent during an unspecified felony. In contrast, 39 percent were killed in lethal arguments, brawls, and romantic triangles and another 22 percent in unspecified noncrime circumstances, most of which involved domestic disputes. The remainder involved gang and drug warfare, gambling, and prostitution. When gun suicides and accidents are added in, the percentage of gun deaths pursuant to felonies shrinks to about 7 percent.[3]

Most murders in the US are committed not by criminal strangers, but by persons known to the victim. A 2014 study found "no robust, statistically significant correlation between gun ownership and stranger firearm homicide rates. However, we found a positive and significant association between gun ownership and nonstranger firearm homicide rates." These "findings challenge the argument that gun ownership deters violent crime, in particular, homicides."[4]

Even seemingly trivial arguments can become lethal when guns are in reach, as demonstrated by Michael David Dunn's murder of Jordan Davis during an argument about loud music in a gas station. Davis's mother, Lucy McBath, is now a member of Congress from Georgia who advocates for gun control. "The pain of losing a child to gun violence never ends," she said. Her son's murder "was about the availability of guns and eagerness to hate."[5]

Contrary to claims by the gun lobby, gun controls do reduce access to firearms by criminals, defuse dangerous situations, and save lives. President Trump admitted before the NRA that tight gun laws in the UK keep criminals from getting guns. As compared to the UK, a resident of the United States was over seventy-five times more likely to suffer a gun murder in 2017 and twelve times more likely to be murdered by all causes. Japan, with its strict gun controls, experienced just twenty-two gun crimes in 2017 that resulted in either death, injury, or property damage. Even members of Japan's notorious organized crime ring, the yakuza, rarely possess guns.[6]

In the United States, ATF traces of guns reveal that in states with stringent gun control laws, criminals rely far more on out-of-state firearms than in states with lax regulations. On average, for five states with the tightest gun control laws as ranked by the pro-gun control Giffords Law Center, 62 percent of firearms traced to crime came from other states. For five states with the weakest gun controls, the percentage of out-of-state guns drops by more than half, to just 27 percent.[7]

Even with firearms skipping across state lines, gun controls at the state level notably reduce gun homicides. Analysis of a state-by-state database with the Giffords Law Center gun control rankings, social, economic, and demographic data, and measures of gun violence and other crimes provides insight into the effectiveness of stringent gun controls. In 2017, the five tightest gun control states, according to Giffords Law Center, had an average firearms homicide rate of 2.4 per 100,000, compared to a nearly tripled rate of 6.3 for the five with loosest gun controls. Nationwide the positive correlation between gun controls and reduced gun homicides holds true when controlling for urbanization, major cities, region, race, wealth, income, and education. For every ten states with decreasing Giffords rankings, the homicide rate from firearms rises by 0.6 persons per 100,000.[8]

With their myopic focus on the bogus distinction between honest citizens and criminals, the gun lobby passes over the effects of gun control laws on reducing suicides by gunfire. The five top gun control states on the Giffords Law Center rating had an average 2017 firearms suicide rate of 2.3 per 100,000, compared to a nearly quadrupled rate of 8.7 for the bottom five states. When controlling for urbanization, major cities, region, race, wealth, income, and education, for every ten states with decreasing Giffords rankings, the suicide rate from firearms rises by 1.4 persons per 100,000.

Gun controls can have a dramatic effect on curing firearms deaths. For firearms deaths from all causes, the five top gun control states had an average 2017 death rate of 5.1 per 100,000. The rate for the bottom five gun control states was more than three times higher, at a rate of 18.2 per 100,000. When similarly controlling for other factors, for every ten states with decreasing Giffords rankings, the death rate from firearms rises by 2.4 per 100,000.

To visualize how gun control saves lives, consider this: If the nationwide gun death rate of 12.0 fell to the average rate of the top five gun control states, some 23,000 fewer Americans would have died in 2017. If, however, the states succumbed to the gun lobby's drive to weaken gun controls, and the gun death rate rose to the average of the bottom five control states, some 20,500 more Americans would have died in 2017. A reduction of America's firearms death rate to 5.1 or lower per 100,000 is hardly beyond reach. The largest firearms death rate for 2017 in the other G7 nations plus Australia was 1.5 per 100,000.[9]

There is no "substitution effect" of violence by other means taking the place of gun violence. The much-lower firearm homicide rates in the tight-gun-control states is accompanied by lower overall homicides as well. On average in 2017, for all homicides, 3.6 persons per 100,000 died in the top five gun control states, compared to a more than doubled rate of 8.0 for the bottom five states. The more guns, the more murders.

The gun lobby has turned much of its wrath against Massachusetts, which adopted strict gun controls in 1998. On the ten-year anniversary of these laws, the NRA sponsored a "Boston Tea Party 2008" to let elected officials "know, just as our forefathers did, that unfair treatment against lawful gun owners will not be tolerated." The NRA's anti-control crusade failed, and a decade later Massachusetts, which ranks fourth on the Giffords gun control score, has the second-lowest firearms death rate in the nation, less than a third of the national rate.[10]

The reforms suggested below, because they are comprehensive and national, should exceed the lower levels of gun homicides, suicides, and overall deaths achieved in the tightest–gun-control states. The proposed reforms fall into two categories. First, are reforms that focus on the people who are authorized to possess guns. Second, are reforms that focus on firearms themselves. Survey researchers have tested most of these proposed reforms, which are backed by impressive majorities of the American people, including gun owners.[11]

The gun control measures work in synergy, reinforcing one another, so that their effectiveness is much greater than the sum of their individual parts. A study of 130 gun control laws in ten nations concluded, "The simultaneous implementation of laws targeting multiple firearms restrictions is associated with reductions in firearm deaths." Taken together, the proposed reforms will bring the United States more closely in line with peer democracies that have far lower incidences of gun violence. With Americans possessing so many guns, reform will take time to work effectively, but the goal of reducing the toll of firearms deaths, injuries, and trauma makes the wait very much worthwhile.[12]

National and state legislators who uphold the gun lobby's distorted version of the Second Amendment as a nearly unlimited right to keep and bear private arms should be warned that they are enabling the private, armed militias that target the governments that the lawmakers represent. Philip Zelikow, who had worked on litigation against private military groups, warned in 2017 that after subsiding in the 1990s "the danger is rising again, as my town, the nation and the world can plainly see."[13]

Lawmakers need not worry that any reforms proposed here involve the confiscation of firearms or will deprive law-abiding citizens of sports shooting, hunting, or legitimate self-defense needs. A study by the RAND Corporation of thirteen gun control measures concluded, "We found no qualifying studies showing that any of the 13 policies we investigated decreased defensive gun use."[14]

Require In-Person Federal Permits for Firearms Possession

This reform directly impacts the possession of firearms and is the single most rigorous means of keeping guns from the hands of criminals and other dangerous people.

Following the precedent of New York's Sullivan Act, some seven states have required people to apply in person for a permit or a license to purchase a firearm from any seller, licensed or not.[15]

Nationally in 2017, the seven in-person PTP (permit-to-purchase) states had an average firearms death rate of 5.9 per 100,000, compared to a two and half times greater rate of 14.7 for all other states. Although the in-person PTP states also had other strict gun laws, after controlling for the overall Giffords Law Center gun control ranking, income, race, urbanization, major city, region, and education, the rate of 2017 gun deaths in in-person PTP states was lower than in other states by 3.7 deaths per 100,000 persons.

A federal permit law that applied nationwide would more substantially reduce gun deaths than state measures because of the flow of guns across state lines. The law should cover the possession of all firearms, acquired by purchase from any source or other means, and should have stiff penalties for violations. Although PTP laws vary, the most effective authorize police discretion in denying permits, cover all firearms, require fingerprint identification, mandate firearms safety training, and specify a sufficient waiting period to complete background checks.

Strengthen Background Checks

A strengthened and expanded background check system would reinforce federal PTP laws, but would cover all firearms transactions, not just for handguns. Background checks under the National Instant Criminal Background Check System (NICS) have kept more than 2.5 million dangerous people from buying handguns from a licensed dealer. But the military, courts, hospitals, states, and local jurisdictions do not report complete or accurate information to the FBI, which must complete background checks in three days or purchasers are free to return and buy the firearms. The system also covers only purchases from licensed firearms dealers, not private sales, including at guns shows, or gifts and transfers.

Devin Patrick Kelley's domestic violence conviction during his military service should have prevented him from purchasing the guns he used to murder twenty-six people at a Baptist church in Sutherland Springs, Texas. The air force had failed to report his crime to the FBI, but even if they had done so, the Bureau might not have flagged him, because the FBI and the military use different terms for the same types of crime.

An arrest for a felony drug charge should have put white supremacist Dylann Roof on the blocked list before he purchased the gun that killed nine worshippers at an African American church in Charleston, South Carolina. The FBI failed to complete its investigation of Roof's pending purchase by the three-day waiting period, enabling him to return and buy the murder weapon, no questions asked.

Researchers at Northeastern and Harvard Universities found that during a two-year period, 50 percent of

244 | REPEAL THE SECOND AMENDMENT

persons purchasing guns bought their firearms without a background check—26 percent in the few states that regulate private firearm sales, and 57 percent in other states. Among 256,400 men imprisoned for gun crimes who reported the source of their weapons, 83,843 bypassed background checks by procuring guns from flea markets, pawnshops, gun shows, family members, friends, and third-party purchasers. In 2018, the online gun advertiser Armslist.com placed 1.2 million ads for gun sales that required no background check.[16]

Simple reforms would upgrade the currently flawed system. Ironically, even leading pro-gun advocate John Lott, when testifying in favor of background checks for voting, admitted, "I can think of problems with the NICS system. But they're all easily fixed."[17]

To fix the system, require all reporting agencies to follow federal standards. Expand the prohibited list to persons under twenty-one years of age, persons with multiple convictions related to alcohol or drug abuse, and those on the federal no-fly list or watch lists. To keep firearms from the hands of domestic abusers, cover persons with violent misdemeanor convictions and domestic protective orders. Conduct a federal audit of agency reporting practices. Require background checks by retailers selling on the internet, in pawnshops, flea markets, and gun shows. Require that all person-to-person transactions, whether purchases, gifts, or transfers, be conducted through federally licensed dealers. Include fingerprint checks to avoid the many errors in the current system. Extend the period for the FBI to complete its investigation to thirty days. Apply background checks to the purchase of firearm components.

Limit Persons Purchasing Firearms to One per Month

No national legislation currently restricts bulk purchases, although under an Obama-era regulation, federally licensed firearms dealers must keep and transmit to the government records of bulk transactions. Law-abiding citizens do not need to purchase arsenals of firearms for hunting, sports shooting, or self-defense. Rather, it's often "straw purchasers" that legally buy guns in bulk, then transfer the weapons to criminals in the United States, Mexico, and Central America. According to the ATF, "the acquisition of handguns in multiple sales can be an important trafficking indicator."[18]

A study of a 1993 Virginia law limiting gun purchases to one per month found that "there was a 55% reduction for guns recovered in the northeast corridor (New York, New Jersey, Connecticut, Rhode Island, and Massachusetts); and a 30% reduction for guns recovered anywhere in the United States." However, in 2012 when pro-gun Republicans gained control of government, they invoked the Second Amendment to repeal Virginia's law. As compared to the five years before repeal, the number of Virginia guns recovered in crimes jumped by 33 percent for New York and Massachusetts in the five years after repeal.[19]

Internationally, arms from the United States are

trafficked to Mexico and Central America. Weapons from the United States accounted for 69.5 percent of 2017 traced firearms recovered by law enforcement in Mexico, 31.0 percent in Guatemala, 43.9 percent in Honduras, and 50.2 percent in El Salvador.[20]

Adopt a National Red Flag Law

Although it has gained popularity in the states, this limited reform authorizes law enforcement officials or family members to petition a court to order the temporary removal of firearms from persons deemed to present a clear and present danger to others or themselves. To fill the gap in state legislation, Congress should enact a national red flag law, enforceable through federal courts.

Beginning with Connecticut in 1999, nearly half the states have adopted red flag laws, despite opposition from the gun lobby. In Connecticut firearms suicides fell by 16 percent from the law's adoption in 1999 through 2017. During this same period, the national firearms suicide rate rose by 15 percent.[21]

Require the Safe Storage of Firearms

Safe-storage laws, which typically require that owners store firearms in gun safes and other secure places or equip their guns with trigger locks, prevent accidents and suicides, especially among children, and reduce firearms theft. Suicides among children under eighteen typically take place at home with a firearm owned by parents. Only eleven states currently have safe-storage laws, nine of which also have permit-to-purchase laws. The stringency of safe-storage requirements varies, with only five states imposing state standards for locking devices.[22]

The eleven safe-storage-law states, which also have other strong gun controls, accounted for 41 percent of the population but only 20 percent of the 2017 accidental gun deaths in the United States. Massachusetts, with the nation's stiffest gun storage laws, had no record of accidental gun deaths from 2013 to 2017 and now has the nation's lowest firearms suicide rate and the third-lowest suicide rate from all causes. A 2018 study of the relationship between access to firearms and suicides concluded, "Safety efforts aimed at reducing accessibility and increasing safe storage of firearms would likely have a dramatic impact on statewide overall suicide rates."[23]

The gun lobby has typically countered by citing the most improbable of circumstances to block a sensible gun control: thwarting a home invasion by an instant access to guns. In return for the illusion of home protection, the presence of a gun makes it 41 percent more likely for a homicide and 244 percent more likely for a suicide to occur in the home. Anyone who feels the need for an instant response to an intruder can legally buy an eight-ounce canister of nonlethal bear spray. It has a range of up to thirty feet, fully discharges in a few seconds, and emits a wide spray that doesn't require the accuracy of a gunshot. And you don't have to worry about accidently killing a family member. If you don't believe that eight ounces of bear spray stops intruders, step outside in an open area, spray a small fraction of the product away from you, and start choking.[24]

Hold the Gun Industry Accountable for Its Products and Sales

Congress should repeal the 2005 Protection of Lawful Commerce in Arms Act (PLCAA), which with limited exceptions grants gunmakers and gun dealers protection from liability lawsuits. It should create a database to track gun sales and make available to the police and the public information on which federally licensed dealers sell the most guns used in crimes. A December 2012 study by the Congressional Research Service found that "plaintiffs who have brought challenges under the predicate exception generally have not been successful." No less than makers and sellers of automobiles, food, toys, cigarettes, and drugs, gun manufacturers and dealers should be held to account for the safety of their products and practices.[25]

In September 2004, survivors and families of the six slain victims of the DC snipers won a lawsuit settlement from the maker of the murder weapon, the Bushmaster AR-15 assault rifle, and the Bull's Eye gun shop in Tacoma, Washington. The snipers had stolen their weapon from Bull's Eye, which according to a federal records search had lost track of 238 guns in the previous three years and had sold more than fifty guns that were traced to criminal acts from 1997 to 2001. Absent the 2005 shield law, similar lawsuits might have imposed tighter controls on manufacturers and dealers.[26]

Lawsuits might have taken the deadly Bushmaster off the market before Adam Lanza used it for the massacre at Sandy Hook Elementary School. Despite its allure for ordinary citizens, the gun's practical application is only as "a combat weapon," said Scott Knight, former chairman of the International Association of Chiefs of Police Firearms Committee. With his Bushmaster and multiple thirty-round magazines, Lanza had enough firepower to kill every student and teacher at the school. The rapid police response likely saved many lives, explained Connecticut State Police lieutenant Paul Vance. Families of slain children sued Remington, the new owner of Bushmaster, the gun wholesaler, and the dealer. In a potentially pathbreaking ruling, the Connecticut Supreme Court authorized the case for trial under the charge that defendants had violated the state's law prohibiting unfair trade practices by marketing a military weapon to civilians. Like the lawsuits against tobacco companies, this litigation could expose damning information about deceptive marketing and distorted or suppressed research by the gun industry.[27]

Ban Assault Weapons and High-Capacity Magazines

These weapons of war are designed to kill as many people as possible in the shortest time. A study of mass shootings at "people in a confined or populated area" from 2000 to 2017 documented the killing power of assault rifles. On average, semiautomatic rifles killed 4.25 people and wounded 5.48 per shooting, compared to 2.49 killed and 3.02 wounded in shootings with other weapons. Studies of assault weapons bans found that "mass-shooting fatalities were 70% less likely to occur during the federal ban period [1994–2003]" and that federal and state assault weapons bans "reduced the number of school shooting victims by 54.4%."[28]

Mass shootings account for only a small fraction of victims shot with semiautomatic weapons, mostly pistols. In Minneapolis, Minnesota, during 2014, "High Volume Gunshot incidents [ten or more shots fired] accounted for 20%–28% of victims and were more likely to involve multiple victims. Most HVG cases seemed likely to have involved a gun with a large capacity magazine though these data were limited." Nationwide, the use of high-capacity semiautomatics in gun crimes has soared since the assault weapons ban lapsed in 2004. Consistent with the Minneapolis results, "assault weapons and other high-capacity semiautomatics together generally account for 22 to 36% of gun crimes," including "13–16% of guns used in murders of police."[29]

Assault weapons defy easy classification. However, a ban on high-capacity magazines would render all semi-automatic rifles and pistols much less deadly. Besides, since adoption of the initial federal ban in 1994, authorities have also learned much about how to draft workable assault weapons bans.[30]

Without repealing the Second Amendment the courts could throttle a national ban on assault weapons and magazines with more than ten rounds. In April 2019, a federal district court reaffirmed a preliminary ruling that struck down California's ban on high-capacity magazines. The judge had ruled that the California law represents "precisely the type of policy choice that the Constitution takes off the table" and that "public safety interests may not eviscerate the Second Amendment."[31]

Buy Back Assault Weapons and High-Capacity Magazines

Buybacks work when adequately funded and targeted to illegal weapons and accessories. Australia's buyback program for assault weapons and other banned firearms pulled more than seven hundred thousand dangerous weapons off the streets, through purchase and voluntary surrender: "The buyback was reported to have resulted in the withdrawal of one-fifth of the stock of civilian firearms," concluded a Library of Congress study. Another study found that the proportion of Australian households reporting private gun ownership declined by 75 percent between 1988 and 2005.[32]

Ban High-Caliber Handguns

A quarter of a century ago, Senator Daniel Patrick Moynihan said, "Guns don't kill people, bullets do." For handguns, unlike assault rifles, large-caliber bullets kill most surely. A study from 2010 to 2014 for Boston found that "shootings with larger-caliber handguns were more deadly but no more sustained or accurate than shootings with smaller-caliber handguns." The correlation between the lethality of assaults and higher-caliber handguns held strong when controlling for the "number of wounds, the location of wounds, circumstances of the assault or victim characteristics. . . . For Boston, in the period studied here, simply replacing larger-caliber guns with small caliber guns with no change in the location or number of wounds would have reduced the gun homicide rate by 39.5 percent." The most common high-caliber firearm was a 9 mm handgun such as the Glock 19.[33]

Regulate 3-D and "Ghost" Guns

You can't quite yet pop a blueprint into your computer, pour some plastic into your 3-D printer, and generate a usable, untraceable firearm, no questions asked. But the time is coming. A proliferation of home-brewed 3-D guns will give criminals and terrorists the gift of unlimited, unregistered weapons, not to mention that it will result in increased impulse homicides, suicides, and accidents. "The first movers will be terrorists and insurrectionists who are determined to destroy our current system of government," said Philip J. Cook, a gun policy expert at Duke University. Eventually, if "this form of manufacturing becomes cheap enough, it may become a major source of supply for street gangs and other criminals."[34]

In July 2018, with little fanfare but grave consequences, lawyers for the Trump administration acquiesced in a legal settlement that perverted the Second Amendment and threatens the safety of every American. The administration, after many years of effort to prevent gunmaker Cody Wilson from distributing computer models of gun parts and replicating them in 3-D printers, reached a settlement that would enable such distribution. Wilson, the founder of a pro-gun group, said, "I believe that I am championing the Second Amendment in the twenty-first century." After the settlement he exulted, "This legal victory is the formal beginning to the era of downloadable guns. Guns are as downloadable as music. There will be streaming services for semiautomatics." In late August 2018, federal district court judge Robert S. Lasnik in Seattle temporarily barred the online distribution of blueprints for 3-D printed guns. However, absent congressional legislation, a court ruling won't be deterrent enough.[35]

Information is unstoppable in the modern age, so other protective measures are needed. The Undetectable Firearms Act bans guns that can't be flagged by walk-through metal detectors, but makers can evade the law by adding a small metal piece. Congress should subject home-brewed guns to the same legal requirements as any other firearm and should work with the makers of 3-D printers to install blocking software for the making of guns.

The government also needs to regulate homemade guns that anyone—teenagers, felons, domestic abusers—can readily assemble without background checks from legally purchased components that are nearly but not quite a finished firearm (known as 80 percent receivers). Like 3-D firearms these "ghost guns" are unregistered and untraceable. One supplier of 80 percent receivers, Ghostguns.com, promotes the assembling of "unserial-ized, unregistered" AR-15 assault rifles as "a practice that stems from the 2nd Amendment of our constitution—and doing so without the government involvement is the idea behind 'shall not be infringed.'"[36]

Ghost guns are becoming increasingly common. "The threat of ghost guns to public safety and to law enforce-ment safety is not abstract," said New Jersey attorney general Gurbir Grewal. "It's real. It highlights the black market that exists among criminals for these untraceable guns." Although a few states such as New Jersey have tried to crack down on ghost guns, the remedy is national legislation that subjects nearly completed gun components to the same laws and restrictions as fully assembled firearms and requires the registration of privately constructed guns.[37]

Promote Research on Gun Violence and Safety

Congress should repeal current restrictions on gun violence research by the federal government and instead sponsor and support such crucial inquiry. The nation needs a research program to develop foolproof and safe smart-gun technology for personalized firearms that can be triggered only by an authorized user. Smart guns could limit suicides and accidents and make stolen firearms useless for criminals and mass killers. Research could advance the nascent development of microwave sensors that can detect firearms remotely and of devices that can instantly detect gunshots, even when fired with a noise suppressor.

Conclusion

For much too long, the lies of the gun lobby, the gun industry, and their dependent politicians have entrapped Americans in an endless cycle of gun violence, unmatched by any peer nation. Lies about our colonial heritage. Lies about America's founders. Lies about the Second Amendment. Lies about gun crimes and gun deaths. Lies about stand-your-ground laws. Lies about mass shootings. Lies about assault weapons. Lies about self-defense with firearms. Lies about gun control.

As the Bible teaches, the truth can set us free. The Second Amendment has no use in today's world other than to perpetuate gun murders and assaults, suicides, and accidents. America is alone among advanced democracies in standing aside while tens of thousands of its people each year are killed or injured by firearms. Since the gun lobby reinvented and distorted the Second Amendment in the late twentieth century, more Americans have perished from gunfire at home than in all of the nation's foreign wars combined. We can have a much safer country, but only if the American people demand repeal. Otherwise the Second Amendment will stand in the way of needed reforms. "Power concedes nothing without a demand," said the abolitionist Frederick Douglass. "It never did and it never will."[38]

Repeal of the Second Amendment and strict but reasonable gun controls would be a precious gift to the young people of America. Aalayah Eastmond, a survivor of the Marjory Stoneman Douglas High School massacre, closed her testimony to the US Senate with an eloquent plea to adult decision-makers in the United States:

> The youth is urging our society to recognize
> the depth and seriousness of our gun violence
> epidemic in America. We are all here today with
> an urgent message to you: if the youth across

the country can fight to eradicate gun violence,
why can't judges, lawmakers, and Donald Trump
understand that young people are dying from this
senseless violence?[39]

ACKNOWLEDGMENTS

I thank first and foremost by wife and soulmate Karyn Strickler, who diligently read earlier drafts of the book and shared invaluable suggestions, both large and small. Much credit for the book goes to Karyn. My extraordinary agent, Bridget Matzie of Aevitas Creative Management, recognized the book's potential and provided essential guidance and encouragement. Michael Flamini, my accomplished editor at St. Martin's Press, combed through every line of book and directed me to many essential improvements. Amanda Brower contributed skillful editing, and Meg Showalter fine research. Sam Lichtman, Jake Assael, and Linden Jennings checked many hundreds of footnotes, Dan Ballentyne provided proofreading assistance, and Paul Macrae conducted extraordinary fact checking. I thank Hannah Phillips for facilitating arrangements at St. Martin's and Steve Boldt for expert copyediting.

All errors, of course, I claim for myself.

NOTES

Introduction: The Book That Must Be Written

1. John Paul Stevens, "Repeal the Second Amendment," *New York Times*, 27 March 2018, https://www.nytimes.com/2018/03/27/opinion/john-paul-stevens-repeal-second-amendment.html.

2. Matthew Grimson, "Port Arthur Massacre: The Shooting Spree That Changed Australia's Gun Laws," NBC News, 25 July 2015, https://www.nbcnews.com/news/world/port-arthur-massacre-shooting-spree-changed-australia-gun-laws-n396476.

3. NRA: America's 1st Freedom, "Australia: There Will Be Blood," 9 July 2015, https://www.americas1stfreedom.org/articles/2015/7/9/australia-there-will-be-blood.

4. CDC Wonder, "Underlying Cause of Death, 1999–2017," https://wonder.cdc.gov/controller/datarequest/D76; Australian Bureau of Statistics, Recorded Crime - Victims, Australia, 2018, https://www.abs.gov.au/ausstats/abs@.nsf/mf/4510.0. The latest reporting years at the time of this writing were 2018 for Australia and 2017 for the US base data for the NRA warning is for the last full year (2014).

5. Ibid.; Global Burden of Disease Study, "GBD Compare," https://vizhub.healthdata.org/gbd-compare; "Underlying Cause of Death, 1999–2017," CDC Wonder, https://wonder.cdc.gov/controller/datarequest/D76; "Gun Crimes in Japan Remain Rare," Nippon.com, 19 April 2018, https://www.nippon.com/en/features/h00178/gun-crimes-in-japan-remain-rare.html. For international comparisons of gun control laws see "Armed Violence and Gun Laws, Country by Country," GunPolicy.org, https://www.gunpolicy.org/firearms/home. The G7 includes Canada, France, Germany, Italy, Japan, the United Kingdom, and the United States.

6. Ibid., "Armed Violence and Gun Laws GBD Compare." Mexico has a constitutional provision limited to keeping arms at home.

7. Center for Responsive Politics, OpenSecrets.org, https://www.opensecrets.org; Jake Novak, "NRA Money Isn't Why Gun Control Efforts Are Failing," CNBC, 16 February 2018, https://www.cnbc.com/2018/02/16/nra-money-isnt-why-gun-control-efforts-are-failing-commentary.html.

8. Jack Basil, "Memorandum to General Edson," 18 June 1955, box 27, Papers of Merritt Austin Edson, Library of Congress, Washington, D.C.; *Fact Book* in US Senate, 97th Cong., 2nd sess., "The Right to Keep and Bear Arms," *Report of the Subcommittee on the Constitution of the Committee on the Judiciary,* February 1982, 29. See also, H. Richard Uviller and William C. Merkel, *The Militia and the Right to Arms, Or How the Second Amendment Fell Silent* (Durham: Duke University Press, 2003).

9. Jonathan Elliot, *The Debates in the Several State Conventions of the Adoption of the Federal Constitution,* 2nd ed., reprinted (New York: Lenox Hill, 1974), 3: 378; *American State Papers: Documents, Legislative and Executive, of the Congress of the United States, Class V: Military Affairs* (Washington, D.C.: Gales & Seaton, 1832), 1:6–7.

10. "Gun Control," Quinnipiac University Poll, 16–20 May 2019, http://www.pollingreport.com/guns.htm.

11. Emily Cochrane, "House Expands Domestic Violence Gun Controls in Rebuke to N.R.A.," *New York Times,* 4 April 2019, https://www.nytimes.com/2019/04/04/us/politics/nra-violence-against-women-act.html.

12. Kris Hundley, "Drug Dealer Used 'Stand Your Ground' to Avoid Charges in Two Killings," *Tampa Bay Times,* 17 February 2013, https://www.tampabay.com/news/courts/criminal/drug-dealer-used-stand-your-ground-to-avoid-charges-in-two-killings/1235650; Tamara Rice Lave, "Shoot to Kill: A Critical Look at Stand Your Ground Laws," *University of Miami Law Review,* 67 (2013): 827–831.

13. Philip J. Cook, "Why Stand Your Ground Laws Are Dangerous," *Gun Policy,* 1 August 2013, https://scholars.org/brief/why-stand-your-ground-laws-are-dangerous.

14. Kevin Fallon, "Shame Them: Everyone Who Endorsed Arming Preschoolers on Sacha Baron Cohen's 'Who Is America?,'" Daily Beast, 16 July 2018, https://www.thedailybeast.com/shame-them

-everyone-who-endorsed-arming-preschoolers-on-sacha-baron
-cohens-who-is-america.

15. Arwa Mahdawi, "Sacha Baron Cohen's Scheme to Arm Toddlers Isn't Far from Reality," *Guardian*, 16 July 2018, https://www
.theguardian.com/us-news/2018/jul/16/sacha-baron-cohen-guns
-children-toddlers-who-is-america-reality; Daniel McElrath,
"Test Fire: Thompson Center HotShot," NRA Family, 2 January 2014, https://www.nrafamily.org/articles/2014/1/2/test-fire
-thompsoncenter-hotshot; Keystone Sporting Arms, "Cricket,
My First Rifle," https://www.keystonesportingarmsllc.com/wp
-content/files/2017/05/Crickett_Catalog.pdf; Karl Knighton,
"Of Course We Should Be Marketing Guns to Children," *Save
My Gun Rights*, 23 February 2016, http://savemyrights.com/author
/karl-knighton.

16. *Economist* Intelligence Unit, "Democracy Index 2018," http://www
.eiu.com/Handlers/WhitepaperHandler.ashx?fi=Democracy
_Index_2018.pdf&mode=wp&campaignid=Democracy2018.
The index is based on dozens of indicators, including freedom
from harassment and surveillance by government and other measures of individual liberty.

17. Linda Greenhouse, "A Call to Arms at the Supreme Court,"
New York Times, 3 January 2019, https://www.nytimes.com/2019
/01/03/opinion/guns-second-amendment-supreme-court.html;
Adam Liptak, "Supreme Court Will Review New York City Gun
Law," *New York Times*, 22 January 2019, https://www.nytimes
.com/2019/01/22/us/politics/supreme-court-guns-nyc-license
.html.

18. Stevens, "Repeal the Second Amendment."

19. Samantha Lachman, "Wayne LaPierre Warns Fellow Gun Rights
Supporters of 'Knockout Gamers,' 'Haters,'" *Huffington Post*, 25
April 2014, https://www.huffpost.com/entry/wayne-lapierre-nra
_n_5214959.

20. Elliott Woods, "How the NRA Sells Guns in America Today,"
New Republic, 16 April 2018, https://newrepublic.com/article
/147804/fear-how-nra-sells-guns-america.

21. NRA, "Form 990, 2017," https://www.documentcloud.org
/documents/5300476-NRA-2017-990.html. For LaPierre's reported
billings see Mark Maremont, "Leaked Letters Revealed Details of
NRA Chief's Alleged Spending," *Wall Street Journal*, 11 May 2019,

https://www.wsj.com/articles/leaked-letters-reveal-details-of-nra
-chiefs-alleged-spending-11557597601.

22. John F. Kennedy Moon Speech—Rice Stadium, 12 September 1962, https://er.jsc.nasa.gov/seh/ricetalk.htm.

1. The Toll of Gun Violence

1. Jonathan Heatt, "A Bullet for Your Thoughts," *Jonathan Heatt's Blog*, https://www.goodreads.com/author/show/8182572.Jonathan _Heatt/blog/tag/horror.

2. Nicole Hockley, "Response to 'Boy Shooting Statue,'" in *Bullets into Bells: Poets and Citizens Respond to Gun Violence*, ed. Brian Clements, Alexandra Teague, and Dean Rader (Boston: Beacon Press, 2017), 30.

3. Amanda Terkel, "Joe Manchin Ready for Gun Control Action: 'Everything Should Be on the Table,'" *Huffington Post*, 17 December 2012, https://www.huffingtonpost.com/2012/12/17/joe -manchin-gun-control_n_2314782.html; Kyle Dargan, "Natural Causes," in Clements, Teague, and Rader, *Bullets into Bells*, 31.

4. Peter Charley, "How to Sell a Massacre: NRA's Playbook Revealed," Al Jazeera, 25 March 2019, https://www.aljazeera .com/news/2019/03/sell-massacre-nra-playbook-revealed -190325111828105.html.

5. Ibid.; Asher Stockler, "NRA Wrote Op-eds Published Under New Mexico Sheriffs' Names to Protest Gun Control Bills, Documents Reveal," *Newsweek*, 24 May 2019, https://www.newsweek .com/nra-lobbying-new-mexico-sheriffs-1431949.

6. "Underlying Cause of Death, 1999–2017," CDC Wonder, https:// wonder.cdc.gov/controller/datarequest/D76.

7. Eric Schlosser, "A Grief Like No Other," *Atlantic*, September 1997, https://www.theatlantic.com/magazine/archive/1997/09/a-grief -like-no-other/376944/; Tammerlin Drummond, "One Oakland Murder Creates Major Ripple Effect," *Mercury News*, 4 March 2015, https://www.mercurynews.com/2015/03/04/drummond-one -oakland-murder-creates-major-ripple-effect/.

8. "Read Testimony of Parkland Shooting Survivor Aalayah Eastmond," CNN, 7 September 2018, https://www.cnn.com/2018/09 /07/politics/parkland-survivor-testimony/index.html. "Underlying

Cause of Death," CDC Wonder. Unless otherwise indicated, the homicide, suicide, and death rates data is age adjusted, although age-adjusted and raw rates for firearms homicides and deaths differ little.

9. "Nonfatal Injury Data," US Centers for Disease Control and Prevention (CDC), https://webappa.cdc.gov/sasweb/ncipc/nfirates.html; David Gambacorta and Helen Ubiñas, "The Hidden Toll of Gun Violence," *Philadelphia Inquirer,* 2 December 2018, http://digital .olivesoftware.com/Olive/ODN/PhiladelphiaInquirer/shared /ShowArticle.aspx?doc=PHQP%2F2018%2F12%2F02&entity =Ar00103&sk=F826C42F&mode=text. The CDC estimated 100,200 emergency room visits for gunshot annually from 2013 to 2017, but with wide error margins.

10. Erin Calabrese et al., "Journey of a Bullet," *NBC News Special,* 20 June 2017, https://www.nbcnews.com/specials/journey-of-a -bullet.

11. Ibid.

12. Katy Reckdahl, "Deborah Cotton, Writer Shot in 2013 Mother's Day Second Line Shooting, Dies at 52," *New Orleans Advocate,* 2 May 2017, https://www.theadvocate.com/new_orleans/news /article_cea430ba-2f4d-11e7-b7bd-ab6733e78453.html.

13. Faiz Gani, Joseph V. Sakran, and Joseph K. Canner, "Emergency Department Visits for Firearm-Related Injuries in the United States, 2006–14," *Health Affairs* 36 (2017): 1729–38.

14. Rachel E. Morgan and Jennifer L. Truman, "Criminal Victimization, 2017," Bureau of Justice Statistics, US Department of Justice, 4, https://www.bjs.gov/content/pub/pdf/cv17.pdf. The survey includes only persons aged twelve or older and excludes commercial crime, which would increase victimizations.

15. David Hemenway, "The Costs of Firearm Violence," in Deepali M. Patel and Rachel M. Taylor, ed. *The Social and Economic Costs of Violence* (Washington, D.C.: National Academies Press, 2012), 60–63; David Finkelhor et al., "Prevalence of Childhood Exposure to Violence, Crime, and Abuse: Results from the National Survey of Children's Exposure to Violence," *Journal of the American Medical Association Pediatrics* 169 (2015): 746–54; Ann Novotny, "What Happens to the Survivors?," *Monitor on Psychology* 49 (2018): 36; Dave Cullen, *Parkland: Birth of a Movement* (New York: Harper, 2019), 4.

16. "Read Testimony of Parkland Shooting Survivor Aalayah East-mond."

17. Tim Adams, "Sandy Hook's Tragic Legacy: Seven Years On, a Loving Father Is the Latest Victim," *Guardian,* 31 March 2019, https://www.theguardian.com/us-news/2019/mar/31/sandy-hook-shooting-suicide-parents-fake-news-conspiracy.

18. Ibid.; Christina Maxouris and Elizabeth Joseph, "Alex Jones Says 'Form of Psychosis' Made Him Believe Events like Sandy Hook Massacre Were Staged," CNN, 1 April 2019, https://www.cnn.com/2019/03/30/us/alex-jones-psychosis-sandy-hook/index.html.

19. Angie Drobnic Holan and Amy Sherman, "PolitiFact's Lie of the Year: Online Smear Machine Tries to Take Down Parkland Students," PolitiFact, 11 December 2018, https://www.politifact.com/truth-o-meter/article/2018/dec/11/politifacts-lie-year-parkland-student-conspiracies; Tonya Alanez and Wayne K. Roustan, "Man Defends NRA, Threatens Mother of Parkland Activist David Hogg, Authorities Say," *South Florida Sun Sentinel,* 21 December 2018, https://www.sun-sentinel.com/local/broward/parkland/florida-school-shooting/fl-ne-david-hogg-threatened-20181221-story.html; Criminal Complaint, US District Court, Southern District of California, *U.S. v. M. Brandon Fleury,* Case No. 19-6026-Snow, 11 January 2019.

20. Marwa Eltagouri, "A Santa Fe Shooting Survivor's Reaction Has Shaken People Around the Country," *Washington Post,* 18 May 2018, https://www.washingtonpost.com/news/post-nation/wp/2018/05/18/i-always-felt-it-would-eventually-happen-here-a-santa-fe-high-school-survivors-reaction-to-the-shooting/?utm_term=.b3334cf9f2d6; Daniel Moritz-Rabson, "Over 4 Million Students Held in School Lockdowns for Threats in 2017–18 School Year: Analysis," *Newsweek,* 27 December 2018, https://www.newsweek.com/school-lockdown-update-4-million-students-held-drill-reports-shooting-1272407.

21. "'No Way to Prevent This,' Says Only Nation Where This Regularly Happens," *Onion,* 27 May 2014, https://www.theonion.com/no-way-to-prevent-this-says-only-nation-where-this-r-1819576527.

22. "Underlying Cause of Death," CDC Wonder.

23. Julie Cerel and Rebecca L. Sanford, "The Impact of Suicide: World

Suicide Prevention Day and Why Suicide Awareness Matters," *Oxford University Press Blog*, 10 September 2016, https://blog.oup .com/2016/09/impact-awareness-suicide-prevention-day/; Julie Cerel and Rebecca L. Sanford, "It's Not Who You Know, It's How You Think You Know Them: Suicide Exposure and Suicide Bereavement," *Psychoanalytic Study of the Child* 71 (2018): 78.

24. Creel and Sanford, "It's Not Who You Know," 82–83.

25. "Fatal Injury Data" and "Nonfatal Injury Data," US Centers for Disease Control and Prevention (CDC). Again, this estimate has a wide error margin of 10,195 to 30,780 at a confidence of 95 percent.

26. Taylor Lorenz, "The Shooter's Manifesto Was Designed to Troll, *Atlantic*, 15 March 2019, https://www.theatlantic.com/technology /archive/2019/03/the-shooters-manifesto-was-designed-to-troll /585058.

27. Lisa Marie Pane, "New Zealand's History of Gun Ownership Could Be Upended," *Detroit News*, 15 March 2019, https://www .detroitnews.com/story/news/world/2019/03/15/new-zealand-gun -laws/39209929; Charlotte Graham-McLay, "New Zealand Passes Law Banning Most Semiautomatic Weapons, Weeks After Massacre," *New York Times*, 10 April 2019, https://www.nytimes.com /2019/04/10/world/asia/new-zealand-guns-jacinda-ardern.html.

28. Dalvin Brown, "'Fact Is I Had No Reason to Do It': Thousand Oaks Gunman Posted to Instagram During Massacre," *USA Today*, 10 November 2018, https://www.usatoday.com/story/news /nation/2018/11/10/thousand-oaks-shooting-gunman-posted -instagram-during-bar-massacre/1958013002.

29. Caryn Shaffer, "Sebring Shooting: Florida Politicians Send Prayers," *Florida Today*, 24 January 2019, https://www.floridatoday .com/story/news/local/2019/01/23/sebring-suntrust-bank -shooting-politicians-twitter/2661840002.

2. Guns in Early America

1. National Humanities Center Resource Toolbox Becoming American: "The British Atlantic Colonies, 1690–1763," "Gachradodow, Pennsylvania, 1744," 8.

2. William C. Davis, *A Way Through the Wilderness: The Natchez Trace and the Civilization of the Southern Frontier* (Baton Rouge: Louisiana State University Press, 1996), 88.

3. Ibid.; Pamela Haag, *The Gunning of America: Business and the Making of American Gun Culture* (New York: Basic Books, 2016), 9.

4. Francis Wharton, *State Trials of the United States During the Administrations of Washington and Adams* (Philadelphia: Carey & Wharton, 1849), 359, 388.

5. Clayton E. Cramer, *Armed America: The Remarkable Story of How and Why Guns Became as American as Apple Pie* (New York: Thomas Nelson, 2006).

6. Colin G. Calloway, *The Indian World of George Washington: The First President, the First Americans, and the Birth of a Nation* (New York: Oxford University Press, 2018), 11, 201.

7. John Grenier, *The First Way of War: American War Making on the Frontier, 1607–1814* (New York: Cambridge University Press, 2005), 12.

8. William L. Ramsey, *The Yamasee War: A Study of Culture, Economy, and Conflict in the Colonial South* (Lincoln: University of Nebraska Press, 2008).

9. R. Alan Stello, Jr., *Arsenal of History: The Powder Magazine of South Carolina* (Charleston, S.C.: History Press, 2013), 45; Peter Charles Hoffer, *Cry Liberty: The Great Stono River Slave Rebellion of 1739* (New York: Oxford University Press, 2010), 126; "Full Text of the Negro Law of South Carolina," 1740, Chapter I, Section 2, https://archive.org/stream/negrolawsouthca00goog /negrolawsouthca00goog_djvu.txt.

10. Benjamin Quarles, "The Colonial Militia and Negro Manpower," *Mississippi Valley Historical Review* 45 (1959): 643.

11. All citations to state constitutions are from Francis Newton Thorpe, ed., *The Federal and State Constitutions* (Washington, D.C.: US Government Printing Office, 1909), 7 vols. The territory of Vermont (less than 3 percent of the free population in 1790) mirrored the Pennsylvania language in its constitution of 1786 but did not become a state until 1791, after Congress adopted the Second Amendment.

12. Nathan R. Kozuskanich, "Pennsylvania, the Militia, and the Second Amendment," *Pennsylvania Magazine of History and Biography* 133 (2009): 122, 146; Wharton, *State Trials*, 375.

13. Mark Anthony Frassetto, "Firearms and Weapons Legislation up to the Early 20th Century," 15 January 2013, https:// www.researchgate.net/publication/256044831_Firearms_and

_Weapons_Legislation_up_to_the_Early_20th_Century; "Repository of Historical Gun Laws," Duke University, https://law.duke.edu/gunlaws.

14. Ibid.; Lois G. Schwoerer, "To Hold and Bear Arms: The English Perspective," *Chicago-Kent Law Review* 76 (January 2000): 32, 34–36, 60.

15. Ibid.

16. "From the Autobiography of John Adams," 14 March 1776, Founders Online, https://founders.archives.gov/documents/Adams/01-03-02-0016-0075; Peter Force, *The Organization and Progress of the North American Colonies,* 5th series, vol. 1 (Washington, D.C.: M. St. Clair Clarke and Peter Force, 1848), 709.

17. Christian G. Fritz, *American Sovereigns: The People and America's Constitutional Tradition Before the Civil War* (New York: Cambridge University Press, 2008), 179; Thomas Paine, *Dissertations on Government, the Affairs of the Bank, and Paper Money* (Philadelphia: Charles Cist, 1786), 2.

18. George Washington to Henry Knox, 26 December 1786, in *The Papers of George Washington, Confederation Series,* ed. W. W. Abbot (Charlottesville: University Press of Virginia, 1992–97), 4:481–83.

19. *Somerset v. Stewart* (1772), 98 ER 499; Douglas R. Egerton, *Death or Liberty: African Americans and Revolutionary America* (New York: Oxford University Press, 2009), 52–53.

20. Ibid., Egerton, generally.

21. Calloway, *Indian World,* 3–14.

22. Ibid.; Edward Countryman, "Indians, the Colonial Order, and the Social Significance of the American Revolution," *William and Mary Quarterly* 53 (1996): 354–62; Thomas Jefferson to George Rogers Clark, 1 January 1780, 25 December 1780, in *The Papers of Thomas Jefferson,* ed. Julian P. Boyd (Princeton, N.J.: Princeton University Press, 1951), 3:258–9, 4:237–38.

3. Adoption of the Second Amendment

1. Hannah Levintova, "The Second Amendment Doesn't Say What You Think it Does," *Mother Jones,* 19 June 2014, https://www.motherjones.com/politics/2014/06/second-amendment-guns-michael-waldman.

2. Jack N. Rakove, "The Second Amendment: The Highest State of Originalism," *Chicago-Kent Law Review* 76 (2000): 129.

3. Max Farrand, *Records of the Federal Convention of 1787* (New Haven, Conn.: Yale University Press, 1911), 2:587–88; James Madison, "Speech to Virginia Ratifying Convention," 20 June 1788, in *The Writings of James Madison,* ed. V. Gaillard Hunt (New York: G. P. Putnam's Sons, 1900–1910), 5:223.

4. *The Annals of Congress,* House of Representatives, 1st Cong., 1st sess., 8 June 1789, 448–60.

5. Herbert J. Storing, ed., *The Complete Anti-Federalist* (Chicago: University of Chicago Press, 1981), 3:145–67.

6. Rakove, "Second Amendment," 120–26.

7. *The Annals of Congress,* House of Representatives, 1st Cong., 1st sess., 15 August 1789, 775. See also, 17 August 1789, 784.

8. Ibid., 21 August 1789, 796.

9. *D.C. v. Heller,* "Brief for Professors of Linguistics," 11 January 2008, 2–3, 15, https://www.scotusblog.com/wp-content/uploads/2008/01/07-290_amicus_linguists1.pdf.

10. George Washington to Lund Washington, 30 September 1776; to William Livingston, 24 January 1777; in *The Papers of George Washington, Revolutionary War Series,* ed. Philander D. Chase and Frank E. Grizzard, Jr. (Charlottesville: University Press of Virginia, 1985–98), 6:440–43, 8:147–48; "Sixth Annual Address to Congress," 19 November 1794, in *The Papers of George Washington, Presidential Series,* ed. Dorothy Twohig (Charlottesville: University Press of Virginia, 1987–2016), 17:181–88.

11. *D.C. v. Heller,* "Brief for Professors of Linguistics," 18–21.

12. Saul Cornell, "The Original Meaning of Original Understanding: A Neo-blackstonian Critique," *Maryland Law Review* 67 (2007): 163–64; Owen McGovern, "The Responsible Gun Ownership Ordinance and Novel Textual Questions About the Second Amendment," *Journal of Criminal Law and Criminology,* 102 (2012): 477. See also Saul Cornell, *A Well-Regulated Militia: The Founding Fathers and the Origins of Gun Control in America* (New York: Oxford University Press, 2006).

13. Nathan Kozuskanich, "Originalism in a Digital Age: An Inquiry into the Right to Bear Arms," *Journal of the Early Republic* 29 (Winter 2009): 587–89.

14. Patrick J. Charles, "The 1792 National Militia Act, the Second Amendment, and Individual Militia Rights: A Legal and Historical Perspective," *Georgetown Journal of Law & Public Policy* 9 (2011): 323–92; "An Act to amend the Act calling forth the Militia," 17 July 1862, https://www.loc.gov/law/help/statutes-at-large /37th-congress/session-2/c37s2ch201.pdf.

15. See, also, Roxanne Dunbar-Ortiz, *Loaded: A Disarming History of the Second Amendment* (San Francisco: City Lights Books, 2018).

16. *D.C. v. Heller*, "Brief of Amicus Curiae Academics for the Second Amendment in Support of the Respondent," 34–35, http://www .scotusblog.com/wp-content/uploads/2008/02/07-290_amicus _academicsforsecondamendment.pdf.

17. Thomas Allen Glenn, *Some Colonial Mansions and Those Who Lived in Them, with Genealogies of the Various Families Mentioned*, vol. 2 (Philadelphia: Henry T. Coates, 1899), 168. The law professors rely on a later source, which incorrectly quotes Glenn as specifying 1789, not 1787, as the year of his election to the assembly.

18. Dan Evon, "Did George Washington Want Citizens Armed Against the Government?," Snopes.com, 7 January 2016, https:// www.snopes.com/fact-check/george-washington-gun-quote.

19. Audrey Bowler, "Did George Washington Offer Support for Individual Gun Rights, as Meme Says?," PolitiFact, 20 February 2015, https://www.politifact.com/truth-o-meter/statements /2015/feb/20/facebook-posts/did-george-washington-offer -support-individual-gun; "Spurious Quotations," George Washington's Mount Vernon, https://www.mountvernon.org/library /digitalhistory/digital-encyclopedia/article/spurious-quotations.

20. "George Washington Quotes," National Liberty Alliance, https:// www.nationallibertyalliance.org/files/quotes/Washington%20 Quotes.pdf; David M. Robertson, *An American Warning* (New York: iUniverse, 2009), 19.

21. "Spurious Quotations," George Washington's Mount Vernon.

22. Dan Evon, "Thomas Jefferson on Gun Rights," Snopes.com, 22 June 2016, https://www.snopes.com/fact-check/thomas -jefferson-gun-quote. See, for example, "The Second Amendment," Restoring America, http://www.restoringamerica.org /second_amendment.htm.

23. "Spurious Quotations," Thomas Jefferson Foundation, https://www.monticello.org/site/jefferson/spurious-quotations.

24. "Thomas Jefferson on the Right to Bear Arms," NRA-ILA, 22 January 2003, https://www.nraila.org/articles/20030122/thomas-jefferson-on-the-right-to-bear-a; 2nd Amendment Defender, https://www.freerepublic.com/~2ndamendmentdefender; Thomas Jefferson to George Washington, 19 June 1796, in *The Papers of Thomas Jefferson*, ed. Barbara B. Oberg (Princeton, N.J.: Princeton University Press, 2002), 29:127–30.

25. Dana Loesch, *Hands Off My Gun: Defeating the Plot to Disarm America* (New York: Center Street, 2014), 177; Stephen P. Halbrook, *A Right to Bear Arms: State and Federal Bills of Rights and Constitutional Guarantees* (Westport, Conn.: Greenwood Press, 1989), 44.

26. John Adams, *A Defence of the Constitutions of Government of the United States of America, 1788*, vol. 3 (London: John Stockdale, 1794), 475.

27. "Buy George Mason to Disarm the People Is to Enslave Them Bumper Sticker: Bumper Stickers, Decals & Magnets," Amazon.com, https://www.amazon.com/George-Disarm-People-Enslave-Sticker/dp/B00SS3VQMM; Tim George, "Gun Control: Its Roots in American History," Off the Grid News, https://www.offthegridnews.com/misc/gun-control-its-roots-in-american-history; Loesch, *Hands Off My Gun*, 177; James Bovard, *Freedom in Chains: The Rise of the State and the Demise of the Citizen* (New York: Palgrave Macmillan, 1999), 43.

28. Loesch, *Hands Off My Gun*, 177; Jonathan Elliot, *The Debates in the Several State Conventions of the Adoption of the Federal Constitution*, 2nd ed. (New York: Lenox Hill, 1974), 3:380.

29. Thomas Jefferson's Monticello, "Laws That Forbid the Carrying of Arms (Spurious Quotation)," https://www.monticello.org/site/research-and-collections/laws-forbid-carrying-armsspurious-quotation; Fred Barbash, "Ben Carson, Author of Book About the Constitution, Incorrectly States That Thomas Jefferson Crafted It," *Washington Post*, 23 November 2015, https://www.washingtonpost.com/news/morning-mix/wp/2015/11/23/no-dr-ben-carson-thomas-jefferson-did-not-craft-our-constitution/?utm_term=.deb04611861c.

30. Kristen Rand, "No Right to Keep and Bear Arms," in Josh Sugarmann, *National Rifle Association: Money, Firepower & Fear* (Washington, D.C.: National Press Books, 1992), 265.

31. Stephen P. Halbrook and David B. Kopel, "Tench Coxe and the Right to Bear Arms, 1787–1823," *William and Mary Bill of Rights Journal* 7 (1999): 347–99.

32. *American State Papers: Class V: Military Affairs*, 1:335.

4. A Century of Gun Controls

1. "Firearms Dangerous," *Baltimore Sun*, 26 February 1898, 9.

2. Charles, "1792 National Militia Act."

3. "Sixth Annual Address to Congress," in Twohig, *Papers of George Washington*, 17:181–88; Jacob E. Cooke, *Tench Coxe and the Early Republic* (Chapel Hill: University of North Carolina Press, 1978), 260; C. Edward Skeen, *Citizen Soldiers in the War of 1812* (Lexington: University Press of Kentucky, 1998), 7.

4. Skeen, *Citizen Soldiers*.

5. Ninth Congress. Sus. I. Cu. 37, 39, 40,41. 1807, Chap. XXXIX.-An Act Authorizing The Employment Of The Land And Naval Forces Of The United States, In Case Of Insurrections; *Martin v. Mott*, 25 U.S. 12 Wheat. 19, 19 (1827).

6. For states that adopted more than one constitution, the latest version prior to 1900 is referenced.

7. Laws are from "Repository of Historical Gun Laws," Duke Law. See also Eric Ruben and Saul Cornell, "Firearm Regionalism and Public Carry: Placing Southern Antebellum Case Law in Context," *Yale Law Journal* 125 (2015): 121–35; and Michael P. O'Shea, "The Second Amendment Wild Card: The Persisting Relevance of the 'Hybrid' Interpretation of the Right to Keep and Bear Arms," *Tennessee Law Review* 81 (2014): 597–631.

8. Matt Jancer, "Gun Control Is as Old as the Old West," Smithsonian.com, 8 February 2018, https://www.smithsonianmag.com/history/gun-control-old-west-180968013.

9. *Barron v. Baltimore*, 32 U.S. (7 Pet.) 243 (1833); *United States v. Cruikshank*, 92 U.S. 542 (1876).

10. *Congressional Record, House*, 52nd Cong., 2nd sess., 13 June 1892, 5253; 6 July 1892, 5788–90. See also Mark Anthony Frassetto,

"The First Congressional Debate on Public Carry and What It Tells Us About Firearm Regionalism," *Campbell Law Review* 20 (2018): 335–59.

11. *American State Papers: Class V: Military Affairs*, 1:44.

12. Ibid.,327–37.

13. Ibid., 337; Mark Pitcavage, "Rope of Sand: Territorial Militias, 1801–1812," *Journal of the Early Republic* 13 (1993): 485.

14. Stephen Skowronek, *Building a New American State: The Expansion of National Administrative Capacities, 1877–1920* (New York: Cambridge University Press, 1982), 315.

15. Larry Isaac, "To Counter 'the Very Devil' and More: The Making of Independent Capitalist Militia in the Gilded Age," *American Journal of Sociology* 108 (2002): 353–405.

16. William C. Church, "Rifle Practice," *Army and Navy Journal* 1 (April 1871): 529–30; George Wood Wingate, *Manual for Rifle Practice: Including a Complete Guide to Instruction in the Use and Care of the Modern Breech-Loader* (New York: W. C. Church, 1874), 2; "A Brief History of the NRA," NRA, https://home.nra .org/about-the-nra.

17. "Senator Morton on Southern Troubles," *Baltimore Sun*, 19 September 1874, 1; "The Louisiana Outrages," *New York Times*, 3 February 1875, 5.

18. Joshua Horwitz and Casey Anderson, *Guns, Democracy, and the Insurrectionist Idea* (Ann Arbor: University of Michigan Press, 2009), 133.

19. *English v. State*, 35 Tex. 473, 14 Am. Rep. 374 (1872).

20. *Presser v. Illinois*, 116 U.S. 252 (1886).

5. Enter the Federal Government

1. US House of Representatives, 73rd Cong., 2nd sess., Hearings Before The Committee On Ways And Means, "On H.R. 9066," April and May 1934, 22.

2. "Revolver Killings Fast Increasing," *New York Times*, 11 January 1911, 4; "Bar Hidden Weapons on Sullivan's Plea," *New York Times*, 11 May 1911, 3. Sullivan was a corrupt machine politician, but had earlier campaigned for gun control, which his biographer says, "sprang from heartfelt conviction." Richard F. Welch, *King of the Bowery* (Albany: State University of New York Press, 2008),

146; Peter Duffy, "100 Years Ago, the Shot That Spurred New York's Gun Control Law," *New York Times*, 23 January 2011.

3. *People ex rel. Darling v. Warden of 18 City Prisons*, 154 A.D. 413, 422 (1st Dep't 1913).

4. US House of Representatives, 65th Cong., 2nd sess., Committee on Ways and Means, *Hearings on the Proposed Revenue Act of 1918*, June 7–July 17, and August 5, 14, and 15, 1918, pt. Ii, Miscellaneous Taxes, 1186.

5. 18 U.S. Code §1715. Firearms as nonmailable.

6. "Plan to Bar Arms to All Criminals," *New York Times*, 29 January 1927, 1.

7. US House of Representatives, 73rd Cong., 2nd sess., *Hearings Before the Committee on Ways And Means, on H.R. 9066*, April and May 1934, 4–31.

8. US Senate, 73rd Cong., 2nd sess., *Hearings Before a Subcommittee of the Committee on Commerce, U.S. Senate, to Regulate Commerce in Firearms*, May 28 and 29, 1934, 33.

9. National Rifle Association, "Annual Report, 1907," 1–2, 211. NRA annual reports from 1905 to 1907 are available at https://babel.hathitrust.org/cgi/pt?id=nyp.33433082499066;view=1up;seq=1; Oral History of Milton A. Reckord, 1974, 561-A-16, 561-A-19, box 14, Papers of Milton A. Reckord, Hornbake Library, University of Maryland, College Park, Maryland.

10. "National Marksman Reserve," Circular no. 20, War Department, 15 July 1904, in NRA, "Annual Report, 1907," 192; US General Accounting Office, Army's Program for Civilian Marksmanship (Washington, D.C.: US Government Printing Office, 1976). See also Jeffrey A. Marlin, "The National Guard, the National Board for the Promotion of Rifle Practice, and the National Rifle Association: Public Institutions and the Rise of a Lobby for Private Gun Ownership" (Ph.D. diss., Georgia State University, 2013).

11. James A. Drain to Theodore Roosevelt, 2 February 1907; Roosevelt to James A. Drain, 18 February 1907; Drain to William Loeb, 25 February 1907; Digital Collection, Theodore Roosevelt Center at Dickinson University, https://www.theodorerooseveltcenter.org/Research/Digital-Library; James A. Drain, Sr., *Single Handed*, ed. Mark L. Bardenwerper, 2nd ed. (Cambridge, Mass.: 2013), 131.

12. Harold W. Glassen, "Report of the President," 29 March 1969, box 1, Papers of Harold W. Glassen, Bentley Historical Library, University of Michigan, Ann Arbor.

13. C. B. Lister to Major General M. A. Edson, 3 January 1950, box 27, "Notes Regarding the National Rifle Association of America," Edson Papers.

14. National Rifle Association, "Annual Report, 1905," 7; "Annual Report, 1907," 211.

15. "Brief History of the NRA," NRA; *Hearings . . . to Regulate Commerce in Firearms*, 70–75.

16. *Hearings . . . to Regulate Commerce in Firearms*, 16; *Hearings . . . on H.R. 9066*, 56; Memorandum on Labor Trouble and Publicity (A) and (B), Minutes of the Employment Relations Committee, National Association of Manufacturers, 1 November 1934, series V, box 1, NAM Papers, Hagley Museum and Library, Wilmington, Del.

17. Oral History of Milton A. Reckord, 561-C-64.

18. Karl T. Frederick, "Pistol Regulation: Its Principles and History. Part III," *Journal of Criminal Law and Criminology* 23 (1932): 541; *Hearings . . . on H.R. 9066*, 53.

19. For the backstory of the *Miller* case, see Brian L. Frye, "The Peculiar Story of *United States v. Miller*," *NYU Journal of Law and Liberty* 3 (2008): 48–82.

20. *United States v. Miller*, 307 U.S. 174 (1939).

21. John T. Young et al., "Trends: Guns." *Public Opinion Quarterly* 60 (1996): 634–49.

6. Assassinations and Debates over Gun Control

1. Amitai Etzioni and Richard Remp, *Technological Shortcuts to Social Change* (New York: Russell Sage, 1973), 105.

2. Everard Munsey, "Bill Drafted to Ban Mail-Order Guns," *Washington Post*, 13 November 1961, D14; 88th Cong., 1st sess., *Congressional Record, Senate*, 18 March 1962, 5249–50, and Subcommittee to Investigate Juvenile Delinquency of the Committee on the Judiciary, "Interstate Traffic in Mail-Order Firearms," January, March, and May 1963.

3. Al Bolin, "Where We Stand on Mail Order Weapons," *India-*

napolis Times, 8 December 1963, 14; *Hearings Before the Committee on Commerce, United States Senate, Eighty-Eighth Congress, First and Second Sessions, a Bill to Amend the Federal Firearms Act and S. 2345,* December 1963, January and March 1964.

4. *Hearings Before the Committee on Commerce,* 105.

5. Ibid., 56.

6. Franklin L. Orth to Senator Hugh Scott, 7 December 1963, box 78, Papers of Hugh Scott, Special Collections, University of Virginia Library, Charlottesville.

7. *Hearings . . . a Bill to Amend the Federal Firearms Act,* 314–15; Paul A. Schuette, "Newsletter Brings Attack on Gun-Curb Bill," *Washington Post,* 2 May 1965, 41; Marquis Childs, "NRA v. Dodd: Stalled Law," *Washington Post,* 14 April 1965, 20.

8. US House of Representatives, 90th Cong., 1st sess., *Hearings, Subcommittee no. 5 of Committee on the Judiciary, Anti-crime Program,* March and April 1967, 603–4.

9. NRA Public Relations Committee, "Report of Chairman," 7–8 December 1968, 3, 10, in "Minutes of the Meeting of the Executive Committee of the National Rifle Association of America," box 1, Glassen Papers.

10. Lyndon B. Johnson, "The Public's Right to Protection," 24 June 1968, *Public Papers of the President, Lyndon B. Johnson, 1968–1969,* 2:553, https://quod.lib.umich.edu/p/ppotpus/4731573.1968 .001/818?rgn=full+text;view=image.

11. Harold W. Glassen, "Dear NRA Member," 14 June 1968, box 1, Glassen Papers.

12. Michael Waldman, *The Second Amendment: A Biography* (New York: Simon & Schuster, 2015), 89–90; Lyndon B. Johnson, "Remarks on Signing the Gun Control Act of 1968," 22 October 1968, *Public Papers of the President,* 1059–60, https://quod.lib.umich.edu/p /ppotpus/4731573.1968.002/365?page=root;rgn=full+text;size =100;view=image;q1=lyndon+johnson.

13. National Commission on the Causes and Prevention of Violence, *To Establish Justice, to Insure Domestic Tranquility: Final Report* (Washington, D.C.: Government Printing Office, 1969), 175.

14. Polls cited, in 90th Cong., 2nd sess., *Congressional Record, Senate,* 23 January 1968, S652-53; National Rifle Association, "Dear Friend," 26 July 1975; Citizens Committee for the Right to Keep

and Bear Arms, "Straight Talk Poll," July 1993, boxes 245 and 130, Papers of Group Research Inc., Rare Book and Manuscript Collections, Butler Library, Columbia University, New York, N.Y.

15. Franklin E. Zimring, "Firearms and Federal Law: The Gun Control Act of 1968," *Journal of Legal Studies* 4 (1975): 159, 161.

16. "Wanted: An Anti-Gun Lobby," *Washington Post*, 15 December 1968, B6.

17. "The House That NRA Built," *Washington Post*, 17 June 1967, 12; "Rifle Group Registers as Lobbyist in Capital," *New York Times*, 13 December 1968, 20.

18. "Rifle Group Registers as Lobbyist," *New York Times*, 20.

19. *Hearings . . . a Bill to Amend the Federal Firearms Act*, 256.

20. Ibid., 22.

21. Ibid., 93.

22. Ibid., 236.

23. John Edgar Hoover, "Message from the Director, to All Law Enforcement Officials," 1 June 1963, FBI File Repository, https://leb.fbi.gov/file-repository/archives/june-1963.pdf/view.

24. *Hearings . . . a Bill to Amend the Federal Firearms Act*, 92.

25. Ibid., 211–12.

26. Ibid., 100, 103, 277.

27. Ibid., 144.

28. Albin Krebs, "Strict Gun Control Practiced Abroad," *New York Times*, 13 June 1968, 20; National Commission on the Causes and Prevention of Violence, *To Establish Justice*, 169, 175.

29. *Hearings . . . a Bill to Amend the Federal Firearms Act*, 38.

30. Ibid., p. 211, US Senate, 88th Cong., 1st sess., Committee on the Judiciary, Subcommittee to Investigate Juvenile Delinquency, "Interstate Traffic in Mail-Order Firearms, Part 14" January, March, and May 1963, 3191; US Senate, 89th Cong., 1st sess., Committee on the Judiciary, Subcommittee to Investigate Juvenile Delinquency, "S. Res. 52," May–July 1965, 356.

31. Subcommittee to Investigate Juvenile Delinquency, "Interstate Traffic in Mail-Order Firearms," 3187.

32. *Hearings . . . Bill to Amend the Federal Firearms Act*, 62–63.

33. Subcommittee to Investigate Juvenile Delinquency, "Interstate Traffic in Mail-Order Firearms, Part 14," 3186.

34. Harold W. Glassen, "Press Release," undated, box 1, Glassen Papers.

35. US Senate, 90th Cong., 2nd sess., *Hearings Before the Committee on the Judiciary, Subcommittee to Investigate Juvenile Delinquency, S. Res. 240,* June and July 1968, 480.

36. 90th Cong., 2nd sess., *Congressional Record, House,* 19 July 1968, 22296; George A. Brautigam, "Don't Let Them Take Your Guns Away," 1954, box 131, Group Research Inc. Papers.

37. 91st Cong., 1st sess., *Congressional Record, Senate,* August 13, 1969, 23697–99.

38. Harold W. Glassen, "Remarks at Stetson University," 14 April 1969, box 1, Glassen Papers.

39. 88th Cong., 2nd sess., *Congressional Record, House,* 27 January 1964, 1164.

40. *Hearings . . . a Bill to Amend the Federal Firearms Act,* 83.

41. Arnold Kotz, Harold Hair, and John K. Scales, "Firearms, Violence, and Civil Disorders," Stanford Research Institute, Project MU-7105, July 1968, 3, https://www.ncjrs.gov/pdffiles1/Photocopy/11802NCJRS.pdf.

42. *Hearings . . . a Bill to Amend the Federal Firearms Act,* 274; "Who Guards America's Homes," *American Rifleman* 115 (May 1967): 16; Ben A. Franklin, "Rifle Club Sees Guns as Riot Control," *New York Times,* 7 May 1967, 1; Harold W. Glassen, "What Is the NRA?," undated, 1960s, box 1, Glassen Papers.

43. Kotz, Hair, and Scales, "Firearms, Violence, and Civil Disorders," 3–4.

44. *Hearings . . . a Bill to Amend the Federal Firearms Act,* 23, 25.

45. Jack Basil, "Memorandum to General Edson," 18 June 1955, box 27, Edson Papers.

46. *Hearings . . . a Bill to Amend the Federal Firearms Act,* 120–24; "WABC Radio Press Conference, Guest: Harold W. Glassen," 22 June 1968, box 1, Glassen Papers.

47. "Riots and Gun Control," *Chicago Daily Defender,* 19 September 1968, 10.

48. Harold W. Glassen, "Speech Notes," December 1970, box 1, Glassen Papers; Thad Morgan, "The NRA Supported Gun Control When the Black Panthers Had the Weapons," *History* 22, March 2018, https://www.history.com/news/black-panthers-gun-control-nra-support-mulford-act.

49. Marquis Childs, "Tydings' Legislative Proposals Stir Up Both Right and Left," *Washington Post,* 22 July 1970, 19.

50. Ben A. Franklin, "Tydings Seeks to Counter Gun Lobby," *New York Times,* 6 September 1970, 26; Jack Limpert, "The Defeat of Joe Tydings: When Pols Learned to Fear the NRA," jacklimpert .com, 17 June 2016, http://jacklimpert.com/2016/06/the-defeat -of-joe-tydings-when-pols-learned-to-fear-the-nra.

51. Philipsburg Rod and Gun Club, "HUNTERS!"; Black Forest Conservation Association, 1968; "1,000,000 Pennsylvania Sportsmen," 1968, box 289, Scott Papers.

52. Staff Memo, "The Gleanings from My Meetings," 13 November 1968, box 289, Scott Papers.

53. Arlen J. Large, "The Gun Lobby Works to Defeat Lawmakers Who Support Controls," *Wall Street Journal,* 11 September 1970, 1.

54. *U.S. v. Synnes,* 438 F.2d 764 (8th 1971). For a list of cases, see Robert J. Spitzer, *The Politics of Gun Control,* 6th ed. (New York: Paradigm, 2015), 213.

7. The NRA Reinvents the Second Amendment

1. Azmat Kahn, "How Conservatives 'Reinvented' the Second Amendment," PBS, 18 December 2012, https://www.pbs.org /wgbh/frontline/article/how-conservatives-reinvented-the -second-amendment.

2. Ben A. Franklin, "Shooting of Wallace Spurs a New Effort to Tighten Gun Controls," *New York Times,* 17 May 1972, 29.

3. US House of Representatives, 92nd Cong., 2nd sess., *Hearings Before Subcommittee No. 5 of the Committee on the Judiciary, on H.R. 8828 and Related Bills,* June 27, 28, and 29, 1972, 285–86.

4. David Gumpert, "To the Arms Industry Control Controversy Is a Business Problem," *Wall Street Journal,* 31 May 1972, 1.

5. *Hearings . . . on H.R. 8828 and Related Bills,* 284–85.

6. US Senate, 97th Cong., 2nd sess.,"The Right to Keep and Bear Arms," Report of the Subcommittee on the Constitution of the Committee on the Judiciary, February 1982, 29. See also "Report of the President to the NRA Board of Directors," 25 March 1974; NRA, Attachment 2 and 2A of the Report of 12

July 1974 by the NRA Firearms Legislative Committee, box 14, Reckord Papers.

7. Kristen A. Goss, "Policy, Politics, and Paradox: The Institutional Origins of the Great American Gun War," *Fordham Law Review* 73 (2004): 690–94.

8. Paul Hoston, "Gun Lobby Seeks Millions to Fight Its Foes at Polls," *Los Angeles Times*, 26 April 1976, 1.

9. Ibid.; "Pro-Gun Groups List Campaign Donations," *Los Angeles Times*, 3 November 1976, B30; "GOP Leading in Campaign Funds," *Los Angeles Times*, 8 September 1978, B11.

10. Pat Buchanan, Graduation Address, Rosemont College, 22 May 1971, box 13, Papers of William A. Rusher, Library of Congress.

11. "Guns: Should They Be in Christian Homes?," *Christianity Today*, 18 August 1989, 42–43.

12. Associated Press, "Pistol-Packin' Santa Angers Lawmakers," *Eugene-Register Guard*, 21 December 1979, 18C; "Yes, Virginia, and He's Armed," *Washington Post*, 24 December 1981, 14; Wayne King, "Decking the Halls with Factional Fighting," *New York Times*, 17 December 1987, B14; "Diana Hears," *Washington Times*, 20 December 1983, B1.

13. Bruce Buursma, "Lobbyist Guns for Patron Saint," *Chicago Tribune*, 18 December 1987, 17; "Gun Saint Group Commemorates Catholic Saint's Feast Day," *Christian News Wire*, 27 February 2007; The Passionates of Holy Cross Province, "St. Gabriel Possenti," https://passionist.org/st-gabriel-possenti; "St. Gabriel Possenti: Patron Saint of Handgunners," 1 November 2012, https://gunowners.wordpress.com/2012/11/01/st-gabriel-possenti-patron-saint-of-gun-owners.

14. US House of Representatives, 94th Cong., 1st sess., *Hearings Before the Committee on the Judiciary, Subcommittee on Crime, Firearms Regulation*, February–October 1975, 2849–88.

15. Ibid., 2850; Art Buchwald, "Gun Power to the People," *Los Angeles Times*, 28 October 1975, 8.

16. *Hearings . . . Firearms Regulation*, 2875.

17. Lawrence Meyer, "NRA Plans Summit on Gun Curbs," *Washington Post*, 2 May 1975, 5.

18. Phyllis Schlafly, "NRA Being Subverted?," *Dixon Evening Telegraph*, 12 May 1977, 4.

19. Ernest B. Furgurson, "NRA Split by Dispute over Policy," *Baltimore Sun,* 15 May 1977, 1.

20. Federal Election Commission, "Independent Expenditure Summary, January 1, 1979–December 31, 1980," https://transition.fec.gov/press/summaries/1980/ElectionCycle/1980DataTitle.shtml#; Allan J. Lichtman, *White Protestant Nation: The Rise of the American Conservative Movement* (New York: Grove/Atlantic 2008), 322.

21. James J. Featherstone, General Counsel, National Rifle Association of America, and Richard E. Gardiner, Robert Dowlut, Office of the General Counsel, "The Second Amendment to the United States Constitution Guarantees an Individual Right to Keep and Bear Arms," in US Senate, "Right to Keep and Bear Arms," 83–109.

22. *Lewis v. United States,* 445 U.S. 55 (1980).

23. US Senate, "Right to Keep and Bear Arms," VIII; *American Rifleman,* August 1982, 37.

24. *Quilici v. Village of Morton Grove,* 695 F.2nd 261 (7th Cir. 1982).

25. Matt Valentine, "Disarmed: How Cities Are Losing the Power to Regulate Guns," *Atlantic,* 6 March 2014, https://www.theatlantic.com/politics/archive/2014/03/disarmed-how-cities-are-losing-the-power-to-regulate-guns/284220.

26. "Handguns USA," *Christian Science Monitor,* 19 November 1985, 24; Rupert Cornwell, "Gun Lobby Lays Down Defensive Barrage," *Independent,* 18 May 1995, 16.

27. Peter Finn, "NRA Money Helped Reshape Gun Law," *Washington Post,* 13 March 2013, 1; Michael Waldman, "How the NRA Rewrote the Second Amendment," Brennan Center for Justice, 20 May 2014, https://www.brennancenter.org/analysis/how-nra-rewrote-second-amendment; Robert J. Spitzer, "Lost and Found: Researching the Second Amendment," *Chicago-Kent Law Review* 76 (2000): 384.

28. Finn, "NRA Money Helped Reshape."

29. Cheryl Arvidson, "Powerful Gun Lobby Rolls over Opposition," *Miami News,* 11 September 1981, 6.

30. 99th Cong., 1st sess., *Congressional Record, Senate,* 24 June 1985, S8686.

31. "Armor-Piercing Bullet Ban," *Congressional Quarterly Almanac,*

1986, https://library.cqpress.com/cqalmanac/document.php?id
=cqal86-1149722#H2_2; Ty Larry, "NRA Loses Firepower:
Legislative Defeats, Strife Has It Reeling," *Boston Globe*, 11
June 1990, 1.

32. *United States v. Verdugo-Urquidez*, 494 U.S. 259 (1990); NRA-
ILA, "Federal Court Cases Regarding the Second Amendment,"
29 July 1999, https://www.nraila.org/articles/19990729/federal
-court-cases-regarding-the-secon-1.

33. American Bar Association, "Policy Statement," February 1994,
https://www.americanbar.org/content/dam/aba/administrative
/gun_violence/1994policy.pdf.

34. Michael Kirkland, "McVeigh Member of the NRA for Nearly
Four Years," UPI, 3 May 1995, https://www.upi.com/Archives
/1995/05/03/McVeigh-member-of-NRA-for-nearly-4-years
/4364799473600.

35. Charles M. Sennott, "NRA Becomes Militias' Beacon," *Boston
Globe*, 13 August 1995, 1.

36. "Letter of Resignation Sent by Bush to Rifle Association," *New
York Times*, 11 May 1995, https://www.nytimes.com/1995/05/11
/us/letter-of-resignation-sent-by-bush-to-rifle-association.html;
Robert McG. Thomas, Jr., "Thomas L. Washington, 58, Head of
Rifle Group," *New York Times*, 6 December 1995, B17.

37. Christine Jamieson, "Gun Violence Research: History of the Federal Funding Freeze," *Psychological Science Agenda*, February 2013,
https://www.apa.org/science/about/psa/2013/02/gun-violence
.aspx.

38. Josh Sugarmann, "Book Review: *The Politics of Gun Control*," *New
England Journal of Medicine* 336 (1997): 74.

39. Dave Gilson, "This Collection of NRA Ads Reveals Its De-
scent into Crazy," *Mother Jones*, 10 April 2013, https://www
.motherjones.com/politics/2013/04/national-rifle-association
-ads-history; "Charlton Heston on the Second Amendment,"
Patriot Post, 11 February 1997, https://patriotpost.us/pages/9;
Charlton Heston, "Winning the Cultural War," Harvard Law
School, 16 February 1999, American Rhetoric, http://www
.americanrhetoric.com/speeches/charltonhestonculturalwar.htm.

40. Center for Responsive Politics, "Top Organization Donors: All Federal Contributions 2000 Election Cycle," Open Secrets.org, https://

www.opensecrets.org/overview/toporgs.php?cycle=2000&view
=fc; "Charlton Heston: From My Cold Dead Hands," https://www
.youtube.com/watch?v=5ju4Gla2odw; Lisa Marie Pane, "NRA Be-
set with Infighting over Whether It Has Strayed Too Far," *AP News*,
24 April 2019, apnews.com/bda97817dabf492e9be8099bdd1a4cd6.

41. Judy Sarasohn, "NRA Lobby Is No. 1 on Capitol Hill," *Fortune*,
17 May 2001, https://www.washingtonpost.com/archive/politics
/2001/05/17/fortune-nra-lobby-is-no-1-on-capitol-hill/8019e21d
-766e-47ab-acaf-d43fcfe2adcd/?utm_term=.a93123a98eb0;
"Bush Owes Presidency to NRA, NRA Says," *Los Angeles Times*,
22 April 2002, http://articles.latimes.com/2002/apr/28/news/mn
-40519.

42. David M. Halbfinger, "Shotgun in Hand Kerry Defines His Gun-
Control Stance," *New York Times*, 1 November 2003, https://www
.nytimes.com/2003/11/01/us/shotgun-in-hand-kerry-defines-his
-gun-control-stance.html.

43. Wayne LaPierre, *Guns, Bush, & Kerry* (Washington, D.C.: NRA,
2004), 29–30; Jeffrey H. Birnbaum, "In Swing States, Kerry
Reaches for Gun Vote," *Washington Post*, 9 August 2004, http://
www.washingtonpost.com/wp-dyn/articles/A50660-2004Aug8
.html.

44. 109th Cong., 1st sess., *Congressional Record, Senate*, 27 July 2005,
9088, 9107.

45. NRA-ILA, "President Bush Signs 'Protection of Lawful Commerce in Arms Act,'" 26 October 2005, Library of Congress, Web
Archive Collection, http://webarchive.loc.gov/all/20051102103902
/http://www.nraila.org.

8. The Original Sin of Justice Scalia's Originalism: *D.C. v. Heller*

1. Josh Horwitz, "Dick Heller in His Own Words," *HuffPost*, 25
May 2011, https://www.huffpost.com/entry/dick-heller-in-his-own
-wo_b_128559.

2. Adam Liptak, "Carefully Plotted Course Propels Gun Case to
the Top," *New York Times*, 3 December 2007, https://www.nytimes
.com/2007/12/03/us/03bar.html; Adam Winkler, *Gunfight: The
Battle over the Right to Bear Arms in America* (New York: W. W.
Norton, 2011), 62.

3. Saul Cornel and Nathan Katzenbach, eds., *The Second Amendment on Trial: Critical Essays on* District of Columbia v. Heller (Boston: University of Massachusetts Press, 2013), 401–10.

4. *D.C. v. Heller,* 554 US 570 (2008).

5. Nelson Lund, "The Second Amendment, *Heller,* and Originalist Jurisprudence," *UCLA Law Review* 56 (2009): 1345.

6. Melissa Quinn, "John Paul Stevens: *Heller* Gun Control Decision the Worst in 35-Year Supreme Court Tenure," *Washington Examiner,* 15 May 2019, https://www.washingtonexaminer.com/policy /courts/john-paul-stevens-heller-gun-control-decision-the-worst -in-35-year-supreme-court-tenure.

7. "Presidential Candidates Respond to *D.C. vs. Heller* Ruling," The Liberty Papers, 26 June 2008, http://www.thelibertypapers .org/2008/06/26/presidential-candidates-respond-to-heller-vs-dc -ruling.

8. Ibid.

9. J. Harvie Wilkinson, "Of Guns, Abortions, and the Unraveling Rule of Law," *Virginia Law Review* 95 (2009): 254.

10. Richard A. Posner, "In Defense of Looseness," *New Republic,* 27 August 2008, https://newrepublic.com/article/62124/defense -looseness; *McDonald v. Chicago,* 561 U.S. 742 (2010).

11. "Warren Burger and NRA: Gun Lobby's Big Fraud on Second Amendment," *Milwaukee Independent,* 11 October 2018, http:// www.milwaukeeindependent.com/external/warren-burger-and -nra-gun-lobbys-big-fraud-on-second-amendment.

9. Iron Triangle: The Gun Lobby, Gun Industry, and Politicians

1. Ravi Somaiya, "Banished for Questioning the Gospel of Guns," *New York Times,* 4 January 2014, https://www.nytimes.com/2014 /01/05/business/media/banished-for-questioning-the-gospel-of -guns.html.

2. "Eisenhower's Farewell Address," 17 January 1961, https://www .pbs.org/wgbh/americanexperience/features/eisenhower-farewell.

3. American Historical Foundation, "Second Amendment Tribute .50 Cal. Revolver," https://www.ahffirearms.com/product/second -amendment-tribute-smith-wesson-50-cal.

4. Patriot Ordnance Factory–USA, "Freedom Tour," https://pof

-usa.com/pof-usa-gives-a-factory-freedom-tour/; "Patriotic to the Core," https://pof-usa.com/; GunsInternational.com, "NRA Commemorative—Rifles for Sale," https://www.gunsinternational .com/guns-for-sale-online/rifles/nra-commemorative-rifles/nra -commemorative-rifles.c206_p1_o6.cfm.

5. Leanna Garfield, "There Are 50,000 More Gun Shops than Mc-Donald's in the US," *Business Insider,* 6 October 2017, https:// www.aol.com/article/finance/2017/10/06/there-are-50000-more -gun-shops-than-mcdonalds-in-the-us/23235335.

6. For a comprehensive definition and enumeration of assault weapons, see Connecticut Code, 943, Offenses Against Public Peace and Safety, Sec. 53-202a. Assault weapons: Definitions, https://www .cga.ct.gov/current/pub/chap_943.htm#sec_53-202a; Lisa Marie Pane, "Did Gunman's 'Silencer' Make a Difference in Virginia Beach Carnage?," Associated Press, 1 June 2019, https://www .apnews.com/1cfdc645dbd54592b685b977e211c99b; NRA-ILA, "'Assault Weapons' and 'Large' Magazines," 8 August 2016, https:// www.nraila.org/get-the-facts/assault-weapons-large-magazines.

7. B. Gil Horman, "A First Look at 2019's New Guns," *American Rifleman,* 29 October 2018, https://www.americanrifleman.org /articles/2018/10/29/a-first-look-at-2019-s-new-guns.

8. David M. Fortier, "*Fallschirmjägergewehr* 42: A Modern Reproduction of the Green Devil's Wonder Weapon," *Firearms News,* November 2018, 6, 10–11, 14–16, 18, 20–22.

9. Horman, "First Look"; "How to Build Your Own AR 15—Legally and Unregistered," 80% Lowers, https://www.80-lower.com /blogs/80-lower-blog/how-to-build-your-own-ar-15-legally-and -unregistered.

10. Damon Arthur, "Sheriff: Tehama Shooter Built His Own Illegal Guns," *Record Searchlight,* 15 November 2017, https://www .redding.com/story/news/2017/11/15/tehama-shooter-built-his -own-illegal-guns/868737001; Zusha Elinson and Ben Kesling, "Coast Guard Officer Accused of Planning Attack Amassed an Arsenal," *Wall Street Journal,* 21 February 2019, https://www .wsj.com/articles/coast-guard-officer-accused-of-planning-terror -attack-amassed-an-arsenal-11550789657.

11. Charles C. W. Cooke, "The AR-15 Is the Musket of Our Era," NRA-ILA News, 19 July 2016, https://www.nraila.org/articles /20160719/the-ar-15-is-the-musket-of-its-era.

12. Gina Kolata and C. J. Chivers, "Wounds from Military-Style Rifles, 'A Ghastly Thing to See,'" *New York Times*, 4 March 2018, https://www.nytimes.com/2018/03/04/health/parkland-shooting-victims-ar15.html.

13. Elzerie de Jager et al., "Lethality of Civilian Active Shooter Incidents With and Without Semiautomatic Rifles in the United States," *Journal of the American Medical Association* 320 (2018): 1034–35.

14. Randolph Roth, *American Homicide* (Cambridge, Mass.: Belknap Press of Harvard University Press, 2009); Mathew Lysiak, "Video of Adam Lanza Confirmed as Newton Parents Sue," *Newsweek*, 23 February 2016, https://www.newsweek.com/sandy-hook-lawsuit-adam-lanza-429526; Peter Kren, Paul Kalaus, and Brett Hall, "Material Culture and Military History: Test Firing Early Modern Small Arms," *Military History Review* 42 (1995): 106.

15. NRA, "IRS Form 990, 2016," https://projects.propublica.org/nonprofits/organizations/530116130/201722619349300507/IRS990.

16. Violence Policy Center, "Blood Money II: How Gun Industry Dollars Fund the NRA," September 2013, http://www.vpc.org/studies/bloodmoney2.pdf; "'Dark Money Illuminated,' One Issue Database of Dark Money Donors," https://docs.google.com/spreadsheets/d/1vpImNT1tSNoBWpSIg7Hx_gqG85hcM70CJ_5DtPcIYBI/edit#gid=27072.

17. Ibid., "'Dark Money Illuminated.'"

18. Iain Overton, "Top Ten Companies Awarded US DOD Small Arms Contracts During the War on Terror," AOAV, 24 August 2016, https://aoav.org.uk/2016/top-ten-companies-awarded-us-dod-small-arms-related-contracts-during-the-war-on-terror; Todd Bookman, "Sig Sauer's New Hampshire Hometown Celebrates Huge Army Contract," NPR, 3 February 2017, https://www.nhpr.org/post/sig-sauers-new-hampshire-hometown-celebrates-huge-army-contract#stream/0. As an indication of the importance of military contracts, Colt's eventual loss of its small-arms sales to the military left the company bankrupt.

19. Katharine Q. Seelye, "National Rifle Association Is Turning to World Stage to Fight Gun Control," *New York Times*, 2 April 1997, 2; US Bureau of Alcohol, Tobacco, Firearms, and Explosives, "Annual Firearms Manufacturing and Export Report, 2017 Final," and "2012 Final," https://www.atf.gov/file/133476

/download, https://www.atf.gov/file/4751/download; Own Greene and Nic Marsh, eds., *Small Arms, Crime, and Conflict: Global Governance and the Threat of Armed Violence* (New York: Routledge, 2011); Jade Moldae, "U.S. Firearms Industry, 2017," Shooting Industry, https://shootingindustry.com/u-s-firearms-industry-2017.

20. Todd Bookman, "CEO of U.S. Gun-Maker Faces Jail in Germany," NPR, 25 February 2019, https://www.npr.org/2019/02/25/696690043/ceo-of-u-s-gun-maker-faces-jail-in-germany; "Human Rights Watch, Colombia, 2012," https://www.hrw.org/sites/default/files/related_material/colombia_2012_0.pdf; Todd Bookman, "SIG Sauer CEO Avoids Jail Time for Role in Illegal Arms Shipment," New Hampshire Public Radio, 3 April 2019, https://www.nhpr.org/post/sig-sauer-ceo-avoids-jail-time-role-illegal-arms-shipment#stream/0.

21. Nicholas Marsh and Matt Schroeder, "Parts for Small Arms and Light Weapons," Small Arms Survey, October 2013, 3,4, https://www.files.ethz.ch/isn/173196/SAS-Research-Note-35.pdf.

22. Neil Weinberg, Polly Mosendz, and Bill Allison, "NRA Goes International in Its Mission to Defend Guns," Bloomberg, 3 January 2019, https://www.bloomberg.com/news/features/2019-01-03/nra-goes-global-with-its-pro-gun-agenda; US Bureau of Alcohol, Tobacco, Firearms, and Explosives, "Firearms Commerce in the United States: Annual Statistical Update 2018," 5, https://www.atf.gov/file/130436/download; Violence Policy Center, "Blood Money II."

23. Barbara Plett, "UN Passes Historic Arms Trade Treaty by Huge Majority," BBC, 2 August 2013, https://www.bbc.com/news/world-us-canada-21998394; "The Arms Trade Treaty," Congress.gov, 2016, https://www.congress.gov/114/cdoc/tdoc14/CDOC-114tdoc14.pdf.

24. "The Arms Trade Treaty," Congress.gov; NRA-ILA, "NRA Delivers Remarks at United Nations," 14 July 2011, Library of Congress, Web Archives Collection, http://webarchive.loc.gov/all/20120518020635/http://www.nraila.org/Legislation/Read.aspx?ID=6993, and "Wayne LaPierre Fights for the Second Amendment Before the United Nations," 11 July 2011, http://webarchive.loc.gov/all/20120715123710/http://www.nraila.org/news-issues/news-from-nra-ila/2012/07/wayne-lapierre-defends-the-second-amendment-before-the-united-nations.aspx; Phillip J. Cook and Kristin A. Goss, *The Gun Debate* (Oxford University Press, 2014), 32.

25. Louis Jacobson, "Chain E-Mail Says U.N. Treaty Would Force U.S. to Ban, Confiscate Guns," *PolitiFact*, 9 June 2010, https://www.politifact.com/truth-o-meter/statements/2010/jun/09/chain-email/chain-e-mail-says-un-treaty-would-force-us-ban-con; David Weigel, "Pro-gun Rights Group: 'Not Preposterous' to Ask Whether Government Was Behind Aurora Shootings," Slate, 25 July 2012, https://slate.com/news-and-politics/2012/07/pro-gun-rights-group-not-preposterous-to-ask-whether-government-was-behind-aurora-shootings.html.

26. Ramsey Cox, "Senate Votes 56 to 43 to Stop U.S. from Joining UN Arms Trade Treaty," The Hill, 23 March 2013, https://thehill.com/blogs/floor-action/senate/290001-senate-votes-to-stop-us-from-joining-un-arms-treaty; Michelle Nicholls, "Kerry Signs UN Arms Control Treaty, Says Won't Harm U.S. Rights," Reuters, 25 September 2013, https://www.reuters.com/article/us-un-assembly-kerry-treaty/kerry-signs-u-n-arms-trade-treaty-says-wont-harm-u-s-rights-idUSBRE98O0WV20130925; NRA-ILA, "Trump Administration's Proposed Rulemakings a Win-Win for America's Firearms Industry, National Security," 25 May 2018, https://www.nraila.org/articles/20180525/trump-administration-s-proposed-rulemakings-a-win-win-for-americas-firearms-industry-national-security.

27. Bill Chappell, "Trump Moves to Withdraw U.S. from U.N. Arms Trade Treaty," NPR, 26 April 2019, https://www.npr.org/2019/04/26/717547741/trump-moves-to-withdraw-u-s-from-u-n-arms-trade-treaty; Roberta Rampton, "Trump Heeds NRA, Pulls U.S. out of U.N. Arms Treaty," AOL.com, 26 April 2019, https://www.aol.com/article/news/2019/04/26/trump-heeds-nra-pulls-us-out-of-un-arms-treaty/23717945.

28. Rev. Rob Lee, https://twitter.com/roblee4?lang=en.

29. Wendy Cukier, "The NRA's Hemispheric Reach," *Americas Quarterly,* Spring 2013, https://www.americasquarterly.org/content/nras-hemispheric-reach; David Morton, "Gunning for the World," Yale Global Online, 13 January 2006, https://yaleglobal.yale.edu/content/gunning-world; Amanda Erickson, "How the NRA Has Shaped the World's Gun Laws," *Washington Post,* 14 March 2018, https://www.washingtonpost.com/news/worldviews/wp/2018/03/14/how-the-nra-has-shaped-the-worlds-gun-laws/?noredirect=on&utm_term=.61f90675d71a.

30. George Rennie, "Australia's NRA-Inspired Gun Lobby Is Trying to Chip Away at Gun Control Laws," Australian Broadcasting Corporation, 18 November 2018, https://www.abc.net.au/news /2018-11-16/how-australias-nra-inspired-gun-lobby/10503790.

31. Weinberg, Mosendz, and Bill Allison, "NRA Goes International"; Betsy Woodruff, "Kremlin Blessed Russia's NRA Operation, U.S. Intel. Report Says," Daily Beast, 13 January 2019, https://www.thedailybeast.com/kremlin-blessed-russias-nra -operation-us-intel-report-says?ref=scroll.

32. Woodruff, "Kremlin Blessed Russia's NRA Operation"; Sharon LaFraniere, Matthew Rosenberg, and Adam Goldman, "Maria Butina Loved Trump, Guns, and Russia. It Was a Cover, Prosecutors Say," New York Times, 17 July 2018, https://www.nytimes .com/2018/07/17/us/maria-butina-russian-agent-charges.html.

10. Follow the Money

1. Dan Zimmerman, "Open Letter to NRA Members From Former Staffer Steve Hoback," The Truth About Guns, 29 April 2019, https://www.thetruthaboutguns.com/open-letter-to-nra -members-from-former-staffer-steve-hoback.

2. Todd Neikirk, "NRA Reportedly Spending $100,000 a Day on Legal Fees," The Hill Reporter, 12 May 2019, https://hillreporter .com/nra-reportedly-spending-100000-a-day-on-legal-fees -35253.

3. Veronica Stracqualursi and Sonia Moghe, "New York Attorney General Investigating NRA Finances amid Group's Internal Dispute," CNN, 29 April 2019, https://www.cnn.com/2019/04/27 /politics/nra-new-york-investigation/index.html; John Gargis, "New NRA President, Cobb Native, Aiming for Higher Membership, Reclaiming Government Offices," Marietta Daily Journal, 5 May 2019, https://www.mdjonline.com/news/new-nra-president -cobb-native-aiming-for-higher-membership-reclaiming/article _6732082c-6dc5-11e9-8018-0fe0132c64d9.html.

4. Open Secret News, 27 November 2018, https://www.opensecrets .org/news/2018/11/nra-in-the-1cd; NRA, "IRS Form 990, 2017." Forms 990 including its schedules for the NRA from 2004 to 2017 can be found at ProPublica, https://projects.propublica.org/nonprofits

/organizations/530116130; for the NRA Special Contributions Fund, https://projects.propublica.org/nonprofits/organizations /237367534; for the NRA Freedom Action Foundation, https:// projects.propublica.org/nonprofits/organizations/261277941; for the NRA Civil Rights Defense Fund, https://projects.propublica.org /nonprofits/organizations/521136665; and for the NRA Foundation, https://projects.propublica.org/nonprofits/organizations/521710886.

5. 26 U.S.C. Section 501(c)(3).

6. "The NRA Foundation: Teach Freedom," https://www .nrafoundation.org/about-us; NRA, "IRS Form 990, 2016"; NRA Foundation, "IRS Form 990, 2016"; Kay Phillips Erb, "Ask the Taxgirl: Is the NRA a Charity?," *Forbes,* 8 March 2018, https:// www.forbes.com/sites/kellyphillipserb/2018/03/08/ask-the-taxgirl -is-the-nra-a-charity/#33daf24117df; NRA Foundation, "Annual Report, 2017," Related Parties, 38, https://www.nrafoundation.org /media/2082/16nrafannualreportweb1.pdf.

7. NRA Foundation, "IRS Form 990, 2017."

8. Stephen Spaulding and Jesse Littlewood, "Power Shift: How People Can Take on the NRA," Common Cause, August 2018, https://takingonthenra.org.

9. NRA Foundation, "IRS Form 990, 2017."

10. Ibid.; Mike Spies, "Secrecy, Self-Dealing, and Greed at the N.R.A.," *New Yorker,* 17 April 2019, https://www.newyorker.com/news/news -desk/secrecy-self-dealing-and-greed-at-the-nra; Mike Spies, "An Internal Memo Raises New Questions About Self-Dealing at the N.R.A.," *New Yorker,* 9 May 2019, https://www.newyorker .com/news/news-desk/an-internal-memo-raises-new-questions -about-self-dealing-at-the-nra; Mark Maremont, "Leaked Letters Revealed Details of NRA Chief's Alleged Spending," *Wall Street Journal,* 11 May 2019, https://www.wsj.com/articles/leaked-letters -reveal-details-of-nra-chiefs-alleged-spending-11557597601.

11. Jeff Knox, "NRA's Dirty Laundry Exposed as Pro-gun Group Cleans House," AmmoLand, 20 April 2019, https://www .ammoland.com/2019/04/nras-dirty-laundry-exposed-as-pro -gun-group-cleans-house/#axzz5neZ9u21Y; and "NRA's Future: Only Two Options: Can the BOD Save Us?," 22 April 2019, https://www.ammoland.com/2019/04/nras-future-only-two -options-can-the-bod-save-us/#axzz5neZ9u21Y.

12. Tim Mak, "As Leaks Show Lavish NRA Spending, Former Staff Detail Poor Conditions At Nonprofit," NPR, 15 May 2019, https://wamu.org/story/19/05/15/as-leaks-show-lavish-nra-spending-former-staff-detail-poor-conditions-at-nonprofit.

13. Ibid.

14. Stracqualursi and Moghe, "New York Attorney General Investigating"; Justin Wise, "New York Attorney General Launches Investigation into NRA's Tax-Exempt Status," The Hill, 28 April 2019, https://thehill.com/blogs/blog-briefing-room/news/441015-new-york-attorney-general-launches-investigation-into-nras-tax.

15. Associated Press, "Trump Says NRA 'Under Siege' by New York Investigation," Snopes.com, 28 Apr. 2019, https://www.snopes.com/ap/2019/04/29/trump-says-nra-under-siege-by-new-york-investigation; Vandana Rambaran, "Washington Attorney General Opens Inquiry Into NRA's Financial Affairs, *Fox News*, 12 July 2019, https://www.foxnews.com/us/washington-ag-opens-inquiry-into-nras-financial-affairs.

16. Robert McGuire, "Audit Shows NRA Spending Surged $100 million Amidst Pro-Trump Push in 2016," Center for Responsive Politics, 15 November 2017, https://www.opensecrets.org/news/2017/11/audit-shows-nra-spending-surged-100-million-amidst-pro-trump-push-in-2016; Harry Enten, "The NRA Used to Be Bipartisan. Now It's Mostly Just a Wing of the Republican Party," CNN, 24 February 2018, https://www.cnn.com/2018/02/24/politics/nra-partisan-bipartisan-republican/index.html. See also the campaign finance database at https://www.opensecrets.org and the NRA's "Form 990 IRS" filings referenced above.

17. US District Court for the District of Columbia, *Giffords v. Federal Election Commission,* Case 1:19-cv-0119, filed 24 April 2019, https://campaignlegal.org/sites/default/files/2019-04/Giffords%20v.%20FEC%20File%20Stamped%20Complaint.pdf.

18. Peter Stone and Ben Wieder, "NRA Spent More than Reported in 2016," McClatchy, 11 October 2017, http://www.mcclatchydc.com/news/politics-government/article177312006.html.

19. Betsy Woodruff, "Ad Agency Fires Back at NRA with $50 Million Lawsuit," Daily Beast, 23 May 2019, https://www.thedailybeast.com/nra-legal-fight-ackerman-mcqueen-ad-agency-fires-back-with-dollar50-million-counterclaim.

20. Dave Gilson, "The NRA's Board Members Are—Shockingly—Mostly White Guys," *Mother Jones*, 1 March 2018, https://www.motherjones.com/politics/2018/03/nra-board-members-tom-selleck.

21. Martin Gilens and Benjamin I. Page, "Testing Theories of American Politics: Elites, Interest Groups, and Average Citizens," *Perspectives on Politics* 12 (2013): 564–81.

22. Robert Kuttner, "Three Reasons Why Liberals Lack Traction with Voters, Despite Conservative Failures," *American Prospect*, 14 June 2014, https://prospect.org/article/three-reasons-liberals-lack-traction-voters-despite-conservative-failures.

23. Matt Stevens, "Cory Booker's Gun Control Plan Calls for National Licensing Program," *New York Times*, 6 May 2019, https://www.nytimes.com/2019/05/06/us/politics/cory-booker-gun-control.html.

11. Debunking the Gun Lobby's Case for Firearms Self-Defense

1. David Hemenway, "Gun Threats and Self-Defense Gun Uses," Harvard Injury Control Research Center, 2000, https://www.hsph.harvard.edu/hicrc/firearms-research/gun-threats-and-self-defense-gun-use-2.

2. "Mass Shootings," Gun Violence Archive, https://www.gunviolencearchive.org/mass-shooting?page=3.

3. Maggie Fox, "Homicides Using Guns Up 31 Percent, CDC Finds," NBC News, 27 July 2018, https://www.aol.com/article/news/2018/07/27/homicides-using-guns-up-31-percent-cdc-finds/23491253; Jay Dickey and Mark Rosenberg, "We Won't Know the Cause of Gun Violence Until We Look for It," *Washington Post*, 27 July 2012, https://www.washingtonpost.com/opinions/we-wont-know-the-cause-of-gun-violence-until-we-look-for-it/2012/07/27/gJQAPfenEX_story.html?utm_term=.bff348b79e28.

4. Dickey and Rosenberg, "We Won't Know the Cause"; David E. Stark and Nigam H. Shah, "Funding and Publication of Research on Gun Violence and Other Leading Causes of Death," *Journal of the American Medical Association* 317 (2017): 84; Scott Jaschik, "Scholars Renew Calls for U.S. to Fund Research on Gun Violence," Inside Higher Ed, 3 October 2017, https://www

.insidehighered.com/news/2017/10/03/mass-shooting-las-vegas
-leads-renewed-calls-lift-limits-studying-gun-violence.

5. Joe Coscarelli, "Real CNN Poll Asks: Did 'Space Aliens, Time Travelers or Beings from Another Dimension' Make Flight 370 Disappear?," Intelligencer, 7 May 2014, http://nymag.com /intelligencer/2014/05/cnn-poll-did-aliens-make-flight-370 -disappear.html?gtm=bottom&gtm=bottom; Joshua Keating, "No, 12 Million Americans Don't Believe the Country Is Run by Shape-Shifting Lizards," Foreign Policy, 2 April 2013, https:// foreignpolicy.com/2013/04/02/no-12-million-americans-dont -believe-the-country-is-run-by-shape-shifting-lizards.

6. "Recent Polls—Belief in Aliens and UFOs," AlienResistance.org, http://www.alienresistance.org/ufo-alien-deception/recent-polls -trends-belief-aliens-ufos.

7. Gary Kleck and Marc Gertz, "Armed Resistance to Crime: The Prevalence and Nature of Self Defense with a Gun," Journal of Criminal Law and Criminology 86 (1995): 150–87.

8. Michael J. Strube, "The Truth Is Out There," Psychological Inquiry 7 (1996): 183–84. See also the stories in Chrissy Stockton, "100+ Alien Abduction Stories That Will Make You Believe," Thought Catalog, 6 June 2018, https://thoughtcatalog.com/christine -stockton/2018/06/alien-abduction-stories.

9. Philip J. Cook and Jens Ludwig, "Guns in America: Results of a Comprehensive National Survey on Firearms Ownership and Use," Police Foundation, 1996, 74.

10. Ibid., 74–75.

11. Ibid., 75–76.

12. David Hemenway, Matthew Miller, and Deborah Azrael, "Gun Use in the United States: Results from Two National Surveys," Injury Prevention 6 (2000): 263–67; David Hemenway and Matthew Miller, "Gun Threats and Self-Defense Gun Use," Harvard Injury Control Center, https://www.hsph.harvard.edu/hicrc /firearms-research/gun-threats-and-self-defense-gun-use-2.

13. "Senator Morton on Southern Troubles," Baltimore Sun, 19 September 1874, 1; "Hendrick's Apology for the Negro Massacre," Chicago Tribune, 6 May 1876, 4.

14. Seni Tienabeso, "'I Was the Victim,' Says Loud Music Trial Shooter in Jailhouse Phone Call," ABC News, 17 February 2014, https://abcnews.go.com/US/victim-loud-music-trial-shooter

-jailhouse-phone-call/story?id=22558295; Angie Jackson, "Man Gets Life in Prison for Shooting Charleston Police Officer in 2013," Charleston, S.C. *Post and Courier,* 15 November 2018, https://www.postandcourier.com/news/man-gets-life-in-prison -for-shooting-charleston-police-officer/article_04cbae08-e93c -11e8-95c5-ab2529060837.html.

15. "Record Number of Handgun Crimes—Nears One Million a Year," press release, US Department of Justice, 15 May 1994, https://www.bjs.gov/content/pub/press/HVFSDAFT.PR. Data on total victimizations between 1987 and 1992 is from *Sourcebook of Criminal Justice Statistics, 1993,* US Department of Justice, 247, https://www.bjs.gov/content/pub/pdf/scjs93.pdf.

16. Michael Planty and Jennifer L. Truman, "Special Report: Firearms Violence, 1993–2011," Bureau of Justice Statistics, US Department of Justice, May 2013, 12, https://www.bjs.gov/content /pub/pdf/fv9311.pdf.

17. For a detailed statistical critique of Kleck's survey see, David Hemenway, "Survey Research and Self-Defense Gun Use: An Explanation of Extreme Overestimates," *Journal of Criminal Law and Criminology* 87 (1997): 1430–45.

18. Kleck and Gertz, "Armed Resistance," 177; Deborah Azrael and David Hemenway, "'In the Safety of Your Own Home': Results from a National Survey on Gun Use at Home," *Social Science & Medicine* 50 (2000): 285–91.

19. See, for example, Cook and Ludwig, "Guns in America," David Hemenway, "Survey Research and Self Defense Gun and *Private Guns, Public Health* (Ann Arbor: University of Michigan Press, 2004); C. J. V. Wellford, and C. V. Pepper Petrie, (2004). *Firearms and Violence: A Critical Review* (Washington, D.C.: The National Academies Press, 2004); Gary Kleck, "The Illegitimacy of One-Sided Speculation: Getting the Defensive Gun Use Estimate Down," *Journal of Criminal Law and Criminology* 87 (1997): 1446–61; Gary Kleck, "Response Errors in Surveys of Defensive Gun Use: A National Internet Survey Experiment," *Crime and Delinquency* 64 (2018): 1119–42; Arthur Kellermann et al., "Weapon Involvement in Home Invasion Crimes," *Journal of the American Medical Association* 273 (1995): 1759–62; and "Injuries and Deaths due to Firearms in the Home," *Journal of Trauma: Injury, Infection, and Critical Care* 45 (1998).

20. Kleck and Gertz, "Armed Resistance," 177; *Crime in the United States, 1995,* Federal Bureau of Investigation, US Department of Justice, https://ucr.fbi.gov/crime-in-the-u.s/1995; "Section II: Crime Index Offenses Reported," 18, 22, https://ucr.fbi.gov/crime-in-the-u.s/1995/95sec2.pdf. The 1995 report covers 1991 to 1995. "Past Summary Ledgers, 2014–2018," Gun Violence Archive, https://www.gunviolencearchive.org/past-tolls.

21. Alex Yablon and Mike Spies, "The NRA Is Selling Insurance to Gun Owners Willing to Shoot in Self Defense," The Trace, 26 April 2017, https://www.thetrace.org/2017/04/nra-insurance-carry-guard-self-defense; Morgan Gstalter, "Washington State Deems NRA-Branded Insurance Program Illegal," The Hill, 16 January 2019, https://thehill.com/homenews/state-watch/425676-washington-state-deems-nra-branded-insurance-program-illegal.

22. "DFS Fines Lockton Companies $7 Million for Underwriting NRA-Branded 'Carry Guard' Insurance Program in Violation of New York Insurance Law," press release, New York State Department of Financial Services, 2 May 2018, https://www.dfs.ny.gov/about/press/pr1805021.htm; NRA Carry Guard, https://lockton.nracarryguard.com.

23. "The Challenge of Defining and Measuring Defensive Gun Use," RAND Corporation, 2016, https://www.rand.org/research/gun-policy/analysis/supplementary/defensive-gun-use.html. Ironically, using survey data from the NCVS, Kleck has written that "resistance with a gun appears to be most effective in preventing injuries," but adds, "this finding is not statistically significant due to the small number of reported gun uses." Jongyeon Tark and Gary Kleck, "Resisting Crime: The Effects of Victim Action on the Outcomes of Crime," *Criminology* 42 (2004): 902.

24. Amy Swearer, "8 Times Law-Abiding Citizens Saved Lives with an AR-15," Daily Signal, 4 March 2018, https://www.dailysignal.com/2018/03/14/8-times-law-abiding-citizens-saved-lives-ar-15.

25. Jacquelyn C. Campbell, et al., "Risk Factors for Femicide in Abusive Relationships: Results From a Multisite Control Study," *American Journal of Public Health* 93 (2003): 1089–97; Jacob Kaplan, "Uniform Crime Reporting (UCR) Program Data: Supplementary Homicide Reports, 1976–2017" (Ann Arbor, Mich.: Inter-university Consortium for Political and Social Research

[distributor], 2018), https://doi.org/10.3886/E100699V6; "Supplemental Homicide Reports," Florida Department of Law Enforcement, http://www.fdle.state.fl.us/FSAC/Crime-Data/SHR. The Florida data on supplemental homicides is tallied separately from the FBI reports.

26. "There Were 500 Workplace Homicides in the United States in 2016," Bureau of Labor Statistics, 23 January 2018, https://www.bls.gov/opub/ted/2018/there-were-500-workplace-homicides-in-the-united-states-in-2016.htm; Meghan Keneally, "Domestic Violence Plays a Role in Many Mass Shootings, but Receives Less Attention: Experts," ABC News, 7 January 2019, https://abcnews.go.com/beta-story-container/US/domestic-violence-plays-role-mass-shootings-receives-attention/story?id=59418186.

27. Keneally, "Domestic Violence"; Melissa Jeltsen, "There Were 2 Mass Shootings in Texas Last Week, but Only 1 on TV," *Huffington Post*, 26 May 2018, https://www.huffingtonpost.com/entry/texas-amanda-painter-mass-shooting_us_5b081ab4e4b0802d69caad89.

28. Linda L. Dahlberg, Robin M. Ikeda, and Marcie-jo Kresnow, "Guns in the Home and the Risk of a Violent Death in the Home: Findings from a National Study," *American Journal of Epidemiology* 160 (2004): 929–36; Andrew Anglemyer, Tara Horvath, and George Rutherford, "The Accessibility of Firearms and Risk for Suicide and Homicide Victimization Among Household Members: A Systematic Review and Meta-analysis," *Annals of Internal Medicine* 160 (2014): 101–10; Charles C. Branas et al., "Investigating the Link Between Gun Possession and Gun Assault," *American Journal of Public Health* 99 (2009): 2034–40.

29. Kaplan, "Uniform Crime Reporting"; "Supplemental Homicide Reports," Florida Department of Law Enforcement; "The Nation's Two Measures of Homicides," Bureau of Justice Statistics, US Department of Justice, July 2014, https://www.bjs.gov/content/pub/pdf/ntmh.pdf.

30. "Harry J. Enten, Gabriel Dance, and Karen McVeigh, "Rise in Justifiable Homicides Linked to Weak Gun Control Laws," *Guardian*, 5 April 2012, https://www.theguardian.com/world/2012/apr/05/stand-your-ground-gun-control-data. Kleck also claims that justifiable homicides do not include "excusable homicides," but the distinction between such homicides with firearms

is that excusable homicides include accidental killings, which would not qualify as killing in self-defense. See Sue Titus Reid, *Criminal Law*, 7th ed. (Los Angeles: Roxbury, 2007), 166; "What Is Excusable Homicide," *Black's Law Dictionary*, https://thelawdictionary.org/excusable-homicide-1; and *Florida Criminal Jury Instructions Handbook* (LexisNexis, 2018), instruction 7.1.

31. Susan Ferriss, "NRA Pushed 'Stand Your Ground' Laws Across the Nation," *The Center for Public Integrity*, 26 March 2012, https://publicintegrity.org/education/nra-pushed-stand-your-ground-laws-across-the-nation; David K. Humphreys, Antonio Gasparrini, and Douglas J. Wiebe, "Association Between Enactment of a 'Stand Your Ground' Self Defense Law and Unlawful Homicides in Florida," *Journal of the American Medical Association*, Research Letter, October 2017; Chandler McClellan and Erdel Tekin, "Stand Your Ground Laws, Homicides and Injuries," *Journal of Human Resources* 52 (2017): 621–653; Susan Taylor Martin, Florida Stand Your Ground Yields Some Shocking Examples Depending on How the Law is Applied," *Tampa Bay Times*, 17 February 2013, http://www.tampabay.com/news/publicsafety/crime/florida-stand-your-ground-law-yields-some-shocking-outcomes-depending-on/1233133

32. Jeffrey L. Rodengen, *NRA: An American Legend* (Fort Lauderdale, Fla.: Write Stuff Enterprises, 2002), 239; Connie Humburg, "Many Killers Who Go Free with Florida 'Stand Your Ground' Law Have History of Violence," *Tampa Bay Times*, 17 February 2013, http://www.tampabay.com/news/courts/criminal/many-killers-who-go-free-with-florida-stand-your-ground-law-have-history/1241378.

33. Humburg, "Many Killers."

34. Kris Hundley, "Drug Dealer Used 'Stand Your Ground' to Avoid Charges in Two Killings," *Tampa Bay Times*, 17 February 2013, https://www.tampabay.com/news/courts/criminal/drug-dealer-used-stand-your-ground-to-avoid-charges-in-two-killings/1235650.

35. "Four 'Stand Your Ground' Cases in the US," BBC News, 12 April 2012, https://www.bbc.com/news/world-us-canada-17693084; Thomas Gabor, *Confronting Gun Violence in America* (New York: Palgrave Macmillan, 2016), 174.

36. David Ovalle, "Stand Your Ground Law Helps Free Miami Teens Accused of MLK Day Shooting That Wounded 8," *Miami Herald*, 23 February 2017, https://www.miamiherald.com/news/local /crime/article134526664.html.

37. Data compiled from "Supplemental Homicide Reports," Florida Department of Law Enforcement.

38. Michael Spanbauer, "Self-Defense Policy, Justified Homicides, and Race," Working Papers 1708, Tulane University, Department of Economics, revised March 2018, https://ideas.repec.org/p/tul /wpaper/1708.html; "Stand Your Ground," American Bar Association, September 2015, https://www.americanbar.org/groups /diversity/racial_ethnic_justice/projects/SYG.

39. Meg Kelly, "Do 98 Percent of Mass Public Shootings Happen in Gun-Free Zones?," *Washington Post*, 10 May 2018, https://www .washingtonpost.com/news/fact-checker/wp/2018/05/10/do-98 -percent-of-mass-public-shootings-happen-in-gun-free-zones/ ?utm_term=.23c23ef1ff1b.

40. James Silver, Andre Simmons, and Sarah Craun, "A Study of the Pre-attack Behaviors of Active Shooters in the United States, Between 2000 and 2013," Federal Bureau of Investigation, US Department of Justice, June 2018, 23, https://www.fbi.gov/file -repository/pre-attack-behaviors-of-active-shooters-in-us-2000 -2013.pdf/view.

41. "A Study of Active Shooter Incidents in the United States Between 2000 and 2013," Federal Bureau of Investigation, US Department of Justice, 11,12, https://www.fbi.gov/file-repository /active-shooter-study-2000-2013-1.pdf/view; "Active Shooter Incidents in the United States in 2014 and 2015," 3, https://www .fbi.gov/file-repository/activeshooterincidentsus_2014-2015.pdf /view; "Active Shooter Incidents in the United States in 2016 and 2017," 5, https://www.fbi.gov/file-repository/active-shooter -incidents-us-2016-2017.pdf/view.

42. Mathew Haag, "Man Killed by Police at an Alabama Mall Was a 'Good Guy with a Gun' Family's Lawyer Says," *New York Times*, 26 November 2018, https://www.nytimes.com/2018/11 /26/us/black-man-killed-alabama-mall-shooting.html?action =click&module=RelatedCoverage&pgtype=Article&region =Footer; Holly Yan, "'Hero' Security Guard Killed by Police Was

Working Extra Shifts for His Son's Christmas," CNN, 15 November 2018, https://www.cnn.com/2018/11/15/us/chicago-area-security-guard-police-shooting/index.html.

43. "Chicago Mercy Hospital Attack Is 33rd Mass Shooting by a Concealed Handgun Permit Holder," Violence Policy Center, 20 November 2018, http://vpc.org/press/chicago-mercy-hospital-attack-is-33rd-mass-shooting-by-a-concealed-handgun-permit-holder.

44. Enten, Dance, and McVeigh, "Rise in Justifiable Homicides."

12. "More Guns, Less Crime," Another Gun Lobby Myth

1. Melinda Wenner Moyer, "More Guns do not Stop More Crime, Evidence Shows," *Scientific American*, 1 October 2017, https://www.scientificamerican.com/article/more-guns-do-not-stop-more-crimes-evidence-shows.

2. Julia Lurie, "When the Gun Lobby Tries to Justify Firearms Everywhere, It Turns to This Guy," *Mother Jones*, 28 July 2015, https://www.motherjones.com/politics/2015/07/john-lott-guns-crime-data.

3. Ibid.

4. Evan DeFilippis, "Shooting Down the Gun Lobby's Favorite 'Academic': A Lott of Lies," *Armed With Reason*, 1 December 2014, www.armedwithreason.com/shooting-down-the-gun-lobbys-favorite-academic-a-lott-of-lies; Richard Morin, "Writer Admits He's His Own Best Critic," Chron, chron.com/life/article/writer-admits-he-s-his-own-best-critic-2124045.phb.

5. Ibid.

6. "John Lott Exposes Critics Lies," John Lott's Website, 13 September 2015, http://johnrlott.blogspot.com/2015_09_13_archive.html.

7. John Lott, "Violence Policy Center Keeps Using Justifiable Homicide Data to Make False Claims About Defensive Gun Use," Crime Prevention Research Center 24 September 2017, https://crimeresearch.org/2017/09/violence-policy-center-keeps-using-using-justifiable-homicide-data-make-false-claims-defensive-gun-use.

8. Otis Dudley Duncan, "John R. Lott Jr. on Defensive Gun Statistics," *Science Blogs*, 10 April 2003, http://scienceblogs.com/deltoid/2003/04/10/duncan3; James Lindgren, "Comments on Questions About John R. Lott's Claims Regarding a 1997 Survey,"

Way Back Machine 17 January 2003, https://web.archive.org/web /20040803044204/http://www.cse.unsw.edu.au:80/~lambert /guns/lindgren.html; DeFillipis, "Shooting Down the Gun Lobby's Favorite 'Academic'"; John Lott's Website, Response 1997 Survey, "Supplemental Information," http://www.johnlott.org /files/GenDisc97_02surveys.html; "John Lott Exposes Critics Lies: Response to Evan DeFilipis and Devin Hughes' newest claims at ThinkProgress," *Firearms Owners Against Crime*, 19 August 2016, https://foac-pac.org/John-Lott-Exposes-Critics-Lies:-Response -To-Evan-Defilippis-And-Devin-Hughes-Newest-Claims-At -Thinkprogress/News-Item/5385.

9. State of Nebraska, Committee on Judiciary LB465, February 6, 1997, statement of John Lott, Transcript prepared by the Clerk of the Legislature, Transcriber's Office, https:// www.nebraskalegislature.gov/FloorDocs/95/PDF/Transcripts /Judiciary/1997-02-06.pdf; "John R. Lott, Jr.'s Reply to Otis Duncan's Recent Article in The Criminologist," https:// scienceblogs.com/deltoid/2000/09/01/lottduncan; John Lott, "Did I Attribute the 98 Percent Brandishing Number to Others?" https://scienceblogs.com/deltoid/2003/04/05/lottreply9; Ibid., "Supplemental Information;" John Wiener, *Historians in Trouble: Plagiarism, Fraud, and Politics in the Ivory Tower* (New York, The New Press, 2005), 140. There is also an entry for John Lott in Roelf Bolt, *The Encyclopedia of Liars and Deceivers* (London: Reaktion Books, 2004), 132.

10. John R. Lott, Jr., "Presentation to Presidential Advisory Commission on Election Integrity: A Suggestion and Some Evidence," September 2017, https://www.whitehouse.gov/sites/whitehouse .gov/files/docs/pacei-dr-john-lott-presentation.pdf; John Lott, Jr., "Background Checks Are Not the Answer to Gun Violence," *New York Times,* 12 February 2018, https://www.nytimes.com/2018 /02/12/opinion/politics/background-checks-gun-violence.html; "Pro-gun Researcher Uses Trump Voter Fraud Commission to Troll Democrats on Background Checks," The Trace, 12 September 2017, https://www.thetrace.org/rounds/john-lott-trump-voter -fraud-background-checks-nics.

11. National Research Council of the Academies of Science, *Firearms and Violence: A Critical Review* (Washington, D.C.: National Academies Press, 2005), 2.

12. Moyer, "More Guns Do Not Stop More Crime"; John J. Donohue, Abhay Aneja, and Kyle D. Weber, "Right-to-Carry Laws and Violent Crime: A Comprehensive Assessment Using Panel Data, and a State-Level Synthetic Controls Analysis," NBER Working Paper no. 23510, revised November 2018, https://www.nber.org/papers/w23510; John Donohue, "Laws Facilitating Gun Carrying and Homicide," *American Journal of Public Health* 107 (2017): 1864–65.

13. Michael Siegel, Craig S. Ross, and Charles King, "Examining the Relationship Between the Prevalence of Guns and Homicide Rates in the USA Using a New and Improved State-Level Gun Ownership Proxy," *BMJ* 20 (2014): 424–26.

14. "Underlying Cause of Death," CDC Wonder.

15. Charles D. Phillips et al., "When Concealed Handgun Licensees Break Bad: Criminal Convictions of Concealed Handgun Licensees in Texas, 2001–2009," *American Journal of Public Health* 103 (2013): 86–91.

16. David Hemenway, Deborah Azrael, and Matthew Miller, "Whose Guns Are Stolen? The Epidemiology of Gun Theft Victims," *Injury Epidemiology* 4 (2017), 11–15; Brian Freskos, "Missing Pieces," The Trace, 20 November 2017, https://www.thetrace.org/features/stolen-guns-violent-crime-america.

17. Mariel Alper and Lauren Glaze, "Source and Use of Firearms Involved in Crimes: Survey of Prison Inmates, 2016," Bureau of Justice Statistics, United States Department of Justice, January 2019, https://www.bjs.gov/content/pub/pdf/suficspi16.pdf.

18. "Easy Targets," *New Yorker*, 7 February 2019, https://www.newyorker.com/news/news-desk/why-thieves-target-gun-stores.

19. Sam Lichtman, "How UK and US Gangster Rap Show Us the Difference in Each Country's Gun Laws," One Track Mine, 12 December 2018, https://onetrackmine.com/how-uk-and-us-gangster-rap-show-us-the-difference-in-each-countrys-gun-laws.

20. Yu Lu and Jeff R. Temple, "Dangerous Weapons or Dangerous People? The Temporal Associations Between Gun Violence and Mental Health," *Preventive Medicine* 121 (2019): 1–6; Eric B. Elbogen and Sally C. Johnson, "The Intricate Link Between Violence and Mental Disorder," *Archives of General Psychiatry* 66 (2009): 152; Mohit Varshney et al., "Violence and Mental Illness: What Is the True Story?," *BMJ* 70 (2016): 223–25.

21. Hannah Ritchie and Max Roser, "Mental Health," Our World in Data, April 2018, https://ourworldindata.org/mental-health; Shaun Dakin, https://twitter.com/i/web/status/927613084465881089.

22. Chris Harris, "Trump's Knife Crime Claim: How Do the US and the UK Compare?," Euronews, 6 May 2018, https://www.euronews.com/2018/05/05/trump-s-knife-crime-claim-how-do-the-us-and-uk-compare; "GBD Compare, 2017," Global Burden of Disease Study, https://vizhub.healthdata.org/gbd-compare.

23. Brad J. Bushman, "The Tradeoffs of Gun Ownership," *Psychology Today*, 1 August 2012, https://www.psychologytoday.com/us/blog/get-psyched/201208/the-tradeoffs-gun-ownership-0.

24. Michael D. Anestis, *Guns and Suicide: An American Epidemic* (New York: Oxford University Press, 2018), xiii.

25. German Lopez, "Guns Killed More People than Car Crashes in 2017," Vox, 11 December 2018, https://www.vox.com/future-perfect/2018/12/11/18135976/gun-deaths-us-2017-suicide.

26. "Duration of Suicide Crises," Harvard School of Public Health, https://www.hsph.harvard.edu/means-matter/means-matter/duration and "Firearm Access is a Risk Factor for Suicide," https://www.hsph.harvard.edu/means-matter/means-matter/risk; "Fatal Injury Data" and "Nonfatal Injury Data," CDC.

27. Michael D. Anestis and Claire Houtsma, "The Association Between Gun Ownership and Statewide Overall Suicide Rates," *Suicide and Life-Threatening Behavior* 48 (2018): 204–17; Anita Knopov et al., "Household Gun Ownership and Youth Suicide Rates at the State Level, 2005–2015," *American Journal of Preventive Medicine*, in press, 2019, https://www.ncbi.nlm.nih.gov/pubmed/28294383.

28. "GBD Compare, 2017," Global Burden of Disease Study..

29. Niall McCarthy, "The Top 15 Countries for Military Expenditure In 2016," *Forbes*, 24 April 2017, https://www.forbes.com/sites/niallmccarthy/2017/04/24/the-top-15-countries-for-military-expenditure-in-2016-infographic/#11d4f35743f3.

30. Meagan Flynn, "Shot in the Neck at 17," *Seattle Times*, 14 November 2018, https://www.seattletimes.com/nation-world/shot-in-the-neck-at-17-this-is-the-trauma-surgeon-now-leading-doctors-against-gun-violence-and-nra/?utm_source=RSS&utm_medium=Referral&utm_campaign=RSS_all.

31. Bruce Y. Yee, "How Doctors Responded After NRA Told Them to 'Stay in Their Lane,'" *Forbes*, 11 November 2018, https://www

.forbes.com/sites/brucelee/2018/11/11/how-doctors-responded
-after-the-nra-said-stay-in-their-lane/#a9508c1581c6; Lisa Marie Pane, "It's a Twitter War: Doctors Clash with NRA over
Gun Deaths," Associated Press, 22 November 2018, https://www
.apnews.com/ef9238dd2b75447d8fc1c0b3144d508f.

32. "This Is Our Lane: An Open Letter to the NRA from American Healthcare Professionals," Physicians Thrive, 12 November 2018, https://physiciansthrive.com/articles/category/medical
-professionals/2501921/this-is-our-lane-an-open-letter-to-the-nra
-from-american-healthcare-professionals; Jenny Deam, "Over 26K
ER Staff, Paramedics Sign Open Letter to NRA," EMS World, 15
November 2018, https://www.emsworld.com/news/1221714/over
-26k-er-staff-paramedics-sign-open-letter-nra.

33. Jeremy Gorner, "Gunman in Mercy Hospital Shooting Fired
About 40 Shots Before Dying in Shootout with SWAT Officer,"
Chicago Tribune, 21 November 2018, https://www.chicagotribune
.com/news/local/breaking/ct-met-chicago-mercy-hospital
-shooting-details-20181121-story.html.

34. Jamie Ducharme, "Doctor Slam NRA's Directive to 'Stay in Their
Lane,'" *Time,* 20 November 2018, time.com/5460036/this-is-our
-lane-doctors-guns; U.S. Centers for Disease Control and Prevention, "Achievements in Public Health, 1900–1999 Motor-Vehicle
Safety: A 20th Century Public Health Achievement," *MMWR
Weekly,* May 1999, 369, https://www.cdc.gov/mmwr/preview
/mmwrhtml/mm4818a1.htm.

35. Chris Kahn, "Americans Support Gun Control but Doubt
That Lawmakers Will Act," Reuters, 8 February 2019, https://
www.reuters.com/article/us-florida-shooting-anniversary-poll
/americans-support-gun-control-but-doubt-lawmakers-will-act
-reuters-ipsos-poll-idUSKCN1PX11I.

13. A Path to Repeal

1. "Five Years of Prohibition and Its Results," *North American Review,* June–August 1925, 6, http://americainclass.org/sources
/becomingmodern/divisions/text4/prohibitionrepeal.pdf.

2. Lichtman, *White Protestant Nation,* 10.

3. Daniel Okrent, *Last Call: The Rise and Fall of Prohibition* (New
York: Scribner, 2010), 81–82.

4. John Kobler, *Ardent Spirits: The Rise and Fall of Prohibition* (New York: G. P. Putnam's Sons, 1973), 12.

5. Michael S. Patterson, "The Fall of a Bishop: James Cannon, Jr., versus Carter Glass, 1909–1934," *Journal of Southern History* 39 (1973): 493–518, quote on 493.

6. National Commission on Law Observance and Enforcement, "Report on the Enforcement of the Prohibition Laws of the United States," 7 January 1931, https://www.ncjrs.gov/pdffiles1 /Digitization/44540NCJRS.pdf.

7. "Wet Plank Moves Gain in Both Parties," *New York Times,* 7 June 1932, 1.

8. David Kyvig, *Repealing National Prohibition* (Kent, Ohio: Kent State University Press, 1999), 1–3, 123.

9. Z. Byron Wolf, "There's Not 'a Snowflake's Chance in Hell' of Repealing the Second Amendment," CNN, 27 March 2018, https://www.cnn.com/2018/03/27/politics/repealing-the -second-amendment/index.html; Charles Merz, *The Dry Decade* (New York: Doubleday, Doran, 1931), 297; Karyn Strickler, "The Do-Nothing Strategy, an Exposé of Progressive Poli- tics," CounterPunch, 30 June 2003, https://www.counterpunch .org/2003/06/30/the-do-nothing-strategy-an-expose-of -progressive-politics; "Louis D. Brandeis Legacy Fund for Social Justice," Brandeis University, https://www.brandeis.edu /legacyfund/bio.html.

10. Aamar Madhani, "Poll: Approval of Same Sex Marriage in U.S. Reaches New High," *USA Today,* 23 May 2018, https://www .usatoday.com/story/news/nation/2018/05/23/same-sex-marriage -poll-americans/638587002.

11. Jonathan Turley, "Repealing the Second Amendment Isn't Easy but It's What March for Our Lives Students Need," *USA Today,* 28 March 2018, https://www.usatoday.com/story/opinion/2018 /03/28/repealing-second-amendment-march-our-lives-students /463644002.

12. See the recent book by Moms Demand Action founder Shannon Watts, *Fight Like a Mother* (New York: HarperOne, 2019).

13. Frederick E. Allen, "Anheuser-Busch Heir Quits the NRA in Protest," *Forbes,* 19 April 2013, https://www.forbes.com/sites /frederickallen/2013/04/19/anheuser-busch-heir-quits-the-nra -in-protest/#4b2235b9131a.

14. Dan Satherley, "Full List of Companies Cutting Ties with the NRA After the Florida Shooting," Newshub, 25 February 2018, https://www.newshub.co.nz/home/world/2018/02/full-list-of-companies-cutting-ties-with-the-nra-after-the-florida-shooting.html; Sarah Min, "Dick's Sporting Goods to Stop Selling Guns in 125 Stores," CBS News, 12 March 2019, https://www.cbsnews.com/news/dicks-sporting-goods-to-stop-selling-guns-in-125-stores.

15. Elizabeth MacBride, "Business Stood Up Against the NRA Last Year. Here's Why That's Scary," *Forbes*, 20 December 2018, https://www.forbes.com/sites/elizabethmacbride/2018/12/20/the-tiny-nonprofit-that-helped-drive-a-sea-change-in-gun-politics-last-year/#253642333d6e; Yasemin Irvin-Erickson et al., "Gun Violence Affects the Economic Health of Communities," Urban Institute, June 2017, https://www.urban.org/sites/default/files/publication/90666/eigv_brief_3.pdf.

16. Rob Schenck, "I'm an Evangelical Preacher. You Can't Be Pro-Life and Pro-Gun," *Washington Post*, 28 December 2015, https://www.washingtonpost.com/posteverything/wp/2015/12/28/im-evangelical-you-cant-be-pro-life-and-pro-gun/?utm_term=.d01b467e68a5; U.S. Conference of Catholic Bishops, "Responsibility, Rehabilitation, and Restoration: A Catholic Perspective on Crime and Criminal Justice," 15 November 2000, http://www.usccb.org/issues-and-action/human-life-and-dignity/criminal-justice-restorative-justice/crime-and-criminal-justice.cfm#scriptural; Amy E. Schwartz, "Ask the Rabbis: Gun Control," *Moment*, 30 September 2014, https://www.momentmag.com/ask-the-rabbis-gun-control.

17. Victoria Balera, "Fox News Poll: 71 Percent Say Gun Violence a 'Serious Problem' That Government Should Address," Fox News, 4 June 2019, https://www.foxnews.com/politics/fox-news-poll-71-percent-say-gun-violence-a-major-problem-government-should-address; Tim Price, "After Senate's Gun Control Failure, FDR Points the Way Forward," Roosevelt Institute, 19 April 2013, http://rooseveltinstitute.org/after-senates-gun-control-failure-fdr-points-way-forward.

18. "All Disclosed Outside Spending, 2018," OpenSecrets.org, https://www.opensecrets.org/outside-spending/spenders-industries.

19. Bob Bryan, "Something Historic Is Happening with How Americans View the NRA," Business Insider, 21 March 2018, https://www.businessinsider.com/nra-poll-popularity-favorability-more-americans-dislike-2018-3; Vivian Wang, "The N.R.A. Has Declared War on Andrew Cuomo: He Couldn't Be Happier," *New York Times*, 9 August 2018, https://www.nytimes.com/2018/08/09/nyregion/nra-cuomo-insurance-lawsuit.html; Hawaii, Thirtieth Legislature, 2019, Senate Concurrent Resolution no. 42, https://www.capitol.hawaii.gov/session2019/bills/SCR42_.pdf.

14. After Repeal: Gun Control Reforms for a Safer America

1. CNN Staff, "Florida Student Emma Gonzalez To Lawmakers And Gun Advocates: 'We Call BS'," CNN, 17 February 2017.

2. Paul M. Reeping et al., "State Gun Laws, Gun Ownership, and Mass Shootings in the US: Cross Sectional Time Series," *BMJ* 264 (2019): 542–47.

3. "2017 Expanded Homicide Data," Federal Bureau of Investigation, US Department of Justice, https://ucr.fbi.gov/crime-in-the-u.s/2017/crime-in-the-u.s.-2017/topic-pages/expanded-homicide.

4. Ibid.; Michael Siegel, et al., "The Relationship Between Gun Ownership and Stranger and Nonstranger Firearm Homicide Rates in the United States, 1981–2010," *American Journal of Public Health* 104 (20140: 1912–19.

5. Maureen Groppe, "Parkland Shooting Spurred a Grieving Mom to Run for Congress. Now She's Voting for New Gun Laws," *USA Today*, 14 February 2019, https://www.usatoday.com/story/news/politics/2019/02/14/parkland-lucy-mcbath-new-face-gun-control/2850333002.

6. "GBD Compare, 2017," Global Burden of Disease Study; "Gun Crimes in Japan Remain Rare," Nippon.com.

7. "Firearms Trace Data 2017," US Bureau of Alcohol, Tobacco, Firearms, and Explosives, https://www.atf.gov/resource-center/firearms-trace-data-2017; "Annual Gun Control Scorecard," Giffords Law Center, https://lawcenter.giffords.org/scorecard. Giffords Law explains, "We use an exhaustive quantitative rubric to score each state on its gun law strength, adding points for safety

regulations like universal background checks and extreme risk protection orders and subtracting points for reckless policies like 'Stand Your Ground' and permitless carry laws." Its top five gun control states are California, Connecticut, Massachusetts, New Jersey, and New York. The bottom five states are Arizona, Idaho, Kansas, Missouri, and Mississippi.

8. The CDC does not report data on gun homicides for some sparsely populated states: Maine, New Hampshire, North Dakota, South Dakota, Rhode Island, Vermont, and Wyoming. The CDC does report data on gun suicides and gun deaths for all states: "Underlying Cause of Death," CDC Wonder. Unless otherwise indicated all quantitative results are statistically significant at standard levels in social science.

9. "GBD Compare, 2017," Global Burden of Disease Study.

10. NRA-ILA, "Attention Massachusetts Gun Owners: Join in NRA and GOAL's Boston Tea Party 2008!," 11 July 2008, https://www.nraila.org/articles/20080711/attention-massachusetts-gun-owners-joi; "Underlying Cause of Death," CDC Wonder.

11. Colleen L. Barry et al., "Public Support for Gun Violence Prevention Policies Among Gun Owners and Non-Gun Owners in 2017," *American Journal of Public Health* 108 (2018): 878–81.

12. Julian Santaella-Tenorio et al., "What Do We Know About the Association Between Firearm Legislation and Firearm-Related Injuries?," *Epidemiologic Reviews* 38 (2016): 140–57.

13. Philip Zelikow, "The Domestic Terrorism Danger: Focus on Unauthorized Private Military Groups," *Lawfare*, 15 August 2017, https://www.lawfareblog.com/domestic-terrorism-danger-focus-unauthorized-private-military-groups.

14. "How Gun Policies Affect Defensive Gun Use," RAND Corporation, 2016, https://www.rand.org/research/gun-policy/analysis/defensive-gun-use.html.

15. Cassandra K. Crifasi, Alexander McCourt, and Daniel W. Webster, "Policies to Reduce Gun Violence in Illinois," Center for Gun Policy and Research, Johns Hopkins Bloomberg School of Public Health, February 2019, 6–7, https://www.jhsph.edu/research/centers-and-institutes/johns-hopkins-center-for-gun-policy-and-research/publications/jhsph-gun-violence-in-illinois.pdf.

16. Matthew Miller, Lisa Hepburn, and Deborah Azrael, "Firearms

Acquisition Without Background Checks: Results from a National Survey," *Annals of Internal Medicine* 166 (2017): 233–39; Alper and Glaze, "Source and Use of Firearms"; Pete Williams, "The Fight for Universal Gun Background Checks Returns to Congress," 5 February 2019, NBC News, https://www.nbcnews.com/politics/congress/fight-universal-gun-background-checks-returns-congress-now-democrats-have-n967556.

17. "Pro-Gun Researcher Uses Trump Voter Fraud Commission," The Trace.

18. "Crime Gun Trace Reports 1999," US Bureau of Alcohol, Tobacco and Firearms, November 2000, https://www.atf.gov/resource-center/docs/ycgii-report-1999-national-reportpdf-0/download.

19. Douglas S. Weil and Rebecca C. Knox, "Effects of Limiting Handgun Purchases on Interstate Transfer of Firearms," *Journal of the American Medical Association* 275 (1996): 1759–61. Later data is from ATF "Gun Trace Reports," 2007 to 2011 and 2012 to 2017.

20. "Firearms Traces Mexico, 2017," US Bureau of Alcohol, Tobacco, Firearms, and Explosives, 9 March 2018, https://www.atf.gov/resource-center/docs/undefined/tracedatamexicocy1217finalpdf/download; "Firearms Traces: Central America, 2017," 9 March 2018, https://www.atf.gov/resource-center/docs/undefined/tracedatacentralamericacy17finalpdf/download.

21. "Underlying Cause of Death," CDC Wonder.

22. Renee M. Johnson et al., "Who Are the Owners of Firearms Used in Adolescent Suicides," *Suicide and Life Threatening Behavior* 40 (2011): 609–11.

23. Anestis and Houtsma, "Association Between Gun Ownership and Statewide," 204–17; "Preventing Suicide," US Centers for Disease Control and Prevention, 2018, https://www.cdc.gov/violenceprevention/suicide/consequences.html.

24. Azrael and Hemenway, "'In the Safety of Your Own Home,'" 285–91; Douglas J. Wiebe, "Homicide and Suicide Risks Associated with Firearms in the Home: A National Case-Control Study," *Annals of Emergency Medicine* 41 (2003): 771–82.

25. Vivian S. Chu, "The Protection of Lawful Commerce in Arms Act: An Overview of Limiting Tort Liability of Gun Manufacturers," Congressional Research Service, 20 December 2012, https://fas.org/sgp/crs/misc/R42871.pdf.

26. Tom Jackman, "Gunmaker, Store Agree to Payout in Sniper Case," *Washington Post,* 10 September 2004, http://www .washingtonpost.com/wp-dyn/articles/A8763-2004Sep9.html; Erick Erickson, "Setting the Record Straight: Adam Lanza Did Use the Bushmaster AR-15," RedState, 27 December 2012, https://www.redstate.com/erick/2012/12/27/setting-the-record -straight-adam-lanza-did-use-the-bushmaster-ar-15.

27. *Donna L. Soto et al. v. Bushmaster et al.,* (SC 19832) (SC 19833), 2019.

28. de Jager et al., "Lethality of Civilian Active Shooter Incidents," 1034–35; Mark Gius, "The Impact of State and Federal Assault Weapons Bans on Public Mass Shootings," *Applied Economic Letters* 22 (2014): 281–84; Charles DiMaggio, "Changes in US Mass Shooting Deaths Associated with the 1994–2004 Federal Assault Weapon Ban: Analysis of Open-Source Data," *Journal of Acute Care Surgery,* 2018; Mark Gius, "The Effects of Federal and State Gun Control Laws on School Shootings," *Applied Economic Letters* 25 (2018): 317–20.

29. Christopher S. Koper, et al., "Gunshot Victimizations Resulting From High-Volume Gunfire Incidents in Minneapolis, *Injury prevention,* 24 February 2018; Christopher S. Koper et al., "Criminal Use of Assault Weapons and High-Capacity Semiautomatic Firearms: An Updated Examination of Local and National Sources," *Journal of Urban Health* 95 (2017): 313–21.

30. See, for example, "2013 Connecticut General Statutes Title 53—Crimes Chapter 943—Offenses Against Public Peace and Safety, Section 53-202a—Assault weapons: Definitions," https:// law.justia.com/codes/connecticut/2013/title-53/chapter-943 /section-53-202a.

31. *Duncan v. Becerra,* Case no. 3:17-cv-1017-BEN, Order Granting Preliminary Injunction, 29 June 2017; Judgment, 29 March 2019.

32. "Firearms Control Legislation and Policy: Australia," Library of Congress, 30 July 2015, http://www.loc.gov/law/help/firearms -control/australia.php; Simon Chapman, Philip Alpers, and Michael Jones, "Association Between Gun Law Reforms and Intentional Firearm Deaths in Australia, 1979–2013," *Journal of the American Medical Association* 316 (2016): 291–96.

33. Ian Urbina, "California Tries New Tack on Gun Violence: Ammunition Control," *New York Times*, 9 September 2018, https://www.nytimes.com/2018/09/09/us/california-gun-control-ammunition-bullets.html; Anthony A. Braga and Philip J. Cook, "The Association of Firearm Caliber with Likelihood of Death from Gunshot Injury in Criminal Assaults," *Journal of the American Medical Association*, Network Open, 27 July 2018, https://jamanetwork.com/journals/jamanetworkopen/fullarticle/2688536.

34. German Lopez, "The Battle to Stop 3-D Printed Guns, Explained," Vox, 29 August 2018, https://www.vox.com/2018/7/31/17634558/3d-printed-guns-trump-cody-wilson-defcad.

35. David Coldewey, "Court Victory Legalizes 3-D Gun Blueprints," Tech Crunch, 10 July 2018, https://techcrunch.com/2018/07/10/court-victory-legalizes-3d-printable-gun-blueprints; "Man Behind 3D-Printed Gun Blueprints Explains Why He Wants to Post Instructions Online," CBS News, 31 July 2018, https://www.cbsnews.com/news/3d-printed-gun-maker-cody-wilson-explains-why-he-wants-to-post-blueprints-for-ar-15-style-rifles; Marrion Zhou, "3-D Printed Gun Controversy: Everything You Need to Know," CNET, 29 August 2018, https://www.cnet.com/news/the-3d-printed-gun-controversy-everything-you-need-to-know.

36. "About Us," Ghostguns.com, https://www.ghostguns.com/content/4-about-us.

37. Brenda Flanagan, "Law Enforcement Officials Tout First Arrests of 'Ghost Gun' Traffickers," NJTV, 14 May 2019, https://www.njtvonline.org/news/video/law-enforcement-officials-tout-first-arrests-of-ghost-gun-traffickers.

38. "(1857) Frederick Douglass, 'If There Is No Struggle, There Is No Progress,'" BlackPast.org, https://blackpast.org/1857-frederick-douglass-if-there-no-struggle-there-no-progress.

39. "Read Testimony of Parkland Shooting Survivor Aalayah Eastmond," CNN, 7 September 2018, https://www.cnn.com/2018/09/07/politics/parkland-survivor-testimony/index.html.

INDEX